TEXAS LAW
and the
Practice of
Psychology

A Sourcebook

J. RAY HAYS, Ph.D., J.D.
EMILY SUTTER, Ph.D.
ROBERT McPHERSON, Ph.D.

TEXAS PSYCHOLOGICAL ASSOCIATION

TEXAS LAW
and the
Practice of
Psychology

A Sourcebook

EDITED BY

HAYS, SUTTER & McPHERSON

Published by

TEXAS PSYCHOLOGICAL ASSOCIATION

&

BAYOU PUBLISHING · HOUSTON, TX

Copyright © 2005
by Texas Psychological Association

All rights reserved.
No part of this book may be reproduced, stored in a retrieval system, or transmitted in any form or by any means, electronic, mechanical, photocopying, recording or otherwise, without the express written permission of the Author or Publisher, except for brief quotations in critical reviews. Inquiries should be addressed to Permissions, Bayou Publishing, 2524 Nottingham, Houston, TX 77005-1412. Ph: (713) 526-4558. E-mail: permissions@bayoupublishing.com.

This publication is designed to provide accurate and authoritative information in regard to the subject matter covered. It is sold with the understanding that the publisher is not engaged in rendering legal, accounting, psychotherapeutic or other professional service. If expert assistance is required, the services of a competent professional person should be sought. From a Declaration of Principles jointly adopted by a Committee of the American Bar Association and a Committee of Publishers.

Printed in the United States of America
Sixth Edition 10 9 8 7 6

ISBN-10: 1-886298-20-3
ISBN-13: 1-978-1-886298-20-0

Published by:

Texas Psychological Association
1005 Congress Ave., Suite 410
Austin, TX 78701
(512) 280-4099
http://www.texaspsyc.org

Bayou Publishing
2524 Nottingham
Houston, TX 77005-1412
713-526-4558
http://www.bayoupublishing.com

CONTENTS AT A GLANCE

CONTENTS

INTRODUCTION TO THE 2005 EDITION

This project began modestly as an educational effort of the Texas Psychological Association and met exceptional success over the past twenty years as a source for information on the legal aspects of practice with practitioners, students of psychology, and those entering the state. This Sixth Edition continues the tradition to provide a single resource for the legal sources that guide the practice of mental health treatment in Texas. As in past editions, we gathered those statutes that are most directly related to practice so that the practitioner can find in one place the guidance necessary for most legally related practice questions. In addition to statutory material, we included several other sources of legal guidance for the practitioner and student by adding case law, an archive of the Attorney General Opinions and Open Records Opinions related to professional practice, synopses of the opinion letters of the Texas State Board of Examiners of Psychologists, and, new with this edition, a description of the HIPAA security rule that came into effect in the spring of 2005.

Our Licensing Act has been renewed by the legislature after sunset review. The changes in the law are minimal and a summary of the changes is available by accessing the Board's website at "*www.tsbep.state.tx.us*" and clicking on "New Developments and Requirements" in the middle of the home page. That section provides a link where the Act will appear when the linked website is updated. We have provided a summary of the results of the Sunset Review; however, because the changes in the law were minimal we decided not to include the Board's enabling statue in this Edition.

The statutory material in this edition follows the same organization as in the past, that is, we have kept the classification scheme used by the Texas Legislature instead of attempting to organize the material in a more user friendly way. For example, the concept of privacy of mental health information is covered primarily in Chapter 611 of the Health and Safety Code. However, there are several of other Texas Statutes that deal with privacy of information, such as the Communicable Disease Act, Family Code, and alcohol and drug statues. We have included the statutory authority for the regulation of "telehealth" in this edition from the Occupation Code.

The two legal decisions included in this Edition are *Thapar v. Zezulka* and *Abrams v. Jones*. *Thapar v. Zezulka* provides an excellent discussion of the duty to warn and duty to protect doctrine in Texas. We waited over 20 years in Texas to know the status of these duties. The Texas Supreme Court has now given practitioners guidance when a patient threatens another person. In this case, the Texas Supreme Court takes the position that courts should not second-guess the decision by a practitioner to tell law enforcement personnel or medical personnel about the danger presented by a patient. This gives a good deal of discretion to practitioners who are faced with a difficult situation and the decision is certainly pro-therapist. *Abrams v. Jones* concerns the privacy of information between a therapist, a child client, and the child's parents and provides a remedy for parents who request but are denied access to a child's records. Practitioners can draw guidance from this case about record keeping and the duty to parents and child clients.

This Edition updates the archive of Attorney General Opinions and Open Records Opinions that are relevant to practice. These opinions are relatively difficult to research because of the way they are indexed on the website of the Texas Attorney General. We hope that this archive will assist practitioners who have questions related to these decisions, such as whether data and protocols are a part of a patient's file and thus open to the patient (LO 97-073) and the oversight of the TSBEP over employees in exempt agencies (JC-321). We have also included new synopses of TSBEP Opinion Letters. These opinion letters make interesting reading for practitioners to find out what other professionals are thinking and perhaps doing in their practices. Finally, one addition to this Edition is a summary of the disciplinary actions taken by the Board.

Remember lawyers give opinions not answers. There are always "ifs," "ands," or "buts" in the law which most certainly keep lawyers fully employed. When you have a question about the legal aspects of practice use this text for reference but also get the consult from other professionals involved in your type of practice and do not hesitate to ask an attorney or the Board for advice. Your malpractice insurance carrier can provide consultation on matters that relate to many aspects of practice. The Texas Psychological Association maintains a legal consultation service for a modest annual fee and provides a free ethical consultation service through the Director of Professional Services. Each of these entities is interested in keeping you out of trouble; use these resources.

We are fortunate in Texas to be at the stage of professional development that we are. The continued growth of mental health practice is dependent not only on what we do in our offices but the shape of the laws that control practice. This volume represents the state of regulatory development. If you see areas where the rights and prerogatives of our patients and our profession can be enhanced, please take a proactive stance of being involved in positive change by contacting TPA or your local area society.

I am grateful to each person who has made suggestions about inclusion of material in this book and to my co-editors who made this book an excellent resource. Finally, as always, all proceeds from this effort go the Texas Psychological Association; the editors take nothing from this except the satisfaction of providing a resource for the profession.

—Ray Hays, Ph.D., J.D.
Diplomate in Clinical and Forensic Psychology, ABPP
Houston, Texas

ABOUT THE EDITORS

J. Ray Hays, Ph.D., J.D., is a member of the faculty of the Menninger Department of Psychiatry and Behavioral Sciences, Baylor College of Medicine, where he is Chief of the Psychology Service at Ben Taub General Hospital. He has edited this series since its inception in 1985 after proposing the idea for the book to the Texas Psychological Association Executive Committee. He is a Diplomate in both Clinical and Forensic Psychology from the American Board of Professional Psychology and the American Board of Forensic Psychology. His doctorate is from the University of Georgia with an internship at the Texas Research Institute of Mental Sciences. His law degree is from the South Texas College of Law. He is a former Chair of the Texas State Board of Examiners of Psychologists, serving as member from 1975 to 1982, and former President and one of the first Fellows of the American Association of State Psychology Boards, now the Association of State and Provincial Psychology Boards. He has written, edited, or compiled nine books, sixteen book chapters, and over 100 scientific articles on a variety of psychological topics. He is the recipient of the Texas Psychological Association Award for Outstanding Contribution to Education.

Emily G. Sutter, Ph.D., received her doctorate from the University of Texas at Austin and interned at Baylor College of Medicine. She is Professor Emeritus at the University of Houston-Clear Lake (UHCL) where she coordinates the school psychology internships. Prior to retiring from the classroom, she taught classes in the Professional Psychology sequence of programs, including a Professional Practice, Law and Ethics class for twenty years. Twice she served as Interim Dean of the school, first in 1990-1992 and again 2001-2002. She served as a member of the Texas State Board of Examiners of Psychologists from 1993-2002. She chaired the Board for three of those years and was Vice Chair for two more. She has published in child clinical psychology and professional practice issues. Additionally, she has a long history of service to the profession of psychology, chairing many committees and filling elected offices, including the Presidencies of both the Houston and Texas Psychological Associations. She has received Outstanding Service Awards from her University, the Houston

Psychological Association, the Texas Association of School Psychologists, and most recently received the Distinguished Lifetime Achievement Award from the Texas Psychological Association.

Robert H. McPherson, Ph.D., is Executive Associate Dean for the College of Education at the University of Houston, former Chair of the Department of Educational Psychology, and former Director of Training for the counseling psychology program. He completed his doctorate at the University of Houston and his internship at Texas A&M. He teaches the supervision and mental health & public policy courses for the counseling psychology program. His research interests address supervision processes, as well as legal, ethical, and regulatory issues related to professional practice. He is a Fellow of the American Psychological Association, past president of the Texas and Houston Psychological Associations, and former chair of the Council of Counseling Psychology Training Programs. He has been inducted into the National Academies of Practice and is recipient of the American Psychological Association's Karl Heiser Award in recognition for his advocacy contributions on behalf of psychologists and their patients. Recently elected to the APA Council of Representatives, Dr. McPherson also serves as Director of Professional Affairs for the Texas Psychological Association, providing consultation to psychologists, the legislature, and the public on issues related to psychology practice.

STATUTES

CIVIL PRACTICE AND REMEDIES CODE

SEXUAL EXPLOITATION BY MENTAL HEALTH PROVIDER—§81

§81.001. Definitions

In this chapter:

(1) *"Mental health services"* means assessment, diagnosis, treatment, or counseling in a professional relationship to assist an individual or group in:

    (A) alleviating mental or emotional illness, symptoms, conditions, or disorders, including alcohol or drug addiction;

    (B) understanding conscious or subconscious motivations;

    (C) resolving emotional, attitudinal, or relationship conflicts; or

    (D) modifying feelings, attitudes, or behaviors that interfere with effective emotional, social, or intellectual functioning.

(2) *"Mental health services provider"* means an individual, licensed or unlicensed, who performs or purports to perform mental health services, including a:

    (A) licensed social worker as defined by Section 505.002, Occupations Code;

    (B) chemical dependency counselor as defined by Section 504.001, Occupations Code;

    (C) licensed professional counselor as defined by Section 503.002, Occupations Code;

    (D) licensed marriage and family therapist as defined by Section 505.002, Occupations Code;

(E) member of the clergy;

(F) physician who is practicing medicine as defined by Section 151.002, Occupations Code;

(G) psychologist offering psychological services as defined by Section 501.003, Occupations Code; or

(H) special officer for mental health assignment certified under Section 1701.404, Occupations Code.

(3) " *Patient*" means an individual who seeks or obtains mental health services. The term includes a person who has contact with a special officer for mental health assignment because of circumstances relating to the person's mental health.

(4) " *Sexual contact*" means:

(A) " deviate sexual intercourse" as defined by Section 21.01, Penal Code;

(B) "sexual contact" as defined by Section 21.01, Penal Code;

(C) " sexual intercourse" as defined by Section 21.01, Penal Code; or

(D) requests by the mental health services provider for conduct described by Paragraph (A), (B), or (C). "Sexual contact" does not include conduct described by Paragraph (A) or (B) that is a part of a professionally recognized medical treatment of a patient.

(5) " *Sexual exploitation*" means a pattern, practice, or scheme of conduct, which may include sexual contact, that can reasonably be construed as being for the purposes of sexual arousal or gratification or sexual abuse of any person. The term does not include obtaining information about a patient's sexual history within standard accepted practice while treating a sexual or marital dysfunction.

(6) "*Therapeutic deception*" means a representation by a mental health services provider that sexual contact with, or sexual exploitation by, the mental health services provider is consistent with, or a part of, a patient's or former patient's treatment.

(7) "*Mental health services,*" as defined by this section, provided by a member of the clergy does not include religious, moral, and spiritual counseling, teaching, and instruction.

§81.002. Sexual Exploitation Cause of Action

A mental health services provider is liable to a patient or former patient of the mental health services provider for damages for sexual exploitation if the patient or former patient suffers, directly or indirectly, a physical, mental, or emotional injury caused by, resulting from, or arising out of:

(1) sexual contact between the patient or former patient and the mental health

services provider;

(2) sexual exploitation of the patient or former patient by the mental health services provider; or

(3) therapeutic deception of the patient or former patient by the mental health services provider.

§81.003. Liability of Employer

(a) An employer of a mental health services provider is liable to a patient or former patient of the mental health services provider for damages if the patient or former patient is injured as described by Section 81.002 and the employer:

(1) fails to make inquiries of an employer or former employer, whose name and address have been disclosed to the employer and who employed the mental health services provider as a mental health services provider within the five years before the date of disclosure, concerning the possible occurrence of sexual exploitation by the mental health services provider of patients or former patients of the mental health services provider; or

(2) knows or has reason to know that the mental health services provider engaged in the sexual exploitation of the patient or former patient and the employer failed to:

(A) report the suspected sexual exploitation as required by Section 81.006; or

(B) take necessary action to prevent or stop the sexual exploitation by the mental health services provider.

(b) An employer or former employer of a mental health services provider is liable to a patient or former patient of the mental health services provider for damages if the patient or former patient is injured as described by Section 81.002 and the employer or former employer:

(1) knows of the occurrence of the sexual exploitation by the mental health services provider of the patient or former patient;

(2) receives a specific request by an employer or prospective employer of the mental health services provider, engaged in the business of providing mental health services, concerning the possible existence or nature of sexual exploitation by the mental health services provider; and

(3) fails to disclose the occurrence of the sexual exploitation.

(c) An employer or former employer is liable under this section only to the extent that the failure to take the action described by Subsection (a) or (b) was a proximate and actual cause of damages sustained.

(d) If a mental health professional who sexually exploits a patient or former patient is a member of the clergy and the sexual exploitation occurs when the professional is acting as a member of the clergy, liability if any under this section is limited to the church, congregation, or parish in which the member of the clergy carried out the clergy member's pastoral duties:

(1) at the time the sexual exploitation occurs, if the liability is based on a violation of Subsection (a); or

(2) at the time of the previous occurrence of sexual exploitation, if the liability is based on a violation of Subsection (b).

(e) Nothing in Subsection (d) shall prevent the extension of liability under this section beyond the local church, congregation, or parish where the current or previous sexual exploitation occurred, as appropriate under Subsection (d), if the patient proves that officers or employees of the religious denomination in question at the regional, state, or national level:

(1) knew or should have known of the occurrences of sexual exploitation by the mental health services provider;

(2) received reports of such occurrences and failed to take necessary action to prevent or stop such sexual exploitation by the mental health services provider and that such failure was a proximate and actual cause of the damages; or

(3) knew or should have known of the mental health professional's propensity to engage in sexual exploitation.

§81.004. Damages

(a) A plaintiff who prevails in a suit under this section may recover actual damages, including damages for mental anguish even if an injury other than mental anguish is not shown.

(b) In addition to an award under Subsection (a), a plaintiff who prevails in a suit under this section may recover exemplary damages and reasonable attorney fees.

§81.005. Defenses

(a) It is not a defense to an action brought under Section 81.002 or 81.003 that the sexual exploitation of the patient or former patient occurred:

(1) with the consent of the patient or former patient;

(2) outside the therapy or treatment sessions of the patient or former patient; or

(3) off the premises regularly used by the mental health services provider for the therapy or treatment sessions of the patient or former patient.

(b) It is a defense to an action brought under Section 81.002 or 81.003 by a former patient that the person was not emotionally dependent on the mental health services provider when the sexual exploitation began and the mental health services provider terminated mental health services with the patient more than two years before the date the sexual exploitation began.

(c) A person is considered not emotionally dependent for purposes of this chapter if the nature of the patient's or former patient's emotional condition and the nature of the treatment provided by the mental health services provider are not such that the mental health services provider knows or has reason to believe that the patient or former patient is unable to withhold consent to the sexual exploitation.

§81.006. Reporting therapist-client sexual relationship

(a) If a mental health services provider or the employer of a mental health services provider has reasonable cause to suspect that a patient has been the victim of sexual exploitation by a mental health services provider during the course of treatment, or if a patient alleges sexual exploitation by a mental health services provider during the course of treatment, the mental health services provider or the employer shall report the alleged conduct not later than the 30th day after the date the person became aware of the conduct or the allegations to:

(1) the prosecuting attorney in the county in which the alleged sexual exploitation occurred; and

(2) any state licensing board that has responsibility for the mental health services provider's licensing.

(b) Before making a report under this section, the reporter shall inform the alleged victim of the reporter's duty to report and shall determine if the alleged victim wants to remain anonymous.

(c) A report under this section need contain only the information needed to:

(1) identify the reporter;

(2) identify the alleged victim, unless the alleged victim has requested anonymity; and

(3) express suspicion that sexual exploitation has occurred.

(d) Information in a report is privileged information and is for the exclusive use of the prosecuting attorney or state licensing board that receives the information. A person who receives privileged information may not disclose the information except to the extent that disclosure is consistent with the authorized purposes for which the person first obtained the information. The identity of an alleged victim of sexual exploitation by a mental health services provider may not be disclosed by the reporter, or by a person who has received or has access to a report or record, unless the alleged victim has consented to the disclosure in writing.

(e) A person who intentionally violates Subsection (a) or (d) is subject to disciplinary action by that person's appropriate licensing board and also commits an offense. An offense under this subsection is a Class C misdemeanor.

§81.007. Limited Immunity from Liability

(a) A person who, in good faith, makes a report required by Section 81.006 is immune from civil or criminal liability resulting from the filing of that report.

(b) Reporting under this chapter is presumed to be done in good faith.

(c) The immunity provided by this section does not apply to liability resulting from sexual exploitation by a mental health services provider of a patient or former patient.

§81.008. Admission of Evidence

(a) In an action for sexual exploitation, evidence of the plaintiff's sexual history and reputation is not admissible unless:

(1) the plaintiff claims damage to sexual functioning; or

(2)(A) the defendant requests a hearing before trial and makes an offer of proof of the relevancy of the history or reputation; and

(B) the court finds that the history or reputation is relevant and that the probative value of the evidence outweighs its prejudicial effect.

(b) The court may allow the admission only of specific information or examples of the plaintiff's conduct that are determined by the court to be relevant. The court's order shall detail the information or conduct that is admissible and no other such evidence may be introduced.

§81.009. Limitations

(a) Except as otherwise provided by this section, an action under this chapter must be filed before the third anniversary of the date the patient or former patient understood or should have understood the conduct for which liability is established under Section 81.002 or 81.003.

(b) If a patient or former patient entitled to file an action under this chapter is unable to bring the action because of the effects of the sexual exploitation, continued emotional dependence on the mental health services provider, or threats, instructions, or statements by the mental health services provider, the deadline for filing an action under this chapter is tolled during that period, except that the deadline may not be tolled for more than 15 years.

(c) This section does not apply to a patient or former patient who is a "child" or a "minor" as defined by Section 101.003, Family Code, until that patient or former patient has reached the age of 18. If the action is brought by a parent, guardian, or other person having custody of the child or minor, it must be brought within the period set forth in this section.

DECLARATION FOR MENTAL HEALTH TREATMENT—§137

§137.001. Definition

In this chapter:

(1) 'Adult' means a person 18 years of age or older or a person under 18 years of age who has had the disabilities of minority removed.

(2) 'Attending physician' means the physician, selected by or assigned to a patient, who has primary responsibility for the treatment and care of the patient.

(3) 'Declaration for mental health treatment' means a document making a declaration of preferences or instructions regarding mental health treatment.

(4) 'Emergency' means a situation in which it is immediately necessary to treat a patient to prevent:

    (A) probable imminent death or serious bodily injury to the patient because the patient:

        (i) overtly or continually is threatening or attempting to commit suicide or serious bodily injury to the patient; or

        (ii) is behaving in a manner that indicates that the patient is unable to satisfy the patient's need for nourishment, essential medical care, or self-protection; or

    (B) imminent physical or emotional harm to another because of threats, attempts, or other acts of the patient.

(5) 'Health care provider' means an individual or facility licensed, certified, or otherwise authorized to administer health care or treatment, for profit or otherwise, in the ordinary course of business or professional practice and includes a physician or other health care provider, a residential care provider, or an inpatient mental health facility as defined by Section 571.003, Health and Safety Code.

(6) 'Incapacitated' means that, in the opinion of the court in a guardianship proceeding under Chapter XIII, Texas Probate Code, or in a medication hearing under Section 574.106, Health and Safety Code, a person lacks the ability to understand the nature and consequences of a proposed treatment, including the benefits, risks, and alternatives to the proposed treatment, and lacks the ability to make mental health treatment decisions because of impairment.

(7) 'Mental health treatment' means electroconvulsive or other convulsive treatment, treatment of mental illness with psychoactive medication as defined by Section 574.101, Health and Safety Code, or emergency mental health treatment.

(8) 'Principal' means a person who has executed a declaration for mental health treatment.

§137.002. Eligible Persons; Period of validity

Persons who may execute declaration for mental health treatment; Period of validity.

(a)   An adult who is not incapacitated may execute a declaration for mental health treatment. The preferences or instructions may include consent to or refusal of mental health treatment.

(b)   A declaration for mental health treatment is effective on execution as provided by this chapter. Except as provided by Subsection (c), a declaration for mental health treatment expires on the third anniversary of the date of its execution or when revoked by the principal, whichever is earlier.

(c)   If the declaration for mental health treatment is in effect and the principal is incapacitated on the third anniversary of the date of its execution, the declaration remains in effect until the principal is no longer incapacitated.

§137.003. Execution and witnesses

(a)   A declaration for mental health treatment must be signed by the principal in the presence of two or more subscribing witnesses.

(b)   A witness may not, at the time of execution, be:

(1)   the principal's health or residential care provider or an employee of that provider;

(2)   the operator of a community health care facility providing care to the principal or an employee of an operator of the facility;

(3)   a person related to the principal by blood, marriage, or adoption;

(4)   a person entitled to any part of the estate of the principal on the death of the principal under a will, trust, or deed in existence or who would be entitled to any part of the estate by operation of law if the principal died intestate; or

(5)   a person who has a claim against the estate of the principal.

(c)   For a witness's signature to be effective, the witness must sign a statement affirming that, at the time the declaration for mental health treatment was signed, the principal:

(1)   appeared to be of sound mind to make a mental health treatment decision;

(2)   has stated in the witness's presence that the principal was aware of the nature of the declaration for mental health treatment and

that the principal was signing the document voluntarily and free from any duress; and

(3)   requested that the witness serve as a witness to the principal's execution of the document.

§137.004. Health care provider

Health care provider is to act in accordance with declaration for mental health treatment.

A physician or other health care provider shall act in accordance with the declaration for mental health treatment when the principal has been found to be incapacitated. A physician or other provider shall continue to seek and act in accordance with the principal's informed consent to all mental health treatment decisions if the principal is capable of providing informed consent.

§137.005 Limitation on liability

(a) An attending physician, health or residential care provider, or person acting for or under an attending physician's or health or residential care provider's control is not subject to criminal or civil liability and has not engaged in professional misconduct for an act or omission if the act or omission is done in good faith under the terms of a declaration for mental health treatment.

(b) An attending physician, health or residential care provider, or person acting for or under an attending physician's or health or residential care provider's control does not engage in professional misconduct for:

(1) failure to act in accordance with a declaration for mental health treatment if the physician, provider, or other person:

(A) was not provided with a copy of the declaration; and

(B) had no knowledge of the declaration after a good faith attempt to learn of the existence of a declaration; or

(2) acting in accordance with a directive for mental health treatment after the directive has expired or has been revoked if the physician, provider, or other person does not have knowledge of the expiration or revocation.

§137.006 Discrimination in relation to execution of declaration for mental health treatment

A health or residential care provider, health care service plan, insurer issuing disability insurance, self-insured employee benefit plan, or nonprofit hospital service plan may not:

(1) charge a person a different rate solely because the person has executed a declaration for mental health treatment;

(2) require a person to execute a declaration for mental health treatment

before:

    (A) admitting the person to a hospital, nursing home, or residential care home;

    (B) insuring the person; or

    (C) allowing the person to receive health or residential care;

(3) refuse health or residential care to a person solely because the person has executed a declaration for mental health treatment; or

(4) discharge the person solely because the person has or has not executed a declaration for mental health treatment.

§137.007 Use and effect of declaration for mental health treatment

(a) On being presented with a declaration for mental health treatment, a physician or other health care provider shall make the declaration a part of the principal's medical record. When acting in accordance with a declaration for mental health treatment, a physician or other health care provider shall comply with the declaration to the fullest extent possible.

(b) If a physician or other provider is unwilling at any time to comply with a declaration for mental health treatment, the physician or provider may withdraw from providing treatment consistent with the exercise of independent medical judgment and must promptly:

    (1) make a reasonable effort to transfer care for the principal to a physician or provider who is willing to comply with the declaration;

    (2) notify the principal, or principal's guardian, if appropriate, of the decision to withdraw; and

    (3) record in the principal's medical record the notification and, if applicable, the name of the physician or provider to whom the principal is transferred.

§137.008 Disregard of declaration for mental health treatment

(a) A physician or other health care provider may subject the principal to mental health treatment in a manner contrary to the principal's wishes as expressed in a declaration for mental health treatment only:

    (1) if the principal is under an order for temporary or extended mental health services under Section 574.034 or 574.035, Health and Safety Code, and treatment is authorized in compliance with Section 574.106, Health and Safety Code; or

    (2) in case of an emergency when the principal's instructions have not been effective in reducing the severity of the behavior that has caused the emergency.

(b) A declaration for mental health treatment does not limit any authority provided by Chapter 573 or 574, Health and Safety Code:

(1) to take a person into custody; or

(2) to admit or retain a person in a mental health treatment facility.

(c) This section does not apply to the use of electroconvulsive treatment or other convulsive treatment.

§137.009. Conflicting or contrary provisions

(a) Mental health treatment instructions contained in a declaration executed in accordance with this chapter supersede any contrary or conflicting instructions given by:

(1) a durable power of attorney under Chapter 135; or

(2) a guardian appointed under Chapter XIII, Texas Probate Code, after the execution of the declaration.

(b) Mental health treatment instructions contained in a declaration executed in accordance with this chapter shall be conclusive evidence of a declarant's preference in a medication hearing under Section 574.106, Health and Safety Code.

§137.010. Revocation

(a) A declaration for mental health treatment is revoked when a principal who is not incapacitated:

(1) notifies a licensed or certified health or residential care provider of the revocation;

(2) acts in a manner that demonstrates a specific intent to revoke the declaration; or

(3) executes a later declaration for mental health treatment.

(b) A principal's health or residential care provider who is informed of or provided with a revocation of a declaration for mental health treatment immediately shall:

(1) record the revocation in the principal's medical record; and

(2) give notice of the revocation to any other health or residential care provider the provider knows to be responsible for the principal's care.

§137.011 Form of declaration for mental health treatment

The declaration for mental health treatment must be in substantially the following form:

DECLARATION FOR MENTAL HEALTH TREATMENT

I, _____, being an adult of sound mind, willfully and voluntarily make this declaration for mental health treatment to be followed if it is determined by a court that my ability to understand the nature and consequences of a proposed treatment, including the benefits, risks, and alternatives to the proposed treatment, is impaired to such an extent that I lack the capacity to make mental health treatment decisions. 'Mental health treatment' means electroconvulsive or other convulsive treatment, treatment of mental illness with psychoactive medication, and preferences regarding emergency mental health treatment.

(OPTIONAL PARAGRAPH) I understand that I may become incapable of giving or withholding informed consent for mental health treatment due to the symptoms of a diagnosed mental disorder. These symptoms may include:

_____

_____

_____

_____

PSYCHOACTIVE MEDICATIONS

If I become incapable of giving or withholding informed consent for mental health treatment, my wishes regarding psychoactive medications are as follows:

_____ I consent to the administration of the following medications:

_____

_____

_____

_____ I do not consent to the administration of the following medications:

_____

_____

_____

_____ I consent to the administration of a federal Food and Drug Administration approved medication that was only approved and in existence after my declaration and that is considered in the same class of psychoactive medications as stated below:

_____

_____

Conditions or limitations:

_____

CONVULSIVE TREATMENT

If I become incapable of giving or withholding informed consent for mental health treatment, my wishes regarding convulsive treatment are as follows:

_____ I consent to the administration of convulsive treatment.

_____ I do not consent to the administration of convulsive treatment.

Conditions or limitations:

_____

PREFERENCES FOR EMERGENCY TREATMENT

In an emergency, I prefer the following treatment FIRST

(circle one)   Restraint/Seclusion/Medication.

In an emergency, I prefer the following treatment SECOND

(circle one)   Restraint/Seclusion/Medication.

In an emergency, I prefer the following treatment THIRD

(circle one)   Restraint/Seclusion/Medication.

_____ I prefer a male/female to administer restraint, seclusion, and/or medications.

Options for treatment prior to use of restraint, seclusion, and/or medications:

_____

_____

Conditions or limitations:

_____

_____

ADDITIONAL PREFERENCES OR INSTRUCTIONS

Conditions or limitations:

_____

_____

Signature of Principal/ Date: _____

STATEMENT OF WITNESSES

I declare under penalty of perjury that the principal's name has been represented to me by the principal, that the principal signed or acknowledged this declaration in my presence, that I believe the principal to be of sound mind, that the principal has affirmed that the principal is aware of the nature of the document and is signing it voluntarily and free from duress, that the principal requested that I serve as witness to the principal's execution of this document, and that I am not a provider of health or residential care to the principal, an employee of a provider of health or residential care to the principal, an operator of a community health care facility providing care to the principal, or an employee of an operator of a community health care facility providing care to the principal.

I declare that I am not related to the principal by blood, marriage, or adoption and that to the best of my knowledge I am not entitled to and do not have a claim against any part of the estate of the principal on the death of the principal under a will or by operation of law.

Witness Signature: _____

Print Name: _____

Date: _____

Address: _____

Witness Signature: _____

Print Name: _____

Date: _____

Address: _____

NOTICE TO PERSON MAKING A DECLARATION FOR MENTAL HEALTH TREATMENT

This is an important legal document. It creates a declaration for mental health treatment. Before signing this document, you should know these important facts:

This document allows you to make decisions in advance about mental health treatment and specifically three types of mental health treatment: psychoactive medication, convulsive therapy, and emergency mental health treatment. The instructions that you include in this declaration will be followed only if a court believes that you are incapacitated to make treatment decisions. Otherwise, you will be considered able to give or withhold consent for the treatments.

This document will continue in effect for a period of three years unless you become incapacitated to participate in mental health treatment decisions.

If this occurs, the directive will continue in effect until you are no longer incapacitated.

You have the right to revoke this document in whole or in part at any time you have not been determined to be incapacitated. YOU MAY NOT REVOKE THIS DECLARATION WHEN YOU ARE CONSIDERED BY A COURT TO BE INCAPACITATED. A revocation is effective when it is communicated to your attending physician or other health care provider.

If there is anything in this document that you do not understand, you should ask a lawyer to explain it to you. This declaration is not valid unless it is signed by two qualified witnesses who are personally known to you and who are present when you sign or acknowledge your signature.

CODE OF CRIMINAL PROCEDURE

ICOMPETENCY TO STAND TRIAL—§46B

§46B.003. Incompetency; presumptions

(a) A person is incompetent to stand trial if the person does not have:

    (1) sufficient present ability to consult with the person's lawyer with a reasonable degree of rational understanding; or

    (2) a rational as well as factual understanding of the proceedings against the person.

(b) A defendant is presumed competent to stand trial and shall be found competent to stand trial unless proved incompetent by a preponderance of the evidence.

§46B.004. Raising the Issue of Incompetency to Stand Trial

(a) Either party may suggest by motion, or the trial court may suggest on its own motion, that the defendant may be incompetent to stand trial. A motion suggesting that the defendant may be incompetent to stand trial may be supported by affidavits setting out the facts on which the suggestion is made.

(b) If evidence suggesting the defendant may be incompetent to stand trial comes to the attention of the court, the court on its own motion shall suggest that the defendant may be incompetent to stand trial.

(c) On suggestion that the defendant may be incompetent to stand trial, the court shall determine by informal inquiry whether there is some evidence from any source that would support a finding that the defendant may be incompetent to stand trial.

(d) If the court determines there is evidence to support a finding of incompetency, the court, except as provided by Article 46B.005(d), shall stay all other

41

proceedings in the case.

§46B.005. Determining incompetency to stand trial

(a) If after an informal inquiry the court determines that evidence exists to support a finding of incompetency, the court shall order an examination under Subchapter B to determine whether the defendant is incompetent to stand trial.

(b) Except as provided by Subsection (c), the court shall hold a hearing under Subchapter C before determining whether the defendant is incompetent to stand trial.

(c) The court is not required to hold a hearing if:

(1) neither party requests a jury trial on the issue of incompetency;

(2) neither party opposes a finding of incompetency; and

(3) the court does not, on its own motion, determine that a hearing is necessary to determine incompetency.

(d) If the issue of the defendant's incompetency to stand trial is raised after the trial begins, the court may determine the issue at any time before sentencing. If the determination is delayed until after the return of a verdict, the court shall make the determination as soon as reasonably possible after the return. If a verdict of not guilty is returned, the court may not determine the issue of incompetency.

§46B.007. Admissibility of Statements and Certain Other Evidence

A statement made by a defendant during an examination or hearing on the defendant's incompetency, the testimony of an expert based on that statement, and evidence obtained as a result of that statement may not be admitted in evidence against the defendant in any criminal proceeding, other than at:

(1) a hearing on the defendant's incompetency; or

(2) any proceeding at which the defendant first introduces into evidence a statement, testimony, or evidence described by this section.

SUBCHAPTER B. EXAMINATION

§46B.021. Appointment of experts

(a) On a suggestion that the defendant may be incompetent to stand trial, the court may appoint one or more disinterested experts to:

(1) examine the defendant and report to the court on the competency or incompetency of the defendant; and

(2) testify as to the issue of competency or incompetency of the defendant at any trial or hearing involving that issue.

(b) On a determination that evidence exists to support a finding of incompetency to stand trial, the court shall appoint one or more experts to perform the duties described by Subsection (a).

(c) An expert involved in the treatment of the defendant may not be appointed to examine the defendant under this article.

(d) The movant or other party as directed by the court shall provide to experts appointed under this article information relevant to a determination of the defendant's competency, including copies of the indictment or information, any supporting documents used to establish probable cause in the case, and previous mental health evaluation and treatment records.

(e) The court may appoint as experts under this chapter qualified psychiatrists or psychologists employed by the local mental health authority or local mental retardation authority. The local mental health authority or local mental retardation authority is entitled to compensation and reimbursement as provided by Article 46B.027.

(f) If a defendant wishes to be examined by an expert of the defendant's own choice, the court on timely request shall provide the expert with reasonable opportunity to examine the defendant.

§46B.022. Experts: qualifications

(a) To qualify for appointment under this subchapter as an expert, a psychiatrist or psychologist must:

(1) as appropriate, be a physician licensed in this state or be a psychologist licensed in this state who has a doctoral degree in psychology; and

(2) have the following certification or experience or training:

(A) as appropriate, certification by:

(i) the American Board of Psychiatry and Neurology with added or special qualifications in forensic psychiatry; or

(ii) the American Board of Professional Psychology in forensic psychology; or

(B) experience or training consisting of:

(i) at least 24 hours of specialized forensic training relating to incompetency or insanity evaluations;

(ii) for an appointment made before January 1, 2005, at least five years of experience before January 1, 2004, in performing criminal forensic evaluations for courts; or

(iii) for an appointment made on or after January 1, 2005, at least five years of experience before January 1, 2004, in performing criminal forensic evaluations for courts and eight or more hours of continuing education relating to forensic evaluations, completed in the 12 months preceding the appointment and documented with the court.

(b) In addition to meeting qualifications required by Subsection (a), to be appointed as an expert a psychiatrist or psychologist must have completed six hours of required continuing education in courses in forensic psychiatry or psychology, as appropriate, in either of the reporting periods in the 24 months preceding the appointment.

(c) A court may appoint as an expert a psychiatrist or psychologist who does not meet the requirements of Subsections (a) and (b) only if exigent circumstances require the court to base the appointment on professional training or experience of the expert that directly provides the expert with a specialized expertise to examine the defendant that would not ordinarily be possessed by a psychiatrist or psychologist who meets the requirements of Subsections (a) and (b).

§46B.024. Factors considered in examination

During an examination under this subchapter and in any report based on that examination, an expert shall consider, in addition to other issues determined relevant by the expert, the following:

(1) the capacity of the defendant during criminal proceedings to:

(A) rationally understand the charges against the defendant and the potential consequences of the pending criminal proceedings;

(B) disclose to counsel pertinent facts, events, and states of mind;

(C) engage in a reasoned choice of legal strategies and options;

(D) understand the adversarial nature of criminal proceedings;

(E) exhibit appropriate courtroom behavior; and

(F) testify;

(2) whether the defendant has a diagnosable mental illness or is a person with mental retardation;

(3) the impact of the mental illness or mental retardation, if existent, on the defendant's capacity to engage with counsel in a reasonable and rational manner; and

(4) if the defendant is taking psychoactive or other medication:

(A) whether the medication is necessary to maintain the defendant's competency; and

(B) the effect, if any, of the medication on the defendant's appearance, demeanor, or ability to participate in the proceedings.

§46B.025. Expert's report

(a) An expert's report to the court must state an opinion on a defendant's competency or incompetency to stand trial or explain why the expert is unable to state such an opinion and must also:

(1) identify and address specific issues referred to the expert for evaluation;

(2) document that the expert explained to the defendant the purpose of the evaluation, the persons to whom a report on the evaluation is provided, and the limits on rules of confidentiality applying to the relationship between the expert and the defendant;

(3) in general terms, describe procedures, techniques, and tests used in the examination and the purpose of each procedure, technique, or test; and

(4) state the expert's clinical observations, findings, and opinions on each specific issue referred to the expert by the court, and state specifically any issues on which the expert could not provide an opinion.

(b) If in the opinion of an expert appointed under Article 46B.021 the defendant is incompetent to proceed, the expert shall state in the report:

(1) the exact nature of the deficits resulting from the defendant's mental illness or mental retardation, if any, that impact the factors listed in Article 46B.024, contributing to the defendant's incompetency; and

(2) prospective treatment options, if any, appropriate for the defendant.

(c) An expert's report may not state the expert's opinion on the defendant's sanity at the time of the alleged offense, if in the opinion of the expert the defendant is incompetent to proceed.

§46B.026. Report deadline

(a) Except as provided by Subsection (b), an expert examining the defendant shall provide the report on the defendant' s competency or incompetency to stand trial to the court, the attorney representing the state, and the attorney representing the defendant not later than the 30th day after the date on which the expert was ordered to examine the defendant and prepare the report.

(b) For good cause shown, the court may permit an expert to complete the examination and report and provide the report to the court and attorneys at a date later than the date required by Subsection (a).

SUBCHAPTER C

COURT-ORDERED EXAMINATION AND REPORT

§46C.101. Appointment of experts

(a) If notice of intention to raise the insanity defense is filed under Article 46C.051, the court may, on its own motion or motion by the defendant, the defendant's counsel, or the attorney representing the state, appoint one or more disinterested experts to:

(1) examine the defendant with regard to the insanity defense; and

(2) testify as to the issue of insanity at any trial or hearing involving that issue.

(b) The court shall advise an expert appointed under this article of the facts and circumstances of the offense with which the defendant is charged and the elements of the insanity defense.

§46C.102. Experts qualifications

(a) The court may appoint qualified psychiatrists or psychologists as experts under this chapter. To qualify for appointment under this subchapter as an expert, a psychiatrist or psychologist must:

(1) as appropriate, be a physician licensed in this state or be a psychologist licensed in this state who has a doctoral degree in psychology; and

(2) have the following certification or experience or training:

(A) as appropriate, certification by:

(i) the American Board of Psychiatry and Neurology with added or special qualifications in forensic psychiatry; or

(ii) the American Board of Professional Psychology in forensic psychology; or

(B) experience or training consisting of:

(i) at least 24 hours of specialized forensic training relating to incompetency or insanity evaluations;

(ii) at least five years of experience in performing criminal forensic evaluations for courts; and

(iii) eight or more hours of continuing education relating to forensic evaluations, completed in the 12 months preceding the appointment and documented with the court.

(b) In addition to meeting qualifications required by Subsection (a), to be appointed as an expert a psychiatrist or psychologist must have completed six hours of required continuing education in courses in forensic psychiatry or psychology, as appropriate, in the 24 months preceding the appointment.

(c) A court may appoint as an expert a psychiatrist or psychologist who does not meet the requirements of Subsections (a) and (b) only if exigent circumstances require the court to base the appointment on professional training or experience of the expert that directly provides the expert with a specialized expertise to examine the defendant that would not ordinarily be possessed by a psychiatrist or psychologist who meets the requirements of Subsections (a) and (b).

§46C.103. Competency to stand trail: concurrent appointment

(a) An expert appointed under this subchapter to examine the defendant with regard to the insanity defense also may be appointed by the court to examine the defendant with regard to the defendant's competency to stand trial under Chapter 46B, if the expert files with the court separate written reports concerning the defendant's competency to stand trial and the insanity defense.

(b) Notwithstanding Subsection (a), an expert may not examine the defendant for purposes of determining the defendant's sanity and may not file a report regarding the defendant's sanity if in the opinion of the expert the defendant is incompetent to proceed.

§46C.104. Order compelling defendant to submit to examination

(a) For the purposes described by this chapter, the court may order any defendant to submit to examination, including a defendant who is free on bail. If the defendant fails or refuses to submit to examination, the court may order the defendant to custody for examination for a reasonable period not to exceed 21 days. Custody ordered by the court under this subsection may include custody at a facility operated by the department.

(b) If a defendant who has been ordered to a facility operated by the department for examination remains in the facility for a period that exceeds 21 days, the head of that facility shall cause the defendant to be immediately transported to the committing court and placed in the custody of the sheriff of the county in which the committing court is located. That county shall reimburse the facility for the mileage and per diem expenses of the personnel required to transport the defendant, calculated in accordance with the state travel rules in effect at that time.

(c) The court may not order a defendant to a facility operated by the department for examination without the consent of the head of that facility.

§46C.105. Reports submitted by experts

(a) A written report of the examination shall be submitted to the court not later than the 30th day after the date of the order of examination. The court shall provide copies of the report to the defense counsel and the attorney representing the state.

(b) The report must include a description of the procedures used in the examination and the examiner's observations and findings pertaining to the insanity defense.

(c) The examiner shall submit a separate report stating the examiner's observations and findings concerning:

    (1) whether the defendant is presently a person with a mental illness and requires court-ordered mental health services under Subtitle C, Title 7, Health and Safety Code; or

(2) whether the defendant is presently a person with mental retardation.

§46C.106. Compensation of experts

(a) The appointed experts shall be paid by the county in which the indictment was returned or information was filed.

(b) The county in which the indictment was returned or information was filed shall reimburse a facility operated by the department that accepts a defendant for examination under this subchapter for expenses incurred that are determined by the department to be reasonably necessary and incidental to the proper examination of the defendant.

§46C.107. Examination by expert of defendant's choice

If a defendant wishes to be examined by an expert of the defendant's own choice, the court on timely request shall provide the examiner with reasonable opportunity to examine the defendant.

EDUCATION CODE

§29.001. Statewide Plan

The agency shall develop, and modify as necessary, a statewide design, consistent with federal law, for the delivery of services to children with disabilities in this state that includes rules for the administration and funding of the special education program so that a free appropriate public education is available to all of those children between the ages of three and 21. The statewide design shall include the provision of services primarily through school districts and shared services arrangements, supplemented by regional education service centers. The agency shall also develop and implement a statewide plan with programmatic content that includes procedures designed to:

(1) ensure state compliance with requirements for supplemental federal funding for all state-administered programs involving the delivery of instructional or related services to students with disabilities;

(2) facilitate interagency coordination when other state agencies are involved in the delivery of instructional or related services to students with disabilities;

(3) periodically assess statewide personnel needs in all areas of specialization related to special education and pursue strategies to meet those needs through a consortium of representatives from regional education service centers, local education agencies, and institutions of higher education and through other available alternatives;

(4) ensure that regional education service centers throughout the state maintain a regional support function, which may include direct service delivery and a component designed to facilitate the placement of students with disabilities who cannot be appropriately served in their resident districts;

(5) allow the agency to effectively monitor and periodically conduct site visits

of all school districts to ensure that rules adopted under this section are applied in a consistent and uniform manner, to ensure that districts are complying with those rules, and to ensure that annual statistical reports filed by the districts and not otherwise available through the Public Education Information Management System under Section 42.006, are accurate and complete;

(6) ensure that appropriately trained personnel are involved in the diagnostic and evaluative procedures operating in all districts and that those personnel routinely serve on district admissions, review, and dismissal committees;

(7) ensure that an individualized education program for each student with a disability is properly developed, implemented, and maintained in the least restrictive environment that is appropriate to meet the student's educational needs;

(8) ensure that, when appropriate, each student with a disability is provided an opportunity to participate in career and technology and physical education classes, in addition to participating in regular or special classes; and

(9) ensure that each student with a disability is provided necessary related services; and

(10) ensure that an individual assigned to act as a surrogate parent for a child with a disability, as provided by 20 U.S.C. Section 1415(b) and its subsequent amendments, is required to:

(A) complete a training program that complies with minimum standards established by agency rule;

(B) visit the child and the child's school;

(C) consult with persons involved in the child's education, including teachers, caseworkers, court-appointed volunteers, guardians ad litem, attorneys ad litem, foster parents, and caretakers;

(D) review the child's educational records;

(E) attend meetings of the child's admission, review, and dismissal committee;

(F) exercise independent judgment in pursuing the child's interests; and

(G) exercise the child's due process rights under applicable state and federal law.

§29.002. Definition

In this subchapter, "special services" means:

(1) special instruction, which may be provided by professional and paraprofessional personnel in the regular classroom or in an instructional arrangement described by Section 42.151; or

(2) related services, which are developmental, corrective, supportive, or

evaluative services, not instructional in nature, that may be required for the proper development and implementation of a student's individualized education program.

§29.003. Eligibility Criteria

(a) The agency shall develop specific eligibility criteria based on the general classifications established by this section with reference to contemporary diagnostic or evaluative terminologies and techniques. Eligible students with disabilities shall enjoy the right to a free appropriate public education, which may include instruction in the regular classroom, instruction through special teaching, or instruction through contracts approved under this subchapter. Instruction shall be supplemented by the provision of related services when appropriate.

(b) A student is eligible to participate in a school district's special education program if the student:

(1) is not more than 21 years of age and has a visual or auditory impairment that prevents the student from being adequately or safely educated in public school without the provision of special services; or

(2) is at least three but not more than 21 years of age and has one or more of the following disabilities that prevents the student from being adequately or safely educated in public school without the provision of special services:

(A) physical disability;

(B) mental retardation;

(C) emotional disturbance;

(D) learning disability;

(E) autism;

(F) speech disability; or

(G) traumatic brain injury.

§29.004. Comprehensive Assessment

A written report of a comprehensive individual assessment of a student for purposes of special education services shall be completed not later than the 60th calendar day following the date on which the referral for assessment was initiated by school personnel, the student's parent or legal guardian, or another appropriate person. The assessment shall be conducted using procedures that are appropriate for the student's most proficient method of communication.

§29.005. Individualized Education Program

(a) Before a child is enrolled in a special education program of a school district, the district shall establish a committee composed of the persons required under 20 U.S.C. Section 1401(20) to develop the child's individualized education program.

(b) The committee shall develop the individualized education program by agreement of the committee members or, if those persons cannot agree, by an alternate method provided by the agency. Majority vote may not be used to determine the individualized education program.

(c) If the individualized education program is not developed by agreement, the written statement of the program required under 20 U.S.C. Section 1401(20) must include the basis of the disagreement.

(d) If the child's parent is unable to speak English, the district shall:

(1) provide the parent with a written or audiotaped copy of the child's individualized education program translated into Spanish if Spanish is the parent's native language; or

(2) if the parent's native language is a language other than Spanish, make a good faith effort to provide the parent with a written or audiotaped copy of the child's individualized education program translated into the parent's native language.

§30.001. Coordination of Services to Children with Disabilities

(a) In this section, "children with disabilities" means students eligible to participate in a school district's special education program under Section 29.003.

(b) The commissioner, with the approval of the State Board of Education, shall develop and implement a plan for the coordination of services to children with disabilities in each region served by a regional education service center. The plan must include procedures for:

(1) identifying existing public or private educational and related services for children with disabilities in each region;

(2) identifying and referring children with disabilities who cannot be appropriately served by the school district in which they reside to other appropriate programs;

(3) assisting school districts to individually or cooperatively develop programs to identify and provide appropriate services for children with disabilities;

(4) expanding and coordinating services provided by regional education service centers for children with disabilities; and

(5) providing for special services, including special seats, books, instructional media, and other supplemental supplies and services required for proper instruction.

(c) The commissioner may allocate appropriated funds to regional education service centers or may otherwise spend those funds, as necessary, to implement this section.

§37.0021. Use of confinement, restraint, seclusion and time-out.

(a) It is the policy of this state to treat with dignity and respect all students, including students with disabilities who receive special education services under Subchapter A, Chapter 29. A student with a disability who receives special education services under Subchapter A, Chapter 29, may not be confined in a locked box, locked closet, or other specially designed locked space as either a discipline management practice or a behavior management technique.

(b) In this section:

(1) "Restraint" means the use of physical force or a mechanical device to significantly restrict the free movement of all or a portion of a student's body.

(2) "Seclusion" means a behavior management technique in which a student is confined in a locked box, locked closet, or locked room that:

(A) is designed solely to seclude a person; and

(B) contains less than 50 square feet of space.

(3) "Time-out" means a behavior management technique in which, to provide a student with an opportunity to regain self-control, the student is separated from other students for a limited period in a setting:

(A) that is not locked; and

(B) from which the exit is not physically blocked by furniture, a closed door held shut from the outside, or another inanimate object.

(c) A school district employee or volunteer or an independent contractor of a district may not place a student in seclusion. This subsection does not apply to the use of seclusion in a court-ordered placement, other than a placement in an educational program of a school district, or in a placement or facility to which the following law, rules, or regulations apply:

(1) the Children's Health Act of 2000, Pub. L. No. 106-310, any subsequent amendments to that Act, any regulations adopted under that Act, or any subsequent amendments to those regulations;

(2) 40 T.A.C. Sections 720.1001-720.1013; or

(3) 25 T.A.C. Section 412.308(e).

(d) The commissioner by rule shall adopt procedures for the use of restraint and time-out by a school district employee or volunteer or an independent contractor of a district in the case of a student with a disability receiving special education services under Subchapter A, Chapter 29. A procedure adopted under this subsection must:

(1) be consistent with:

(A) professionally accepted practices and standards of student discipline and techniques for behavior management; and

    (B) relevant health and safety standards; and

(2) identify any discipline management practice or behavior management technique that requires a district employee or volunteer or an independent contractor of a district to be trained before using that practice or technique.

(e) In the case of a conflict between a rule adopted under Subsection

(d) and a rule adopted under Subchapter A, Chapter 29, the rule adopted under Subsection (d) controls.

(f) For purposes of this subsection, "weapon" includes any weapon described under Section 37.007(a)(1). This section does not prevent a student's locked, unattended confinement in an emergency situation while awaiting the arrival of law enforcement personnel if:

(1) the student possesses a weapon; and

(2) the confinement is necessary to prevent the student from causing bodily harm to the student or another person.

(g) This section and any rules or procedures adopted under this section do not apply to:

(1) a peace officer while performing law enforcement duties;

(2) juvenile probation, detention, or corrections personnel; or

(3) an educational services provider with whom a student is placed by a judicial authority, unless the services are provided in an educational program of a school district.

§38.016 Psychotropic drugs and psychiatric evaluations or examinations

(a) In this section:

(1) "Parent" includes a guardian or other person standing in parental relation.

(2) "Psychotropic drug" means a substance that is:

    (A) used in the diagnosis, treatment, or prevention of a disease or as a component of a medication; and

    (B) intended to havean altering effect on perception, emotion, or behavior.

(b) A school district employee may not:

(1) recommend that a student use a psychotropic drug; or

(2) suggest any particular diagnosis; or

(3) use the refusal by a parent to consent to administration of a psychotropic drug to a student, or to a psychiatric evaluation or

examination of a student as grounds, by itself, for prohibiting the child from attending a class or participating in a school-related activity.

(c) Subsection (b) does not:

(1) prevent an appropriate referral under the child find system required under 20 U.S.C. Section 1412, as amended; or

(2) prohibit a school district employee who is a registered nurse, advanced nurse practitioner, physician, or certified or appropriately credentialed mental health professional from recommending that a child be evaluated by an appropriate medical practitioner; or

3) prohibit a school employee from discussing any aspect of a child's behavior or academic progress with the child's parent or another school district employee.

(d) The board of trustees of each school district shall adopt a policy to ensure implementation and enforcement of this section.

(e) An act in violation of Subsection (b) does not override the immunity from personal liability granted in Section 22.051 or other law or the district's sovereign and governmental immunity.

TEXAS ADMINISTRATIVE CODE

(Title 19, Part 2, Chapter 89, Subchapter 89, Subchapter AA, Division 2)

RULE 89.1053 PROCEDURES FOR USE OF RESTRAINT AND TIME-OUT

(a) Requirement to implement. In addition to the requirements of 34 Code of Federal Regulations (CFR), §300.346(a)(2)(i) and (c), school districts and charter schools must implement the provisions of this section regarding the use of restraint and time-out. In accordance with the provisions of Texas Education Code (TEC), §37.0021 (Use of Confinement, Restraint, Seclusion, and Time-Out), it is the policy of the state to treat with dignity and respect all students, including students with disabilities who receive special education services under TEC, Chapter 29, Subchapter A.

(b) Definitions.

(1) "Emergency" means a situation in which a student's behavior poses a threat of:

(A) imminent, serious physical harm to the student or others; or

(B) imminent, serious property destruction.

(2) "Restraint" means the use of physical force or a mechanical device to significantly restrict the free movement of all or a portion of the student's body.

(3) "Time-out" means a behavior management technique in which, to provide a student with an opportunity to regain self-control, the student is separated from other students for a limited period in a setting:

(A) that is not locked; and

(B) from which the exit is not physically blocked by furniture, a closed door held shut from the outside, or another inanimate object.

(c) Use of restraint. A school employee, volunteer, or independent contractor may use restraint only in an emergency as defined in subsection (b) of this section and with the following limitations.

(1) Restraint shall be limited to the use of such reasonable force as is necessary to address the emergency.

(2) Restraint shall be discontinued at the point at which the emergency no longer exists.

(3) Restraint shall be implemented in such a way as to protect the health and safety of the student and others.

(4) Restraint shall not deprive the student of basic human necessities.

(d) Training on use of restraint. Training for school employees, volunteers, or independent contractors shall be provided according to the following requirements.

(1) Not later than April 1, 2003, a core team of personnel on each campus must be trained in the use of restraint, and the team must include a campus administrator or designee and any general or special education personnel likely to use restraint.

(2) After April 1, 2003, personnel called upon to use restraint in an emergency and who have not received prior training must receive training within 30 school days following the use of restraint.

(3) Training on use of restraint must include prevention and de-escalation techniques and provide alternatives to the use of restraint.

(4) All trained personnel shall receive instruction in current professionally accepted practices and standards regarding behavior management and the use of restraint.

(e) Documentation and notification on use of restraint. In a case in which restraint is used, school employees, volunteers, or independent contractors shall implement the following documentation requirements.

(1) On the day restraint is utilized, the campus administrator or designee must be notified verbally or in writing regarding the use of restraint.

(2) On the day restraint is utilized, a good faith effort shall be made to verbally notify the parent(s) regarding the use of restraint.

(3) Written notification of the use of restraint must be placed in the mail or otherwise provided to the parent within one school day of the use of restraint.

(4) Written documentation regarding the use of restraint must be placed in the student's special education eligibility folder in a timely manner so the information is available to the ARD committee when it considers the impact of the student's behavior on the student's learning and/or the creation or revision of a behavioral intervention plan (BIP).

(5) Written notification to the parent(s) and documentation to the student's special education eligibility folder shall include the following:

(A) name of the student;

(B) name of the staff member(s) administering the restraint;

(C) date of the restraint and the time the restraint began and ended;

(D) location of the restraint;

(E) nature of the restraint;

(F) a description of the activity in which the student was engaged immediately preceding the use of restraint;

(G) the behavior that prompted the restraint;

(H) the efforts made to de-escalate the situation and alternatives to restraint that were attempted; and

(I) information documenting parent contact and notification.

(f) Clarification regarding restraint. The provisions adopted under this section do not apply to the use of physical force or a mechanical device which does not significantly restrict the free movement of all or a portion of the student's body. Restraint that involves significant restriction as referenced in subsection (b)(2) of this section does not include:

(1) physical contact or appropriately prescribed adaptive equipment to promote normative body positioning and/or physical functioning;

(2) limited physical contact with a student to promote safety (e.g., holding a student's hand), prevent a potentially harmful action (e.g., running into the street), teach a skill, redirect attention, provide guidance to a location, or provide comfort;

(3) limited physical contact or appropriately prescribed adaptive equipment to prevent a student from engaging in ongoing, repetitive self-injurious behaviors, with the expectation that instruction will be reflected in the individualized education program (IEP) as required by 34 CFR §300.346(a)(2)(i) and (c) to promote student learning and reduce and/or prevent the need for ongoing intervention; or

(4) seat belts and other safety equipment used to secure students during transportation.

(g) Use of time-out. A school employee, volunteer, or independent contractor may use time-out in accordance with subsection (b)(3) of this section with the following limitations.

(1) Physical force or threat of physical force shall not be used to place a student in time-out.

(2) Time-out may only be used in conjunction with an array of positive behavior intervention strategies and techniques and must be included in the

student's IEP and/or BIP if it is utilized on a recurrent basis to increase or decrease a targeted behavior.

(3) Use of time-out shall not be implemented in a fashion that precludes the ability of the student to be involved in and progress in the general curriculum and advance appropriately toward attaining the annual goals specified in the student's IEP.

(h) Training on use of time-out. Training for school employees, volunteers, or independent contractors shall be provided according to the following requirements.

(1) Not later than April 1, 2003, general or special education personnel who implement time-out based on requirements established in a student's IEP and/or BIP must be trained in the use of time-out.

(2) After April 1, 2003, newly-identified personnel called upon to implement time-out based on requirements established in a student's IEP and/or BIP must receive training in the use of time-out within 30 school days of being assigned the responsibility for implementing time-out.

(3) Training on the use of time-out must be provided as part of a program which addresses a full continuum of positive behavioral intervention strategies, and must address the impact of time-out on the ability of the student to be involved in and progress in the general curriculum and advance appropriately toward attaining the annual goals specified in the student's IEP.

(4) All trained personnel shall receive instruction in current professionally accepted practices and standards regarding behavior management and the use of time-out.

(i) Documentation on use of time-out. Necessary documentation or data collection regarding the use of time-out, if any, must be addressed in the IEP or BIP. The admission, review, and dismissal (ARD) committee must use any collected data to judge the effectiveness of the intervention and provide a basis for making determinations regarding its continued use.

(j) Student safety. Any behavior management technique and/or discipline management practice must be implemented in such a way as to protect the health and safety of the student and others. No discipline management practice may be calculated to inflict injury, cause harm, demean, or deprive the student of basic human necessities.

(k) Data reporting. Beginning with the 2003-2004 school year, with the exception of actions covered by subsection (f) of this section, data regarding the use of restraint must be electronically reported to the Texas Education Agency in accordance with reporting standards specified by the Agency.

(l) The provisions adopted under this section do not apply to:

(1) a peace officer while performing law enforcement duties;

(2) juvenile probation, detention, or corrections personnel; or

(3) an educational services provider with whom a student is placed by a judicial authority, unless the services are provided in an educational program of a school district.

Family Code

Court Ordered Counseling in Divorce—§6

§6.505. Counseling

(a) While a divorce suit is pending, the court may direct the parties to counsel with a person named by the court.

(b) The person named by the court to counsel the parties shall submit a written report to the court and to the parties before the final hearing. In the report, the counselor shall give only an opinion as to whether there exists a reasonable expectation of reconciliation of the parties and, if so, whether further counseling would be beneficial. The sole purpose of the report is to aid the court in determining whether the suit for divorce should be continued pending further counseling.

(c) A copy of the report shall be furnished to each party.

(d) If the court believes that there is a reasonable expectation of the parties' reconciliation, the court may by written order continue the proceedings and direct the parties to a person named by the court for further counseling for a period fixed by the court not to exceed 60 days, subject to any terms, conditions, and limitations the court considers desirable. In ordering counseling, the court shall consider the circumstances of the parties, including the needs of the parties' family and the availability of counseling services. At the expiration of the period specified by the court, the counselor to whom the parties were directed shall report to the court whether the parties have complied with the court's order. Thereafter, the court shall proceed as in a divorce suit generally.

(e) If the court orders counseling under this section and the parties to the marriage are the parents of a child under 18 years of age born or adopted during the marriage, the counseling shall include counseling on issues that confront children who are the subject of a suit affecting the parent-child relationship.

CONSENT TO TREATMENT OF CHILD BY NON-PARENT OR CHILD—§32

§32.001. Consent by Non-Parent

(a) The following persons may consent to medical, dental, psychological, and surgical treatment of a child when the person having the right to consent as otherwise provided by law cannot be contacted and that person has not given actual notice to the contrary:

(1) a grandparent of the child;

(2) an adult brother or sister of the child;

(3) an adult aunt or uncle of the child;

(4) an educational institution in which the child is enrolled that has received written authorization to consent from a person having the right to consent;

(5) an adult who has actual care, control, and possession of the child and has written authorization to consent from a person having the right to consent;

(6) a court having jurisdiction over a suit affecting the parent-child relationship of which the child is the subject;

(7) an adult responsible for the actual care, control, and possession of a child under the jurisdiction of a juvenile court or committed by a juvenile court to the care of an agency of the state or county; or

(8) a peace officer who has lawfully taken custody of a minor, if the peace officer has reasonable grounds to believe the minor is in need of immediate medical treatment.

(b) The Texas Youth Commission may consent to the medical, dental, psychological, and surgical treatment of a child committed to it under Title 3 when the person having the right to consent has been contacted and that person has not given actual notice to the contrary.

(c) This section does not apply to consent for the immunization of a child.

(d) A person who consents to the medical treatment of a minor under Subsection (a)(7) or (8) is immune from liability for damages resulting from the examination or treatment of the minor, except to the extent of the person's own acts of negligence. A physician or dentist licensed to practice in this state, or a hospital or medical facility at which a minor is treated is immune from liability for damages resulting from the examination or treatment of a minor under this section, except to the extent of the person's own acts of negligence.

§32.002. Consent Form

(a) Consent to medical treatment under this subchapter must be in writing, signed by the person giving consent, and given to the doctor, hospital, or other medical facility that administers the treatment.

(b) The consent must include:

(1) the name of the child;

(2) the name of one or both parents, if known, and the name of any managing conservator or guardian of the child;

(3) the name of the person giving consent and the person's relationship to the child;

(4) a statement of the nature of the medical treatment to be given; and

(5) the date the treatment is to begin.

Section 4 of Acts 1995, 74th Leg., ch. 123, eff. Sept. 1, 1995, amends subsec. (a) of V.T.C.A., Family Code §35.02 [now this section] without reference to the repeal of said section by Acts 1995, 74th Leg., ch. 20, §2(1). As so amended, subsec. (a) reads:

"Consent to medical treatment under Sections 35.01 and 35.011 of this code shall be in writing, signed by the person giving consent, and given to the doctor, hospital, or other medical facility that administers the treatment."

§32.003. Consent to Treatment by Child

(a) A child may consent to medical, dental, psychological, and surgical treatment for the child by a licensed physician or dentist if the child:

(1) is on active duty with the armed services of the United States of America;

(2) is:

(A) 16 years of age or older and resides separate and apart from the child's parents, managing conservator, or guardian, with or without the consent of the parents, managing conservator, or guardian and regardless of the duration of the residence; and

(B) managing the child's own financial affairs, regardless of the source of the income;

(3) consents to the diagnosis and treatment of an infectious, contagious, or communicable disease that is required by law or a rule to be reported by the licensed physician or dentist to a local health officer or the Texas Department of Health, including all diseases within the scope of Section 81.041, Health and Safety Code;

(4) is unmarried and pregnant and consents to hospital, medical, or surgical treatment, other than abortion, related to the pregnancy;

(5) consents to examination and treatment for drug or chemical addiction, drug or chemical dependency, or any other condition directly related to drug or chemical use; or

(6) is unmarried and has actual custody of the child's biological child and

consents to medical, dental, psychological, or surgical treatment for the child.

(b) Consent by a child to medical, dental, psychological, and surgical treatment under this section is not subject to disaffirmance because of minority.

(c) Consent of the parents, managing conservator, or guardian of a child is not necessary in order to authorize hospital, medical, surgical, or dental care under this section.

(d) A licensed physician, dentist, or psychologist may, with or without the consent of a child who is a patient, advise the parents, managing conservator, or guardian of the child of the treatment given to or needed by the child.

(e) A physician, dentist, psychologist, hospital, or medical facility is not liable for the examination and treatment of a child under this section except for the provider's or the facility's own acts of negligence.

(f) A physician, dentist, psychologist, hospital, or medical facility may rely on the written statement of the child containing the grounds on which the child has capacity to consent to the child's medical treatment.

§32.004. Consent to Counseling

(a) A child may consent to counseling for:

(1) suicide prevention;

(2) chemical addiction or dependency; or

(3) sexual, physical, or emotional abuse.

(b) A licensed or certified physician, psychologist, counselor, or social worker having reasonable grounds to believe that a child has been sexually, physically, or emotionally abused, is contemplating suicide, or is suffering from a chemical or drug addiction or dependency may:

(1) counsel the child without the consent of the child's parents or, if applicable, managing conservator or guardian;

(2) with or without the consent of the child who is a client, advise the child's parents or, if applicable, managing conservator or guardian of the treatment given to or needed by the child; and

(3) rely on the written statement of the child containing the grounds on which the child has capacity to consent to the child's own treatment under this section.

(c) Unless consent is obtained as otherwise allowed by law, a physician, psychologist, counselor, or social worker may not counsel a child if consent is prohibited by a court order.

(d) A physician, psychologist, counselor, or social worker counseling a child under this section is not liable for damages except for damages resulting from the person's negligence or willful misconduct.

(e) A parent, or, if applicable, managing conservator or guardian, who has not consented to counseling treatment of the child is not obligated to compensate a physician, psychologist, counselor, or social worker for counseling services rendered under this section.

§32.005. Examination Without Consent of Abuse or Neglect of Child

(a) Except as provided by Subsection (c), a physician, dentist, or psychologist having reasonable grounds to believe that a child's physical or mental condition has been adversely affected by abuse or neglect may examine the child without the consent of the child, the child's parents, or other person authorized to consent to treatment under this subchapter.

(b) An examination under this section may include X-rays, blood tests, photographs, and penetration of tissue necessary to accomplish those tests.

(c) Unless consent is obtained as otherwise allowed by law, a physician, dentist, or psychologist may not examine a child:

(1) 16 years of age or older who refuses to consent; or

(2) for whom consent is prohibited by a court order.

(d) A physician, dentist, or psychologist examining a child under this section is not liable for damages except for damages resulting from the physician's or dentist's negligence.

WAIVER OF JURISDICTION AND DISCRETIONARY TRANSFER—§54.02

§54.02. Waiver of Jurisdiction and Discretionary Transfer to Criminal Court

(a) The juvenile court may waive its exclusive original jurisdiction and transfer a child to the appropriate district court or criminal district court for criminal proceedings if:

(1) the child is alleged to have violated a penal law of the grade of felony;

(2) the child was:

(A) 14 years of age or older at the time he is alleged to have committed the offense, if the offense is a capital felony, an aggravated controlled substance felony, or a felony of the first degree, and no adjudication hearing has been conducted concerning that offense; or

(B) 15 years of age or older at the time the child is alleged to have committed the offense, if the offense is a felony of the second or third degree or a state jail felony, and no adjudication hearing has been conducted concerning that offense; and

(3) after a full investigation and a hearing, the juvenile court determines that there is probable cause to believe that the child before the court committed the offense alleged and that because of the seriousness of the offense alleged

or the background of the child the welfare of the community requires criminal proceedings.

(b) The petition and notice requirements of Sections 53.04, 53.05, 53.06, and 53.07 of this code must be satisfied, and the summons must state that the hearing is for the purpose of considering discretionary transfer to criminal court.

(c) The juvenile court shall conduct a hearing without a jury to consider transfer of the child for criminal proceedings.

(d) Prior to the hearing, the juvenile court shall order and obtain a complete diagnostic study, social evaluation, and full investigation of the child, his circumstances, and the circumstances of the alleged offense.

(e) At the transfer hearing the court may consider written reports from probation officers, professional court employees, or professional consultants in addition to the testimony of witnesses. At least one day prior to the transfer hearing, the court shall provide the attorney for the child with access to all written matter to be considered by the court in making the transfer decision. The court may order counsel not to reveal items to the child or his parent, guardian, or guardian ad litem if such disclosure would materially harm the treatment and rehabilitation of the child or would substantially decrease the likelihood of receiving information from the same or similar sources in the future.

(f) In making the determination required by Subsection (a) of this section, the court shall consider, among other matters:

(1) whether the alleged offense was against person or property, with greater weight in favor of transfer given to offenses against the person;

(2) the sophistication and maturity of the child;

(3) the record and previous history of the child; and

(4) the prospects of adequate protection of the public and the likelihood of the rehabilitation of the child by use of procedures, services, and facilities currently available to the juvenile court.

(g) If the petition alleges multiple offenses that constitute more than one criminal transaction, the juvenile court shall either retain or transfer all offenses relating to a single transaction. A child is not subject to criminal prosecution at any time for any offense arising out of a criminal transaction for which the juvenile court retains jurisdiction.

(h) If the juvenile court waives jurisdiction, it shall state specifically in the order its reasons for waiver and certify its action, including the written order and findings of the court, and shall transfer the person to the appropriate court for criminal proceedings and cause the results of the diagnostic study of the person ordered under Subsection (d), including psychological information, to be transferred to the appropriate criminal prosecutor. On transfer of the person for criminal proceedings, the person shall be dealt with as an adult and in accordance with the Code of Criminal Procedure. The transfer of custody is an arrest.

(i) A waiver under this section is a waiver of jurisdiction over the child and the criminal court may not remand the child to the jurisdiction of the juvenile court.

(j) The juvenile court may waive its exclusive original jurisdiction and transfer a person to the appropriate district court or criminal district court for criminal proceedings if:

(1) the person is 18 years of age or older;

(2) the person was:

(A) 10 years of age or older and under 17 years of age at the time the person is alleged to have committed a capital felony or an offense under Section 19.02, Penal Code;

(B) 14 years of age or older and under 17 years of age at the time the person is alleged to have committed an aggravated controlled substance felony or a felony of the first degree other than an offense under Section 19.02, Penal Code; or

(C) 15 years of age or older and under 17 years of age at the time the person is alleged to have committed a felony of the second or third degree or a state jail felony;

(3) no adjudication concerning the alleged offense has been made or no adjudication hearing concerning the offense has been conducted;

(4) the juvenile court finds from a preponderance of the evidence that:

(A) for a reason beyond the control of the state it was not practicable to proceed in juvenile court before the 18th birthday of the person; or

(B) after due diligence of the state it was not practicable to proceed in juvenile court before the 18th birthday of the person because:

(i) the state did not have probable cause to proceed in juvenile court and new evidence has been found since the 18th birthday of the person;

(ii) the person could not be found; or

(iii) a previous transfer order was reversed by an appellate court or set aside by a district court; and

(5) the juvenile court determines that there is probable cause to believe that the child before the court committed the offense alleged.

(k) The petition and notice requirements of Sections 53.04, 53.05, 53.06, and 53.07 of this code must be satisfied, and the summons must state that the hearing is for the purpose of considering waiver of jurisdiction under Subsection (j) of this section.

(l) The juvenile court shall conduct a hearing without a jury to consider waiver of jurisdiction under Subsection (j) of this section.

(m) Notwithstanding any other provision of this section, the juvenile court shall waive its exclusive original jurisdiction and transfer a child to the appropriate district court or criminal court for criminal proceedings if:

  (1) the child has previously been transferred to a district court or criminal district court for criminal proceedings under this section, unless:

    (A) the child was not indicted in the matter transferred by the grand jury;

    (B) the child was found not guilty in the matter transferred;

    (C) the matter transferred was dismissed with prejudice; or

    (D) the child was convicted in the matter transferred, the conviction was reversed on appeal, and the appeal is final; and

  (2) the child is alleged to have violated a penal law of the grade of felony.

(n) A mandatory transfer under Subsection (m) may be made without conducting the study required in discretionary transfer proceedings by Subsection (d). The requirements of Subsection (b) that the summons state that the purpose of the hearing is to consider discretionary transfer to criminal court does not apply to a transfer proceeding under Subsection (m). In a proceeding under Subsection (m), it is sufficient that the summons provide fair notice that the purpose of the hearing is to consider mandatory transfer to criminal court.

(o) If a respondent is taken into custody for possible discretionary transfer proceedings under Subsection (j), the juvenile court shall hold a detention hearing in the same manner as provided by Section 54.01, except that the court shall order the respondent released unless it finds that the respondent:

  (1) is likely to abscond or be removed from the jurisdiction of the court;

  (2) may be dangerous to himself or herself or may threaten the safety of the public if released; or

  (3) has previously been found to be a delinquent child or has previously been convicted of a penal offense punishable by a term of jail or prison and is likely to commit an offense if released.

(p) If the juvenile court does not order a respondent released under Subsection (o), the court shall, pending the conclusion of the discretionary transfer hearing, order that the respondent be detained in:

  (1) a certified juvenile detention facility as provided by Subsection (q); or

  (2) an appropriate county facility for the detention of adults accused of criminal offenses.

(q) The detention of a respondent in a certified juvenile detention facility must comply with the detention requirements under this title, except that, to the extent practicable, the person shall be kept separate from children detained in the same facility.

(r) If the juvenile court orders a respondent detained in a county facility under Subsection (p), the county sheriff shall take custody of the respondent under the juvenile court's order. The juvenile court shall set or deny bond for the respondent as required by the Code of Criminal Procedure and other law applicable to the pretrial detention of adults accused of criminal offenses.

§71.003. Family

" Family" includes individuals related by consanguinity or affinity, as determined under Sections 573.022 and 573.024, Government Code, individuals who are former spouses of each other, individuals who are the biological parents of the same child, without regard to marriage, and a foster child and foster parent, without regard to whether those individuals reside together.

FAMILY VIOLENCE—§71

§71.0021. Dating violence

(a) "Dating violence" means an act by an individual that is against another individual with whom that person has or has had a dating relationship and that is intended to result in physical harm, bodily injury, assault, or sexual assault or that is a threat that reasonably places the individual in fear of imminent physical harm, bodily injury, assault, or sexual assault, but does not include defensive measures to protect oneself.

(b) For purposes of this title, "dating relationship" means a relationship between individuals who have or have had a continuing relationship of a romantic or intimate nature. The existence of such a relationship shall be determined based on consideration of:

(1) the length of the relationship;

(2) the nature of the relationship; and

(3) the frequency and type of interaction between the persons involved in the relationship.

(c) A casual acquaintanceship or ordinary fraternization in a business or social context does not constitute a "dating relationship" under Subsection (b).

§71.003. Family

"Family" includes individuals related by consanguinity or affinity, as determined under Sections 573.022 and 573.024, Government Code, individuals who are former spouses of each other, individuals who are the biological parents of the same child, without regard to marriage, and a foster child and foster parent, without regard to whether those individuals reside together.

§71.004. Family Violence

"Family violence" means:

(1) an act by a member of a family or household against another member of the family or household that is intended to result in physical harm, bodily injury, assault, or sexual assault or that is a threat that reasonably places the member in fear of imminent physical harm, bodily injury, assault, or sexual assault, but does not include defensive measures to protect oneself; or

(2) abuse, as that term is defined by Sections 261.001(1)(C), (E), and (G) by a member of a family or household toward a child of the family or household.

PROTECTIVE ORDERS—§81

§81.001. Entitlement to protective order

A court shall render a protective order as provided by Section 85.001(b) if the court finds that family violence has occurred and is likely to occur in the future.

§81.002. No fee for applicant

An applicant for a protective order or an attorney representing an applicant may not be assessed a fee, cost, charge, or expense by a district or county clerk of the court or a sheriff, constable, or other public official or employee in connection with the filing, serving, or entering of a protective order or for any other service described by this subsection, including:

(1) a fee to dismiss, modify, or withdraw a protective order;

(2) a fee for certifying copies;

(3) a fee for comparing copies to originals;

(4) a court reporter fee;

(5) a judicial fund fee;

(6) a fee for any other service related to a protective order; or

(7) a fee to transfer a protective order.

§81.003. Fees and costs paid by party found to have committed family violence.

a) Except on a showing of good cause or of the indigence of a party found to have committed family violence, the court shall require in a protective order that the party against whom the order is rendered pay the $16 protective order fee, the standard fees charged by the clerk of the court in a general civil proceeding for the cost of serving the order, the costs of court, and all other fees, charges, or expenses incurred in connection with the protective order.

(b) The court may order a party against whom an agreed protective order is rendered under Section 85.005 to pay the fees required in Subsection (a).

REPORTING FAMILY VIOLENCE—§91

§91.001. Definitions

In this subtitle:

(1) "Family violence" has the meaning assigned by Section 71.004.

(2) "Medical professional" means a licensed doctor, nurse, physician assistant, or emergency medical technician.

§91.002. Reporting by witnesses encouraged

A person who witnesses family violence is encouraged to report the family violence to a local law enforcement agency.

§91.003. Information provided by medical professionals

A medical professional who treats a person for injuries that the medical professional has reason to believe were caused by family violence shall:

(1) immediately provide the person with information regarding the nearest family violence shelter center;

(2) document in the person's medical file:

(A) the fact that the person has received the information provided under Subdivision (1); and

(B) the reasons for the medical professional's belief that the person's injuries were caused by family violence; and

(3) give the person a written notice in substantially the following form, completed with the required information, in both English and Spanish:

"It is a crime for any person to cause you any physical injury or harm even if that person is a member or former member of your family or household.

"NOTICE TO ADULT VICTIMS OF FAMILY VIOLENCE

"You may report family violence to a law enforcement officer by calling the following telephone numbers: _____.

"If you, your child, or any other household resident has been injured or if you feel you are going to be in danger after a law enforcement officer investigating family violence leaves your residence or at a later time, you have the right to:

"Ask the local prosecutor to file a criminal complaint against the person committing family violence; and

"Apply to a court for an order to protect you. You may want to consult with a legal aid office, a prosecuting attorney, or a private attorney. A court can enter an order that:

"(1) prohibits the abuser from committing further acts of violence;

"(2) prohibits the abuser from threatening, harassing, or contacting you at home;

"(3) directs the abuser to leave your household; and

"(4) establishes temporary custody of the children or any property.

"A VIOLATION OF CERTAIN PROVISIONS OF COURT-ORDERED PROTECTION MAY BE A FELONY.

"CALL THE FOLLOWING VIOLENCE SHELTERS OR SOCIAL ORGANIZATIONS IF YOU NEED PROTECTION: _____."

Conservatorship, Possession, and Access—§153

§153.001. Public policy

(a) The public policy of this state is to:

(1) assure that children will have frequent and continuing contact with parents who have shown the ability to act in the best interest of the child;

(2) provide a safe, stable, and nonviolent environment for the child; and

(3) encourage parents to share in the rights and duties of raising their child after the parents have separated or dissolved their marriage.

(b) A court may not render an order that conditions the right of a conservator to possession of or access to a child on the payment of child support.

§153.002. Best interest of child

The best interest of the child shall always be the primary consideration of the court in determining the issues of conservatorship and possession of and access to the child.

§153.0072. Collaborative law

(a) On a written agreement of the parties and their attorneys, a suit affecting the parent-child relationship may be conducted under collaborative law procedures.

(b) Collaborative law is a procedure in which the parties and their counsel agree in writing to use their best efforts and make a good faith attempt to resolve the suit affecting the parent-child relationship on an agreed basis without resorting to judicial intervention except to have the court approve the settlement agreement, make the legal pronouncements, and sign the orders required by law to effectuate the agreement of the parties as the court determines appropriate. The parties' counsel may not serve as litigation counsel except to ask the court to approve the settlement agreement.

(c) A collaborative law agreement must include provisions for:

(1) full and candid exchange of information between the parties and their attorneys as necessary to make a proper evaluation of the case;

(2) suspending court intervention in the dispute while the parties are using collaborative law procedures;

(3) hiring experts, as jointly agreed, to be used in the procedure;

(4) withdrawal of all counsel involved in the collaborative law procedure if the collaborative law procedure does not result in settlement of the dispute; and

(5) other provisions as agreed to by the parties consistent with a good faith effort to collaboratively settle the matter.

§153.073. Rights of parent at all times

(a) Unless limited by court order, a parent appointed as a conservator of a child has at all times the right:

(1) to receive information from any other conservator

of the child concerning the health, education, and welfare of the child;

(2) to confer with the other parent to the extent possible before making a decision concerning the health, education, and welfare of the child;

(3) of access to medical, dental, psychological, and educational records of the child;

(4) to consult with a physician, dentist, or psychologist of the child;

(5) to consult with school officials concerning the child's welfare and educational status, including school activities;

(6) to attend school activities;

(7) to be designated on the child's records as a person to be notified in case of an emergency;

(8) to consent to medical, dental, and surgical treatment during an emergency involving an immediate danger to the health and safety of the child; and

(9) to manage the estate of the child to the extent the estate has been created by the parent or the parent's family.

(b) The court shall specify in the order the rights that a parent retains at all times.

§153.074. Rights and duties during period of possession

Unless limited by court order, a parent appointed as a conservator of a child has the following rights and duties during the period that the parent has possession of the child:

(1) the duty of care, control, protection, and reasonable discipline of the child;

(2) the duty to support the child, including providing the child with clothing, food, shelter, and medical and dental care not involving an invasive procedure;

(3) the right to consent for the child to medical and dental care not involving an invasive procedure; and

(4) the right to direct the moral and religious training of the child.

§153.075. Duties of parent not appointed conservator

The court may order a parent not appointed as a managing or a possessory conservator to perform other parental duties, including paying child support.

§153.010. Order for family counseling

(a) If the court finds at the time of a hearing that the parties have a history of conflict in resolving an issue of conservatorship or possession of or access to the child, the court may order a party to:

(1) participate in counseling with a mental health professional who:

(A) has a background in family therapy;

(B) has a mental health license that requires as a minimum a master's degree; and

(C) has training in domestic violence if the court determines that the training is relevant to the type of counseling needed; and

(2) pay the cost of counseling.

(b) If a person possessing the requirements of Subsection (a)(1) is not available in the county in which the court presides, the court may appoint a person the court believes is qualified to conduct the counseling ordered under Subsection (a).

§153.132. Rights and duties of parent appointed sole managing conservator

Unless limited by court order, a parent appointed as sole managing conservator of a child has the rights and duties provided by Subchapter B and the following exclusive rights:

(1) the right to designate the primary residence of the child;

(2) the right to consent to medical, dental, and surgical treatment involving invasive procedures, and to consent to psychiatric and psychological treatment;

(3) the right to receive and give receipt for periodic payments for the support of the child and to hold or disburse these funds for the benefit of the child;

(4) the right to represent the child in legal action and to make other decisions of substantial legal significance concerning the child;

(5) the right to consent to marriage and to enlistment in the armed forces of the United States;

(6) the right to make decisions concerning the child's education;

(7) the right to the services and earnings of the child; and

(8) except when a guardian of the child's estate or a guardian or attorney *ad litem* has been appointed for the child, the right to act as an agent of the child in relation to the child's estate if the child's action is required by a state, the United States, or a foreign government.

§153.133. Agreement for joint managing conservatorship

(a) If a written agreement of the parents is filed with the court, the court shall render an order appointing the parents as joint managing conservators only if the agreement:

(1) designates the conservator who has the exclusive right to designate the primary residence of the child and:

(A) establishes, until modified by further order, the geographic area within which the conservator shall maintain the child's primary residence; or

(B) specifies that the conservator may designate the child's primary residence without regard to geographic location;

(2) specifies the rights and duties of each parent regarding the child's physical care, support, and education;

(3) includes provisions to minimize disruption of the child's education, daily routine, and association with friends;

(4) allocates between the parents, independently, jointly, or exclusively, all of the remaining rights and duties of a parent provided by Chapter 151;

(5) is voluntarily and knowingly made by each parent and has not been repudiated by either parent at the time the order is rendered; and

(6) is in the best interest of the child.

(b) The agreement may contain an alternative dispute resolution procedure that the parties agree to use before requesting enforcement or modification of the terms and conditions of the joint conservatorship through litigation, except in an emergency.

§153.192. Right and duties of parent appointed possessory conservator

(a) Unless limited by court order, a parent appointed as possessory conservator of a child has the rights and duties provided by Subchapter B and any other right or duty expressly granted to the possessory conservator in the order.

(b) In ordering the terms and conditions for possession of a child by a parent appointed possessory conservator, the court shall be guided by the guidelines in Subchapter E.

CHILD ABUSE OR NEGLECT—§261

§261.001. Definitions

In this chapter:

(1) " Abuse" includes the following acts or omissions by a person:

(A) mental or emotional injury to a child that results in an observable and material impairment in the child's growth, development, or psychological functioning;

(B) causing or permitting the child to be in a situation in which the child sustains a mental or emotional injury that results in an observable and material impairment in the child's growth, development, or psychological functioning;

(C) physical injury that results in substantial harm to the child, or the genuine threat of substantial harm from physical injury to the child, including an injury that is at variance with the history or explanation given and excluding an accident or reasonable discipline by a parent, guardian, or managing or possessory conservator that does not expose the child to a substantial risk of harm;

(D) failure to make a reasonable effort to prevent an action by another person that results in physical injury that results in substantial harm to the child;

(E) sexual conduct harmful to a child's mental, emotional, or physical welfare;

(F) failure to make a reasonable effort to prevent sexual conduct harmful to a child;

(G) compelling or encouraging the child to engage in sexual conduct as defined by Section 43.01, Penal Code;

(H) causing, permitting, encouraging, engaging in, or allowing the photographing, filming, or depicting of the child if the person knew or should have known that the resulting photograph, film, or depiction of the child is obscene as defined by Section 43.21, Penal Code, or pornographic;

(I) the current use by a person of a controlled substance as defined by Chapter 481, Health and Safety Code, in a manner or to the extent that the use results in physical, mental, or emotional injury to a child; or

(J) causing, expressly permitting, or encouraging a child to use a controlled substance as defined by Chapter 481, Health and Safety Code.

(2) "Department" means the Department of Protective and Regulatory Services.

(3) "Designated agency" means the agency designated by the court as responsible for the protection of children.

(4) " Neglect" includes:

(A) the leaving of a child in a situation where the child would be exposed to a substantial risk of physical or mental harm, without arranging for necessary care for the child, and the demonstration of an intent not to return by a parent, guardian, or managing or possessory conservator of the child;

(B) the following acts or omissions by a person:

(i) placing a child in or failing to remove a child from a situation that a reasonable person would realize requires judgment or actions beyond the child's level of maturity, physical condition, or mental abilities and that results in bodily injury or a substantial risk of immediate harm to the child;

(ii) failing to seek, obtain, or follow through with medical care for a child, with the failure resulting in or presenting a substantial risk of death, disfigurement, or bodily injury or with the failure resulting in an observable and material impairment to the growth, development, or functioning of the child;

(iii) the failure to provide a child with food, clothing, or shelter necessary to sustain the life or health of the child, excluding failure caused primarily by financial inability unless relief services had been offered and refused; or

(iv) placing a child in or failing to remove the child from a situation in which the child would be exposed to a substantial risk of sexual conduct harmful to the child; or

(C) the failure by the person responsible for a child's care, custody, or welfare to permit the child to return to the child's home without arranging for the necessary care for the child after the child has been absent from the home for any reason, including having been in residential placement or having run away.

(5) "Person responsible for a child's care, custody, or welfare" means a person who traditionally is responsible for a child's care, custody, or welfare, including:

(A) a parent, guardian, managing or possessory conservator, or foster parent of the child;

(B) a member of the child's family or household as defined by Chapter 71;

(C) a person with whom the child's parent cohabits;

(D) school personnel or a volunteer at the child's school; or

(E) personnel or a volunteer at a public or private child-care facility that provides services for the child or at a public or private residential institution or facility where the child resides.

(6) " Report" means a report that alleged or suspected abuse or neglect of a child has occurred or may occur.

(7) "Board" means the Board of Protective and Regulatory Services.

(8) "Born addicted to alcohol or a controlled substance" means a child:

(A) who is born to a mother who during the pregnancy used a controlled substance, as defined by Chapter 481, Health and Safety Code, other than a controlled substance legally obtained by prescription, or alcohol; and

(B) who, after birth as a result of the mother's use of the controlled substance or alcohol:

(i) experiences observable withdrawal from the alcohol or controlled substance;

(ii) exhibits observable or harmful effects in the child's physical appearance or functioning; or

(iii) exhibits the demonstrable presence of alcohol or a controlled substance in the child's bodily fluids.

§261.101. Persons Required to Report; Time to Report

(a) A person having cause to believe that a child's physical or mental health or welfare has been adversely affected by abuse or neglect by any person shall immediately make a report as provided by this subchapter.

(b) If a professional has cause to believe that a child has been abused or neglected or may be abused or neglected or that a child is a victim of an offense under Section 21.11, Penal Code, the professional shall make a report not later than the 48th hour after the hour the professional first suspects that the child has been or may be abused or neglected or is a victim of an offense under Section 21.11, Penal Code. A professional may not delegate to or rely on another person to make the report. In this subsection, "professional" means an individual who is licensed or certified by the state or who is an employee of a facility licensed, certified, or operated by the state and who, in the normal course of official duties or duties for which a license or certification is required, has direct contact with children. The term includes teachers, nurses, doctors, day-care employees, employees of a clinic or health care facility that provides reproductive services, juvenile probation officers, and juvenile detention or correctional officers.

(c) The requirement to report under this section applies without exception to an individual whose personal communications may otherwise be privileged, including an attorney, a member of the clergy, a medical practitioner, a social worker, a mental health professional, and an employee of a clinic or health care facility that provides reproductive services.

(d) Unless waived in writing by the person making the report, the identity of an individual making a report under this chapter is confidential and may be disclosed only:

(1) as provided by Section 261.201; or

(2) to a law enforcement officer for the purposes of conducting a criminal investigation of the report.

§261.102. Matters to be Reported

A report should reflect the reporter's belief that a child has been or may be abused or neglected or has died of abuse or neglect.

§261.103. Report Made to Appropriate Agency

(a) Except as provided by Subsection (b), a report shall be made to:

(1) any local or state law enforcement agency;

(2) the department if the alleged or suspected abuse involves a person responsible for the care, custody, or welfare of the child;

(3) the state agency that operates, licenses, certifies, or registers the facility in which the alleged abuse or neglect occurred; or

(4) the agency designated by the court to be responsible for the protection of children.

(b) A report may be made to the Texas Youth Commission instead of the entities listed under Subsection (a) if the report is based on information provided by a child while under the supervision of the commission concerning the child's alleged abuse of another child.

§261.104. Contents of Report

The person making a report shall identify, if known:

(1) the name and address of the child;

(2) the name and address of the person responsible for the care, custody, or welfare of the child; and

(3) any other pertinent information concerning the alleged or suspected abuse or neglect.

§261.106. Immunities

(a) A person acting in good faith who reports or assists in the investigation of a report of alleged child abuse or neglect or who testifies or otherwise participates in a judicial proceeding arising from a report, petition, or investigation of alleged child abuse or neglect is immune from civil or criminal liability that might otherwise be incurred or imposed.

(b) Immunity from civil and criminal liability extends to an authorized volunteer of the department or a law enforcement officer who participates at the request of the department in an investigation of alleged or suspected abuse or neglect or in an action arising from an investigation if the person was acting in good faith and in the scope of the person's responsibilities.

(c) A person who reports the person's own abuse or neglect of a child or who acts in bad faith or with malicious purpose in reporting alleged child abuse or neglect is not immune from civil or criminal liability.

§261.107. False Report; Penalty

(a) A person commits an offense if the person knowingly or intentionally makes a report as provided in this chapter that the person knows is false or lacks factual foundation. An offense under this section is a Class A misdemeanor unless it is shown on the trial of the offense that the person has previously been convicted under this section, in which case the offense is a state jail felony.

(b) A finding by a court in a suit affecting the parent-child relationship that a report made under this chapter before or during the suit was false or lacking factual foundation may be grounds for the court to modify an order providing for possession of or access to the child who was the subject of the report by restricting further access to the child by the person who made the report.

(c) The appropriate county prosecuting attorney shall be responsible for the prosecution of an offense under this section.

§261.108. Frivolous Claims Against Person Reporting

(a) In this section:

(1) "Claim" means an action or claim by a party, including a plaintiff, counterclaimant, cross-claimant, or third-party plaintiff, requesting recovery of damages.

(2) "Defendant" means a party against whom a claim is made.

(b) A court shall award a defendant reasonable attorney's fees and other expenses related to the defense of a claim filed against the defendant for damages or other relief arising from reporting or assisting in the investigation of a report under this chapter or participating in a judicial proceeding resulting from the report if:

(1) the court finds that the claim is frivolous, unreasonable, or without foundation because the defendant is immune from liability under Section 261.106; and

(2) the claim is dismissed or judgment is rendered for the defendant.

(c) To recover under this section, the defendant must, at any time after the filing of a claim, file a written motion stating that:

(1) the claim is frivolous, unreasonable, or without foundation because the defendant is immune from liability under Section 261.106; and

(2) the defendant requests the court to award reasonable attorney's fees and other expenses related to the defense of the claim.

§261.109. Failure to Report; Penalty

(a) A person commits an offense if the person has cause to believe that a child's physical or mental health or welfare has been or may be adversely affected by abuse or neglect and knowingly fails to report as provided in this chapter.

(b) An offense under this section is a Class B misdemeanor.

§261.201. Confidentiality and Disclosure of Information

(a) The following information is confidential, is not subject to public release under Chapter 552, Government Code, and may be disclosed only for purposes consistent with this code and applicable federal or state law or under rules adopted by an investigating agency:

(1) a report of alleged or suspected abuse or neglect made under this chapter and the identity of the person making the report; and

(2) except as otherwise provided in this section, the files, reports, records, communications, audiotapes, videotapes, and working papers used or developed in an investigation under this chapter or in providing services as a result of an investigation.

(b) A court may order the disclosure of information that is confidential under this section if:

(1) a motion has been filed with the court requesting the release of the information;

(2) a notice of hearing has been served on the investigating agency and all other interested parties; and

(3) after hearing and an in camera review of the requested information, the court determines that the disclosure of the requested information is:

(A) essential to the administration of justice; and

(B) not likely to endanger the life or safety of:

(i) a child who is the subject of the report of alleged or suspected abuse or neglect;

(ii) a person who makes a report of alleged or suspected abuse or neglect; or

(iii) any other person who participates in an investigation of reported abuse or neglect or who provides care for the child.

(c) In addition to Subsection (b), a court, on its own motion, may order disclosure of information that is confidential under this section if:

(1) the order is rendered at a hearing for which all parties have been given notice;

(2) the court finds that disclosure of the information is:

(A) essential to the administration of justice; and

(B) not likely to endanger the life or safety of:

(i) a child who is the subject of the report of alleged or suspected abuse or neglect;

(ii) a person who makes a report of alleged or suspected abuse or neglect; or

(iii) any other person who participates in an investigation of reported abuse or neglect or who provides care for the child; and

(3) the order is reduced to writing or made on the record in open court.

(d) The adoptive parents of a child who was the subject of an investigation and an adult who was the subject of an investigation as a child are entitled to examine and make copies of any report, record, working paper, or other information in the possession, custody, or control of the state that pertains to the history of the child. The department may edit the documents to protect the identity of the biological parents and any other person whose identity is confidential.

(e) Before placing a child who was the subject of an investigation, the department shall notify the prospective adoptive parents of their right to examine any report, record, working paper, or other information in the possession, custody, or control of the state that pertains to the history of the child.

(f) The department shall provide prospective adoptive parents an opportunity to examine information under this section as early as practicable before placing a child.

(g) Notwithstanding Subsection (b), the department, on request and subject to department rule, shall provide to the parent, managing conservator, or other legal representative of a child who is the subject of reported abuse or neglect information concerning the reported abuse or neglect that would otherwise be confidential under this section if the department has edited the information to protect the confidentiality of the identity of the person who made the report and any other person whose life or safety may be endangered by the disclosure.

(h) This section does not apply to an investigation of child abuse or neglect in a home or facility regulated under Chapter 42, Human Resources Code.

§261.202. Privileged Communication

In a proceeding regarding the abuse or neglect of a child, evidence may not be excluded on the ground of privileged communication except in the case of communications between an attorney and client.

§261.301. Investigation of Report

(a) With assistance from the appropriate state or local law enforcement agency, the department or designated agency shall make a prompt and thorough investigation of a report of child abuse or neglect allegedly committed by a person responsible for a child's care, custody, or welfare. The investigation shall be conducted without regard to any pending suit affecting the parent-child relationship.

(b) A state agency shall investigate a report that alleges abuse or neglect occurred in a facility operated, licensed, certified, or registered by that agency as provided by Subchapter E. In conducting an investigation for a facility operated, licensed, certified, registered, or listed by the department, the department shall perform the investigation as provided by:

(1) Subchapter E; and

(2) the Human Resources Code.

(c) The department is not required to investigate a report that alleges child abuse or neglect by a person other than a person responsible for a child's care, custody, or welfare. The appropriate state or local law enforcement agency shall investigate that report if the agency determines an investigation should be conducted.

(d) The department may by rule assign priorities and prescribe investigative procedures for investigations based on the severity and immediacy of the alleged harm to the child. The primary purpose of the investigation shall be the protection of the child.

(e) As necessary to provide for the protection of the child, the department or designated agency shall determine:

(1) the nature, extent, and cause of the abuse or neglect;

(2) the identity of the person responsible for the abuse or neglect;

(3) the names and conditions of the other children in the home;

(4) an evaluation of the parents or persons responsible for the care of the child;

(5) the adequacy of the home environment;

(6) the relationship of the child to the persons responsible for the care, custody, or welfare of the child; and

(7) all other pertinent data.

(f) An investigation of a report to the department of serious physical or sexual abuse of a child shall be conducted jointly by an investigator from the appropriate local law enforcement agency and the department or agency responsible for conducting an investigation under Subchapter E.

(g) The inability or unwillingness of a local law enforcement agency to conduct a joint investigation under Subsection (f) does not constitute grounds to prevent or prohibit the department from performing its duties under this subtitle. The department shall document any instance in which a law enforcement agency is unable or unwilling to conduct a joint investigation under Subsection (f).

§261.303. Interference With Investigation; Court Order

(a) A person may not interfere with an investigation of a report of child abuse or neglect conducted by the department or designated agency.

(b) If admission to the home, school, or any place where the child may be cannot be obtained, then for good cause shown the court having family law jurisdiction shall order the parent, the person responsible for the care of the children, or the person in charge of any place where the child may be to allow entrance for the interview, examination, and investigation.

(c) If a parent or person responsible for the child's care does not consent to release of the child's prior medical, psychological, or psychiatric records or to a medical, psychological, or psychiatric examination of the child that is requested by the department or designated agency, the court having family law jurisdiction shall, for good cause shown, order the records to be released or the examination to be made at the times and places designated by the court.

(d) A person, including a medical facility, that makes a report under Subchapter B1 shall release to the department or designated agency, as part of the required report under Section 261.103, records that directly relate to the suspected abuse or neglect without requiring parental consent or a court order.

§261.305. Access to Mental Health Records

(a) An investigation may include an inquiry into the possibility that a parent or a person responsible for the care of a child who is the subject of a report under Subchapter B1 has a history of medical or mental illness.

(b) If the parent or person does not consent to an examination or allow the department or designated agency to have access to medical or mental health records requested by the department or agency, the court having family law jurisdiction, for good cause shown, shall order the examination to be made or that the department or agency be permitted to have access to the records under terms and conditions prescribed by the court.

(c) If the court determines that the parent or person is indigent, the court shall appoint an attorney to represent the parent or person at the hearing. The fees for the appointed attorney shall be paid as provided by Chapter 107.

(d) A parent or person responsible for the child's care is entitled to notice and a hearing when the department or designated agency seeks a court order to allow a medical, psychological, or psychiatric examination or access to medical or mental health records.

(e) This access does not constitute a waiver of confidentiality.

§261.316. Exemption From Fees for Medical Records

The department is exempt from the payment of a fee otherwise required or authorized by law to obtain a medical record from a hospital or health care provider if the request for a record is made in the course of an investigation by the department.

HEALTH AND SAFETY CODE

HIV TESTING, CONFIDENTIALITY, AND CONSENT—§81

§81.103. Confidentiality; Criminal Penalty

(a) A test result is confidential. A person that possesses or has knowledge of a test result may not release or disclose the test result or allow the test result to become known except as provided by this section.

(b) A test result may be released to:

(1) the department under this chapter;

(2) a local health authority if reporting is required under this chapter;

(3) the Centers for Disease Control of the United States Public Health Service if reporting is required by federal law or regulation;

(4) the physician or other person authorized by law who ordered the test;

(5) a physician, nurse, or other health care personnel who have a legitimate need to know the test result in order to provide for their protection and to provide for the patient's health and welfare;

(6) the person tested or a person legally authorized to consent to the test on the person's behalf;

(7) the spouse of the person tested if the person tests positive for AIDS or HIV infection, antibodies to HIV, or infection with any other probable causative agent of AIDS;

(8) a person authorized to receive test results under Article 21.31, Code of Criminal Procedure, concerning a person who is tested as required or authorized under that article; and

(9) a person exposed to HIV infection as provided by Section 81.050.

(c) The court shall notify persons receiving test results under Subsection (b)(8) of the requirements of this section.

(d) A person tested or a person legally authorized to consent to the test on the person's behalf may voluntarily release or disclose that person's test results to any other person, and may authorize the release or disclosure of the test results. An authorization under this subsection must be in writing and signed by the person tested or the person legally authorized to consent to the test on the person's behalf. The authorization must state the person or class of persons to whom the test results may be released or disclosed.

(e) A person may release or disclose a test result for statistical summary purposes only without the written consent of the person tested if information that could identify the person is removed from the report.

(j) A person commits an offense if, with criminal negligence and in violation of this section, the person releases or discloses a test result or other information or allows a test result or other information to become known. An offense under this subsection is a Class A misdemeanor.

§81.104. Injunction; Civil Liability

(a) A person may bring an action to restrain a violation or threatened violation of Section 81.102 or 81.103.

(b) A person who violates Section 81.102 or who is found in a civil action to have negligently released or disclosed a test result or allowed a test result to become known in violation of Section 81.103 is liable for:

(1) actual damages;

(2) a civil penalty of not more than $5,000; and

(3) court costs and reasonable attorney's fees incurred by the person bringing the action.

(c) A person who is found in a civil action to have willfully released or disclosed a test result or allowed a test result to become known in violation of Section 81.103 is liable for:

(1) actual damages;

(2) a civil penalty of not less than $5,000 nor more than $10,000; and

. (3) court costs and reasonable attorney's fees incurred by the person bringing the action.

(d) Each release or disclosure made, or allowance of a test result to become known, in violation of this subchapter constitutes a separate offense.

(e) A defendant in a civil action brought under this section is not entitled to claim any privilege as a defense to the action.

§81.105. Informed Consent

(a) Except as otherwise provided by law, a person may not perform a test designed to identify HIV or its antigen or antibody without first obtaining the informed consent of the person to be tested.

(b) Consent need not be written if there is documentation in the medical record that the test has been explained and the consent has been obtained.

§81.106. General Consent

(a) A person who has signed a general consent form for the performance of medical tests or procedures is not required to also sign or be presented with a specific consent form relating to medical tests or procedures to determine HIV infection, antibodies to HIV, or infection with any other probable causative agent of AIDS that will be performed on the person during the time in which the general consent form is in effect.

(b) Except as otherwise provided by this chapter, the result of a test or procedure to determine HIV infection, antibodies to HIV, or infection with any probable causative agent of AIDS performed under the authorization of a general consent form in accordance with this section may be used only for diagnostic or other purposes directly related to medical treatment.

§81.107. Consent to Test for Accidental Exposures

(a) In a case of accidental exposure to blood or other body fluids under Section 81.102(a)(4)(D), the health care agency or facility may test a person who may have exposed the health care worker to HIV without the person's specific consent to the test.

§81.109. Counseling Required for Positive Test Results

(a) A positive test result may not be revealed to the person tested without giving that person the immediate opportunity for individual, face-to-face post-test counseling about:

(1) the meaning of the test result;

(2) the possible need for additional testing;

(3) measures to prevent the transmission of HIV;

(4) the availability of appropriate health care services, including mental health care, and appropriate social and support services in the geographic area of the person's residence;

(5) the benefits of partner notification; and

(6) the availability of partner notification programs.

(b) Post-test counseling should:

(1) increase a person's understanding of HIV infection;

(2) explain the potential need for confirmatory testing;

(3) explain ways to change behavior conducive to HIV transmission;

(4) encourage the person to seek appropriate medical care; and

(5) encourage the person to notify persons with whom there has been contact capable of transmitting HIV.

(c) Subsection (a) does not apply if:

(1) a report of a test result is used for statistical or research purposes only and any information that could identify the person is removed from the report; or

(2) the test is conducted for the sole purpose of screening blood, blood products, bodily fluids, organs, or tissues to determine suitability for donation.

(d) A person who is injured by an intentional violation of this section may bring a civil action for damages and may recover for each violation from a person who violates this section:

(1) $1,000 or actual damages, whichever is greater; and

(2) reasonable attorney fees.

(e) This section does not prohibit disciplinary proceedings from being conducted by the appropriate licensing authorities for a health care provider's violation of this section.

(f) A person performing a test to show HIV infection, antibodies to HIV, or infection with any other probable causative agent of AIDS is not liable under Subsection (d) for failing to provide post-test counseling if the person tested does not appear for the counseling.

TREATMENT FACILITIES MARKETING PRACTICES ACT—§164

§164.002. Legislative Purpose

The purpose of this chapter is to safeguard the public against fraud, deceit, and misleading marketing practices and to foster and encourage competition and fair dealing by mental health facilities and chemical dependency treatment facilities by prohibiting or restricting practices by which the public has been injured in connection with the marketing and advertising of mental health services and the admission of patients. Nothing in this chapter should be construed to prohibit a mental health facility from advertising its services in a general way or promoting its specialized services. However, the public should be able to distinguish between the marketing activities of the facility and its clinical functions.

§164.003. Definitions

In this chapter:

(1) " *Advertising*" or "advertise" means a solicitation or inducement, through print or electronic media, including radio, television, or direct mail, to purchase the services provided by a treatment facility.

(2) " *Chemical dependency*" has the meaning assigned by Section 462.001.

(3) *"Chemical dependency facility"* means a treatment facility as that term is defined by Section 462.001.

(4) *"Intervention and assessment service"* means a service that offers assessment, counseling, evaluation, intervention, or referral services or makes treatment recommendations to an individual with respect to mental illness or chemical dependency.

(5) *" Mental health facility"* means:

(A) a "mental health facility" as defined by Section 571.003;

(B) a residential treatment facility, other than a mental health facility, in which persons are treated for emotional problems or disorders in a 24-hour supervised living environment; and

(C) an adult day-care facility or adult day health care facility as defined by Section 103.003, Human Resources Code.

(6) *"Mental health professional"* means a:

(A) *" physician"* as defined by Section 571.003;

(B) *" licensed professional counselor"* as defined by Section 503.002, Occupations Code;

(C) *" chemical dependency counselor"* as defined by Section 504.001, Occupations Code;

(D) *" psychologist"* offering *"psychological services"* as defined by Section 501.003, Occupations Code;

(E) *"registered nurse"* licensed under Chapter 301, Occupations Code;

(F) *"vocational nurse"* licensed under Chapter 301, Occupations Code;

(G) *"licensed marriage and family therapist"* as defined by Section 502.002, Occupations Code; and

(H) *" social worker"* as defined by Section 505.002, Occupations Code.

(7) *" Mental health services"* has the meaning assigned by Section 531.002.

(8) *" Mental illness"* has the meaning assigned by Section 571.003.

(9) *" Referral source"* means a person who is in a position to refer or who refers a person to a treatment facility. "Referral source" does not include a physician, an insurer, a health maintenance organization (HMO), a preferred provider arrangement (PPA), or other third party payor or discount provider organization (DPO) where the insurer, HMO, PPA, third party payor, or DPO pays in whole or in part for the treatment of mental illness or chemical dependency.

(10) *" Treatment facility"* means a chemical dependency facility and a mental health facility.

§164.004. Exemptions

This chapter does not apply to:

(1) a treatment facility

(A) operated by the Texas Department of Mental Health and Mental Retardation, a federal agency, or a political subdivision;

(B) funded by the Texas Commission on Alcohol and Drug Abuse;

(2) a community center established under Subchapter A, Chapter 534, or a facility operated by a community center; or

(3) a facility owned and operated by a nonprofit or not-for-profit organization offering counseling concerning family violence, help for runaway children, or rape.

§164.005. Conditioning Employee or Agent Relationships on Patient Revenue

A treatment facility may not permit or provide compensation or anything of value to its employees or agents, condition employment or continued employment of its employees or agents, set its employee or agent performance standards, or condition its employee or agent evaluations, based on:

(1) the number of patient admissions resulting from an employee's or agent's efforts;

(2) the number or frequency of telephone calls or other contacts with referral sources or patients if the purpose of the telephone calls or contacts is to solicit patients for the treatment facility; or

(3) the existence of or volume of determinations made respecting the length of patient stay.

§164.006. Soliciting and Contracting with Certain Referral Sources

A treatment facility or a person employed or under contract with a treatment facility, if acting on behalf of the treatment facility, may not:

(1) contact a referral source or potential client for the purpose of soliciting, directly or indirectly, a referral of a patient to the treatment facility without disclosing its soliciting agent's, employee's, or contractor's affiliation with the treatment facility;

(2) offer to provide or actually provide mental health or chemical dependency services to a public or private school in this state, on a part-time or full-time basis, the services of any of its employees or agents who make, or are in a position to make, a referral, if the services are provided on an individual basis to individual students or their families. Nothing herein prohibits a treatment facility from:

(A) offering or providing educational programs in group settings to public schools in this state if the affiliation between the educational program and the treatment facility is disclosed;

(B) providing counseling services to a public school in this state in an emergency or crisis situation if the services are provided in response to a specific request by a school; provided that, under no circumstances may a student be referred to the treatment facility offering the services; or

(C) entering into a contract with the board of trustees of a school district with an alternative education program under Section 464.020, or with the board's designee, for the provision of chemical dependency treatment services;

(3) provide to an entity of state or local government, on a part-time or full-time basis, the mental health or chemical dependency services of any of its employees, agents, or contractors who make or are in a position to make referrals unless:

(A) the treatment facility discloses to the governing authority of the entity:

(i) the employee's, agent's, or contractor's relationship to the facility; and

(ii) the fact that the employee, agent, or contractor might make a referral, if permitted, to the facility; and

(B) the employee, agent, or contractor makes a referral only if:

(i) the treatment facility obtains the governing authority's authorization in writing for the employee, agent, or contractor to make the referrals; and

(ii) the employee, agent, or contractor discloses to the prospective patient the employee's, agent's, or contractor's relationship to the facility at initial contact; or

(4) in relation to intervention and assessment services, contract with, offer to remunerate, or remunerate a person who operates an intervention and assessment service that makes referrals to a treatment facility for inpatient treatment of mental illness or chemical dependency unless the intervention and assessment service is:

(A) operated by a community mental health and mental retardation center funded by the Texas Department of Mental Health and Mental Retardation;

(B) operated by a county or regional medical society;

(C) a qualified mental health referral service as defined by Section 164.007; or

(D) owned and operated by a nonprofit or not-for-profit organization offering counseling concerning family violence, help for runaway children, or rape.

§164.007. Qualified Mental Health Referral Service: Definition and Standards

(a) A qualified mental health referral service means a service that conforms to all of the following standards:

(1) the referral service does not exclude as a participant in the referral service an individual who meets the qualifications for participation and qualifications for participation cannot be based in whole or in part on an individual's or entity's affiliation or nonaffiliation with other participants in the referral service;

(2) a payment the participant makes to the referral service is assessed equally against and collected equally from all participants, and is only based on the cost of operating the referral service and not on the volume or value of any referrals to or business otherwise generated by the participants of the referral service;

(3) the referral service imposes no requirements on the manner in which the participant provides services to a referred person, except that the referral service may require that the participant charge the person referred at the same rate as it charges other persons not referred by the referral service, or that these services be furnished free of charge or at a reduced charge;

(4) a referral made to a mental health professional or chemical dependency treatment facility is made only in accordance with Subdivision (1) and the referral service does not make referrals to mental health facilities other than facilities maintained or operated by the Texas Department of Mental Health and Mental Retardation, community mental health and mental retardation centers, or other political subdivisions, provided that a physician may make a referral directly to any mental health facility;

(5) the referral service is staffed by appropriately licensed and trained mental health professionals and a person who makes assessments for the need for treatment of mental illness or chemical dependency is a mental health professional as defined by this chapter;

(6) in response to each inquiry or after personal assessment, the referral service makes referrals, on a clinically appropriate, rotational basis, to at least three mental health professionals or chemical dependency treatment facilities whose practice addresses or facilities are located in the county of residence of the person seeking the referral or assessment, but if there are not three providers in the inquirer's county of residence, the referral service may include additional providers from other counties nearest the inquirer's county of residence;

(7) no information that identifies the person seeking a referral, such as name, address, or telephone number, is used, maintained, distributed, or provided for a purpose other than making the requested referral or for administrative functions necessary to operating the referral service;

(8) the referral service makes the following disclosures to each person seeking a referral:

(A) the manner in which the referral service selects the group of providers participating in the referral service;

(B) whether the provider participant has paid a fee to the referral service;

(C) the manner in which the referral service selects a particular provider from its list of provider participants to which to make a referral;

(D) the nature of the relationship or any affiliation between the referral service and the group of provider participants to whom it could make a referral; and

(E) the nature of any restriction that would exclude a provider from continuing as a provider participant;

(9) the referral service maintains each disclosure in a written record certifying that the disclosure has been made and the record certifying that the disclosure has been made is signed by either the person seeking a referral or by the person making the disclosure on behalf of the referral service; and

(10) if the referral service refers callers to a 1-900 telephone number or another telephone number that requires the payment of a toll or fee payable to or collected by the referral service, the referral service discloses the per minute charge.

(b) A qualified mental health referral service may not limit participation by a person for a reason other than:

(1) failure to have a current, valid license without limitation to practice in this state;

(2) failure to maintain professional liability insurance while participating in the service;

(3) a decision by a peer review committee that the person has failed to meet prescribed standards or has not acted in a professional or ethical manner;

(4) termination of the contract between the participant and the qualified mental health referral service by either party under the terms of the contract; or

(5) significant dissatisfaction of consumers that is documented and verifiable.

§164.010. Prohibited Acts

It is a violation of this chapter, in connection with the marketing of mental health services, for a person to:

(1) advertise, expressly or impliedly, the services of a treatment facility through the use of:

(A) promises of cure or guarantees of treatment results that cannot be substantiated; or

(B) any unsubstantiated claims;

(2) advertise, expressly or impliedly, the availability of intervention and assessment services unless and until the services are available and are provided by mental health professionals licensed or certified to provide the particular service;

(3) fail to disclose before soliciting a referral source or prospective patient to induce a person to use the services of the treatment facility an affiliation between a treatment facility and its soliciting agents, employees, or contractors;

(4) obtain information considered confidential by state or federal law regarding a person for the purpose of soliciting that person to use the services of a treatment facility unless and until consent is obtained from the person or, in the case of a minor, the person's parent, managing conservator, or legal guardian or another person with authority to give that authorization; or

(5) represent that a referral service is a qualified mental health referral service unless and until the referral service complies with Section 164.007.

MEDICAL RECORDS PRIVACY—§181

§181.001. Definitions

(a) Unless otherwise defined in this chapter, each term that is used in this chapter has the meaning assigned by the Health Insurance Portability and Accountability Act and Privacy Standards.

(b) In this chapter:

(1) " *Covered entity*" means any person who:

(A) for commercial, financial, or professional gain, monetary fees, or dues, or on a cooperative, nonprofit, or pro bono basis, engages, in whole or in part, and with real or constructive knowledge, in the practice of assembling, collecting, analyzing, using, evaluating, storing, or transmitting protected health information. The term includes a business associate, health care payer, governmental unit, information or computer management entity, school, health researcher, health care facility, clinic, health care provider, or person who maintains an Internet site;

(B) comes into possession of protected health information;

(C) obtains or stores protected health information under this chapter; or

(D) is an employee, agent, or contractor of a person described by Paragraph (A), (B), or (C) insofar as the employee, agent, or contractor creates, receives, obtains, maintains, uses, or transmits protected health information.

(2) " *Health care operations*" has the meaning assigned by the Health Insurance Portability and Accountability Act and Privacy Standards. The term does

not include marketing as described in 45 C.F.R. Section 164.514(e) and any subsequent amendments.

(3) " *Health Insurance Portability and Accountability Act and Privacy Standards* " means the privacy requirements of the Administrative Simplification subtitle of the Health Insurance Portability and Accountability Act of 1996 (Pub. L. No. 104-191) and the final rules adopted on December 28, 2000, and published at 65 Fed. Reg. 82798 et seq., and any subsequent amendments.

(5) " *Protected health information* " means individually identifiable health information, including demographic information collected from an individual, that:

(A) relates to:

(i) the past, present, or future physical or mental health or condition of an individual;

(ii) the provision of health care to an individual; or

(iii) the past, present, or future payment for the provision of health care to an individual; and

(B) identifies the individual or with respect to which there is a reasonable basis to believe the information can be used to identify the individual.

§181.002. Applicability

(a)This chapter does not affect the validity of another statute of this state that provides greater confidentiality for information made confidential by this chapter.

(b) To the extent that this chapter conflicts with another law with respect to protected health information collected by a governmental body or unit, this chapter controls.

§181.004. Rules

A state agency that licenses or regulates a covered entity may adopt rules as necessary to carry out the purposes of this chapter.

§181.057. Information Relating to Offenders with Mental Impairments

This chapter does not apply to an agency described by Section 614.017 with respect to the disclosure, receipt, transfer, or exchange of medical and health information and records relating to individuals in the custody of an agency or in community supervision.

§181.058. Educational Records

In this chapter, protected health information does not include:

(1) education records covered by the Family Educational Rights and Privacy Act of 1974 (20 U.S.C. Section 1232g) and its subsequent amendments; or

(2)records described by 20 U.S.C. Section 1232g(a)(4)(B)(iv) and its subsequent amendments.

§181.101. Compliance with Federal Regulations

A covered entity shall comply with the Health Insurance Portability and Accountability Act and Privacy Standards relating to:

(1) an individual's access to the individual's protected health information;

(2) amendment of protected health information;

(3) uses and disclosures of protected health information, including requirements relating to consent; and

(3)notice of privacy practices for protected health information.

§181.102. Information for Research

(a)A covered entity may disclose protected health information to a person performing health research, regardless of the source of funding of the research, for the purpose of conducting health research, only if the person performing health research has obtained:

(1) individual consent or authorization for use or disclosure of protected health information for research required by federal law;

(2) the express written authorization of the individual required by this chapter;

(3) documentation that a waiver of individual consent or authorization required for use or disclosure of protected health information has been granted by an institutional review board or privacy board as required under federal law; or

(4) documentation that a waiver of the individual's express written authorization required by this chapter has been granted by a privacy board established under this section.

(b)A privacy board:

(1) must consist of members with varying backgrounds and appropriate professional competency as necessary to review the effect of the research protocol for the project or projects on the privacy rights and related interests of the individuals whose protected health information would be used or disclosed;

(2) must include at least one member who is not affiliated with the covered entity or an entity conducting or sponsoring the research and not related to any person who is affiliated with an entity described by this subsection; and

(3) may not have any member participating in the review of any project in which the member has a conflict of interest.

(c) A privacy board may grant a waiver of the express written authorization for the use of protected health information if the privacy board obtains the following documentation:

(1) a statement identifying the privacy board and the date on which the waiver of the express written authorization was approved by the privacy board;

(2)a statement that the privacy board has determined that the waiver satisfies the following criteria:

(A) the use or disclosure of protected health information involves no more than minimal risk to the affected individuals;

(B) the waiver will not adversely affect the privacy rights and welfare of those individuals;

(C) the research could not practicably be conducted without the waiver;

(D) the research could not practicably be conducted without access to and use of the protected health information;

(E) the privacy risks to individuals whose protected health information is to be used or disclosed are reasonable in relation to the anticipated benefits, if any, to the individuals and the importance of the knowledge that may reasonably be expected to result from the research;

(F) there is an adequate plan to protect the identifiers from improper use and disclosure;

(G) there is an adequate plan to destroy the identifiers at the earliest opportunity consistent with conduct of the research, unless there is a health or research justification for retaining the identifiers or the retention is otherwise required by law; and

(H) there are adequate written assurances that the protected health information will not be reused or disclosed to another person or entity, except:

(i) as required by law;

(ii) for authorized oversight of the research project; or

(iii) for other research for which the use or disclosure of protected health information would be permitted by state or federal law;

(3) a brief description of the protected health information for which use or access has been determined to be necessary by the privacy board under Subdivision (2)(D); and

(4) a statement that the waiver of express written authorization has been approved by the privacy board following the procedures under Subsection (e).

(d) A waiver must be signed by the presiding officer of the privacy board or the presiding officer's designee.

(e) The privacy board must review the proposed research at a convened meeting at which a majority of the privacy board members are present, including at least one member who satisfies the requirements of Subsection (b)(2). The waiver of express written authorization must be approved by the majority of the privacy board members present at the meeting, unless the privacy board elects to use an expedited review procedure. The privacy board may use an expedited review procedure only if the research involves no more than minimal risk to the privacy of the individual who is the subject of the protected health information of which use or disclosure is being sought. If the privacy board elects to use an expedited review procedure, the review and approval of the waiver of express written authorization may be made by the presiding officer of the privacy board or by one or more members of the privacy board as designated by the presiding officer.

(f) A covered entity may disclose protected health information to a person performing health research if the covered entity obtains from the person performing the health research representations that:

(1) use or disclosure is sought solely to review protected health information as necessary to prepare a research protocol or for similar purposes preparatory to research;

(2) no protected health information is to be removed from the covered entity by the person performing the health research in the course of the review; and

(3) the protected health information for which use or access is sought is necessary for the research purposes.

(g) A person who is the subject of protected health information collected or created in the course of a clinical research trial may access the information at the conclusion of the research trial.

§181.103. Disclosure of Information to Public Health Authority

A covered entity may use or disclose protected health information without the express written authorization of the individual for public health activities or to comply with the requirements of any federal or state health benefit program or any federal or state law. A covered entity may disclose protected health information:

(1) to a public health authority that is authorized by law to collect or receive such information for the purpose of preventing or controlling disease, injury, or disability, including the reporting of disease, injury, vital events such as birth or death, and the conduct of public health surveillance, public health investigations, and public interventions;

(2) to a public health authority or other appropriate government authority authorized by law to receive reports of child or adult abuse, neglect, or exploitation; and

(3) to any state agency in conjunction with a federal or state health benefit

program.

§181.151. Reidentified Information

A person may not reidentify or attempt to reidentify an individual who is the subject of any protected health information without obtaining the individual's consent or authorization if required under this chapter or other state or federal law.

§181.201. Injunctive Relief; Civil Penalty

(a) The attorney general may institute an action for injunctive relief to restrain a violation of this chapter.

(b) In addition to the injunctive relief provided by Subsection (a), the attorney general may institute an action for civil penalties against a covered entity for a violation of this chapter. A civil penalty assessed under this section may not exceed $3,000 for each violation.

(c) If the court in which an action under Subsection (b) is pending finds that the violations have occurred with a frequency as to constitute a pattern or practice, the court may assess a civil penalty not to exceed $250,000.

§181.202. Disciplinary Action

In addition to the penalties prescribed by this chapter, a violation of this chapter by an individual or facility that is licensed by an agency of this state is subject to investigation and disciplinary proceedings, including probation or suspension by the licensing agency. If there is evidence that the violations of this chapter constitute a pattern or practice, the agency may revoke the individual's or facility's license.

§181.203. Exclusion from State Programs

In addition to the penalties prescribed by this chapter, a covered entity shall be excluded from participating in any state-funded health care program if a court finds the covered entity engaged in a pattern or practice of violating this chapter.

§181.204. Availability of Other Remedies

This chapter does not affect any right of a person under other law to bring a cause of action or otherwise seek relief with respect to conduct that is a violation of this chapter.

NURSING HOME RESIDENTS REQUIRING MH OR MR SERVICES— §242.158

§242.158 Identification of Certain Nursing Home Residents Requiring Mental Health or Mental Retardation Services

(a) Each resident of a nursing home who is considering making a transition to a community-based care setting shall be identified to determine the presence of a mental illness or mental retardation, regardless of whether the resident is receiving treatment or services for a mental illness or mental retardation.

(b) In identifying residents having a mental illness or mental retardation, the department shall use an identification process that is at least as effective as the mental health and mental retardation identification process established by federal law. The results of the identification process may not be used to prevent a resident from remaining in the nursing home unless the nursing home is unable to provide adequate care for the resident.

(c) The department shall compile and provide to the Texas Department of Mental Health and Mental Retardation information regarding each resident identified as having a mental illness or mental retardation before the resident makes a transition from the nursing home to a community-based care setting.

(d) The Texas Department of Mental Health and Mental Retardation shall use the information provided under Subsection (c) solely for the purposes of:

(1) determining the need for and funding levels of mental health and mental retardation services for residents making a transition from a nursing home to a community-based care setting;

(2) providing mental health or mental retardation services to an identified resident after the resident makes that transition; and

(3) referring an identified resident to a local mental health or mental retardation authority or private provider for additional mental health or mental retardation services.

(e) This section does not authorize the department to decide for a resident of a nursing home that the resident will make a transition from the nursing home to a community-based care setting.

Reports of Abuse or Neglect of Patients—§464

§464.010. Reports of Abuse or Neglect

(a) A person, including treatment facility personnel, who believes that a client's physical or mental health or welfare has been, is, or will be adversely affected by abuse or neglect caused by any person shall report the facts underlying that belief to the commission. This requirement is in addition to the requirements prescribed by Chapter 261, Family Code, and Chapter 48, Human Resources Code.

(b) The commission shall prescribe procedures for the investigation of reports under Subsection (a) and for coordination with law enforcement agencies or other agencies.

(c) An individual who in good faith reports to the commission under this section is immune from civil or criminal liability based on the report. That immunity extends to participation in a judicial proceeding resulting from the report but does not extend to an individual who caused the abuse or neglect.

(d) The commission may request the attorney general's office to file a petition for temporary care and protection of a client of a residential treatment facility if it appears that immediate removal of the client is necessary to prevent further abuse.

(e) All records made by the commission during its investigation of alleged abuse or neglect are confidential and may not be released except that the release may be made:

(1) on court order;

(2) on written request and consent of the person under investigation or that person's authorized attorney; or

(3) as provided by Section 464.011.

Voluntary Mental Health Services—§571 and 572

§571.019. Limitation of Liability

(a) A person who participates in the examination, certification, apprehension, custody, transportation, detention, treatment, or discharge of any person or in the performance of any other act required or authorized by this subtitle and who acts in good faith, reasonably, and without negligence is not criminally or civilly liable for that action.

(b) A physician performing a medical examination and providing information to the court in a court proceeding held under this subtitle or providing information to a peace officer to demonstrate the necessity to apprehend a person under Chapter 573 is considered an officer of the court and is not liable for the examination or testimony when acting without malice.

(c) A physician or inpatient mental health facility that discharges a voluntary patient is not liable for the discharge if:

(1) a written request for the patient's release was filed and not withdrawn; and

(2) the person who filed the written request for discharge is notified that the person assumes all responsibility for the patient on discharge.

§572.001. Request for Admission

(a) A person 16 years of age or older or a person younger than 16 years of age who is or has been married may request admission to an inpatient mental health facility by filing a request with the administrator of the facility to which admission is requested. The parent, managing conservator, or guardian of a person younger than 16 years of age who is not and has not been married may request the admission of the person to an inpatient mental health facility by filing a request with the administrator of the facility to which admission is requested.

(b) An admission request must be in writing and signed by the person requesting the admission.

(c) A person or agency appointed as the guardian or a managing conservator of a minor younger than 16 years of age and acting as an employee or agent of the state or a political subdivision of the state may request admission of the minor only with the minor's consent.

(d) The administrator of an inpatient mental health facility may admit a minor who is 16 years of age or older or a person younger than 16 years of age who is or has been married to an inpatient mental health facility as a voluntary patient without the consent of the parent, managing conservator, or guardian.

(e) A request for admission as a voluntary patient must state that the person for whom admission is requested agrees to voluntarily remain in the facility until the person's discharge and that the person consents to the diagnosis, observation, care, and treatment provided until the earlier of:

(1) the person's discharge; or

(2) the period prescribed by Section 572.004.

§572.002. Admission

The facility administrator or the administrator's authorized, qualified designee may admit a person for whom a proper request for voluntary inpatient services is filed if the administrator or the designee determines:

(1) from a preliminary examination that the person has symptoms of mental illness and will benefit from the inpatient services;

(2) that the person has been informed of the person's rights as a voluntary patient; and

(3) that the admission was voluntarily agreed to:

(A) by the person, if the person is:

(i) 16 years of age or older; or

(ii) younger than 16 years of age and is or has been married; or

(B) by the person's parent, managing conservator, or guardian, if the person is younger than 16 years of age and is not and has not been married.

§572.0022. Information on Medications

(a) A mental health facility shall provide to a patient in the patient's primary language, if possible, and in accordance with board rules information relating to prescription medication ordered by the patient's treating physician.

(b) The facility shall also provide the information to the patient's family on request, but only to the extent not otherwise prohibited by state or federal confidentiality laws.

§572.0025. Intake, Assessment, and Admission

(a) The board shall adopt rules governing the voluntary admission of a patient to an inpatient mental health facility, including rules governing the intake and assessment procedures of the admission process.

(b) The rules governing the intake process shall establish minimum standards for:

(1) reviewing a prospective patient's finances and insurance benefits;

(2) explaining to a prospective patient the patient's rights; and

(3) explaining to a prospective patient the facility's services and treatment process.

(c) The assessment provided for by the rules may be conducted only by a professional who meets the qualifications prescribed by board rules.

(d) The rules governing the assessment process shall prescribe:

(1) the types of professionals who may conduct an assessment;

(2) the minimum credentials each type of professional must have to conduct an assessment; and

(3) the type of assessment that professional may conduct.

(e) In accordance with board rule, a facility shall provide annually a minimum of eight hours of inservice training regarding intake and assessment for persons who will be conducting an intake or assessment for the facility. A person may not conduct intake or assessments without having completed the initial and applicable annual inservice training.

(f) A prospective voluntary patient may not be formally accepted for treatment in a facility unless:

(1) the facility has a physician's order admitting the prospective patient, which order may be issued orally, electronically, or in writing, signed by the physician, provided that, in the case of an oral order or an electronically transmitted unsigned order, a signed original is presented to the mental health facility within 24 hours of the initial order; the order must be from:

(A) an admitting physician who has conducted an in-person physical and psychiatric examination within 72 hours of the admission; or

(B) an admitting physician who has consulted with a physician who has conducted an in-person examination within 72 hours of the admission; and

(2) the facility administrator or a person designated by the administrator has agreed to accept the prospective patient and has signed a statement to that effect.

(g) An assessment conducted as required by rules adopted under this section does not satisfy a statutory or regulatory requirement for a personal evaluation of a patient or a prospective patient by a physician before admission.

(h) In this section:

(1) " *Admission*" means the formal acceptance of a prospective patient to a facility.

(2) "*Assessment*" means the administrative process a facility uses to gather information from a prospective patient, including a medical history and the problem for which the patient is seeking treatment, to determine whether a prospective patient should be examined by a physician to determine if admission is clinically justified.

(3) " *Intake*" means the administrative process for gathering information about a prospective patient and giving a prospective patient information about the facility and the facility's treatment and services.

§572.003. Rights of Patients

(a) A person's voluntary admission to an inpatient mental health facility under this chapter does not affect the person's civil rights or legal capacity or affect the person's right to obtain a writ of habeas corpus.

(b) In addition to the rights provided by this subtitle, a person voluntarily admitted to an inpatient mental health facility under this chapter has the right:

(1) to be reviewed periodically to determine the person's need for continued inpatient treatment; and

(2) to have an application for court-ordered mental health services filed only as provided by Section 572.005.

(c) A person admitted to an inpatient mental health facility under this chapter shall be informed of the rights provided under this section and Section 572.004:

(1) orally in simple, nontechnical terms, within 24 hours after the time the person is admitted, and in writing in the person's primary language, if possible; or

(2) through the use of a means reasonably calculated to communicate with a hearing impaired or visually impaired person, if applicable.

(d) The patient's parent, managing conservator, or guardian shall also be informed of the patient's rights as required by this section if the patient is a minor.

§572.004. Discharge

(a) A voluntary patient is entitled to leave an inpatient mental health facility in accordance with this section after a written request for discharge is filed with the facility administrator or the administrator's designee. The request must be signed, timed, and dated by the patient or a person legally responsible for the patient and must be made a part of the patient's clinical record. If a patient informs an employee of or person associated with the facility of the patient's desire to leave the facility, the employee or person shall, as soon as possible, assist the patient in creating the written request and present it to the patient for the patient's signature.

(b) The facility shall, within four hours after a request for discharge is filed, notify the physician responsible for the patient's treatment. If that physician is not available during that period, the facility shall notify any available physician of the request.

(c) The notified physician shall discharge the patient before the end of the four-hour period unless the physician has reasonable cause to believe that the patient might meet the criteria for court-ordered mental health services or emergency detention.

(d) A physician who has reasonable cause to believe that a patient might meet the criteria for court-ordered mental health services or emergency detention shall examine the patient as soon as possible within 24 hours after the time the request for discharge is filed. The physician shall discharge the patient on completion of the examination unless the physician determines that the person meets the criteria for court-ordered mental health services or emergency detention. If the physician makes a determination that the patient meets the criteria for court-ordered mental health services or emergency detention, the physician shall, not later than 4 p.m. on the next succeeding business day after the date on which the examination occurs, either discharge the patient or file an application for court-ordered mental health services or emergency detention and obtain a written order for further detention. The physician shall notify the patient if the physician intends to detain the patient under this subsection or intends to file an application for court-ordered mental health services or emergency detention. A decision to detain a patient under this subsection and the reasons for the decision shall be made a part of the patient's clinical record.

(e) If extremely hazardous weather conditions exist or a disaster occurs, the physician may request the judge of a court that has jurisdiction over proceedings brought under Chapter 574 to extend the period during which the patient may be detained. The judge or a magistrate appointed by the judge may by written order made each day extend the period during which the patient may be detained until 4 p.m. on the first succeeding business day. The written order must declare that an emergency exists because of the weather or the occurrence of a disaster.

(f) The patient is not entitled to leave the facility if before the end of the period prescribed by this section:

(1) a written withdrawal of the request for discharge is filed; or

(2) an application for court-ordered mental health services or emergency detention is filed and the patient is detained in accordance with this subtitle.

(g) A plan for continuing care shall be prepared in accordance with Section

574.081 for each patient discharged. If sufficient time to prepare a continuing care plan before discharge is not available, the plan may be prepared and mailed to the appropriate person within 24 hours after the patient is discharged.

(h) The patient or other person who files a request for discharge of a patient shall be notified that the person filing the request assumes all responsibility for the patient on discharge.

§572.005. Application for Court-Ordered Treatment

(a) An application for court-ordered mental health services may not be filed against a patient receiving voluntary inpatient services unless:

(1) a request for release of the patient has been filed with the facility administrator; or

(2) in the opinion of the physician responsible for the patient's treatment, the patient meets the criteria for court-ordered mental health services and:

(A) is absent from the facility without authorization;

(B) is unable to consent to appropriate and necessary psychiatric treatment; or

(C) refuses to consent to necessary and appropriate treatment recommended by the physician responsible for the patient's treatment and that physician completes a certificate of medical examination for mental illness that, in addition to the information required by Section 574.011, includes the opinion of the physician that:

(i) there is no reasonable alternative to the treatment recommended by the physician; and

(ii) the patient will not benefit from continued inpatient care without the recommended treatment.

(b) The physician responsible for the patient's treatment shall notify the patient if the physician intends to file an application for court-ordered mental health services.

COURT ORDERED EMERGENCY SERVICES—§573

§573.001. Apprehension by Peace Officer Without Warrant

(a) A peace officer, without a warrant, may take a person into custody if the officer:

(1) has reason to believe and does believe that:

(A) the person is mentally ill; and

(B) because of that mental illness there is a substantial risk of serious harm to the person or to others unless the person is immediately restrained; and

(2) believes that there is not sufficient time to obtain a warrant before taking the person into custody.

(b) A substantial risk of serious harm to the person or others under Subsection (a)(1)(B) may be demonstrated by:

(1) the person's behavior; or

(2) evidence of severe emotional distress and deterioration in the person's mental condition to the extent that the person cannot remain at liberty.

(c) The peace officer may form the belief that the person meets the criteria for apprehension:

(1) from a representation of a credible person; or

(2) on the basis of the conduct of the apprehended person or the circumstances under which the apprehended person is found.

(d) A peace officer who takes a person into custody under Subsection (a) shall immediately transport the apprehended person to:

(1) the nearest appropriate inpatient mental health facility; or

(2) a facility deemed suitable by the county's mental health authority, if an appropriate inpatient mental health facility is not available.

(e) A jail or similar detention facility may not be deemed suitable except in an extreme emergency.

(f) A person detained in a jail or a nonmedical facility shall be kept separate from any person who is charged with or convicted of a crime.

§573.011. Application for Emergency Detention

(a) An adult may file a written application for the emergency detention of another person.

(b) The application must state:

(1) that the applicant has reason to believe and does believe that the person evidences mental illness;

(2) that the applicant has reason to believe and does believe that the person evidences a substantial risk of serious harm to himself or others;

(3) a specific description of the risk of harm;

(4) that the applicant has reason to believe and does believe that the risk of harm is imminent unless the person is immediately restrained;

(5) that the applicant's beliefs are derived from specific recent behavior, overt acts, attempts, or threats;

(6) a detailed description of the specific behavior, acts, attempts, or threats; and

(7) a detailed description of the applicant's relationship to the person whose

detention is sought.

(c) The application may be accompanied by any relevant information.

§573.021. Preliminary Examination

(a) A facility shall temporarily accept a person for whom an application for detention is filed.

(b) A person accepted for a preliminary examination may be detained in custody for not longer than 24 hours after the time the person is presented to the facility unless a written order for further detention is obtained. If the 24-hour period ends on a Saturday, Sunday, legal holiday, or before 4 p.m. on the first succeeding business day, the person may be detained until 4 p.m. on the first succeeding business day. If extremely hazardous weather conditions exist or a disaster occurs, the presiding judge or magistrate may, by written order made each day, extend by an additional 24 hours the period during which the person may be detained. The written order must declare that an emergency exists because of the weather or the occurrence of a disaster.

(c) A physician shall examine the person as soon as possible within 24 hours after the time the person is apprehended.

(d) A facility must comply with this section only to the extent that the commissioner determines that a facility has sufficient resources to perform the necessary services under this section.

(e) A person may not be detained in a private mental health facility without the consent of the facility administrator.

§573.022. Emergency Admission and Detention

(a) A person may be admitted to a facility for emergency detention only if the physician who conducted the preliminary examination of the person makes a written statement that:

(1) is acceptable to the facility;

(2) states that after a preliminary examination it is the physician's opinion that:

    (A) the person is mentally ill;

    (B) the person evidences a substantial risk of serious harm to himself or others;

    (C) the described risk of harm is imminent unless the person is immediately restrained; and

    (D) emergency detention is the least restrictive means by which the necessary restraint may be accomplished; and

(3) includes:

    (A) a description of the nature of the person's mental illness;

(B) a specific description of the risk of harm the person evidences that may be demonstrated either by the person's behavior or by evidence of severe emotional distress and deterioration in the person's mental condition to the extent that the person cannot remain at liberty; and

(C) the specific detailed information from which the physician formed the opinion in Subdivision (2).

(b) A county mental health facility that has admitted a person for emergency detention under this section may transport the person to:

(1) a facility of the single portal authority for the area;

(2) an appropriate inpatient mental health facility, if no single portal authority serves the area; or

(3) a facility deemed suitable by the county's mental health authority, if no single portal authority serves the area and an appropriate inpatient mental health facility is not available.

§573.023. Release from Emergency Detention

(a) A person apprehended under Subchapter A or detained under Subchapter B shall be released on completion of the preliminary examination unless the person is admitted to a facility under Section 573.022.

(b) A person admitted to a facility under Section 573.022 shall be released if the facility administrator determines at any time during the emergency detention period that one of the criteria prescribed by Section 573.022(2) no longer applies.

§573.025. Rights of Persons Apprehended or Detained

(a) A person apprehended or detained under this chapter has the right:

(1) to be advised of the location of detention, the reasons for the detention, and the fact that the detention could result in a longer period of involuntary commitment;

(2) to a reasonable opportunity to communicate with and retain an attorney;

(3) to be transported to a location as provided by Section 573.024 if the person is not admitted for emergency detention, unless the person is arrested or objects;

(4) to be released from a facility as provided by Section 573.023;

(5) to be advised that communications with a mental health professional may be used in proceedings for further detention; and

(6) to be transported in accordance with Sections 573.026 and 574.045, if the person is detained under Section 573.022 or transported under an order of protective custody under Section 574.023.

(b) A person apprehended or detained under this subtitle shall be informed of the rights provided by this section:

(1) orally in simple, nontechnical terms, within 24 hours after the time the person is admitted to a facility, and in writing in the person's primary language if possible; or

(2) through the use of a means reasonably calculated to communicate with a hearing or visually impaired person, if applicable.

TEMPORARY AND EXTENDED MENTAL HEALTH SERVICES—§574

§574.010. Independent Psychiatric Evaluation and Expert Testimony

(a) The court may order an independent evaluation of the proposed patient by a psychiatrist chosen by the proposed patient if the court determines that the evaluation will assist the finder of fact. The psychiatrist may testify on behalf of the proposed patient.

(b) If the court determines that the proposed patient is indigent, the court may authorize reimbursement to the attorney ad litem for court-approved expenses incurred in obtaining expert testimony and may order the proposed patient's county of residence to pay the expenses.

§574.034. Order for Temporary Mental Health Services

(a) The judge may order a proposed patient to receive court-ordered temporary inpatient mental health services only if the judge or jury finds, from clear and convincing evidence, that:

(1) the proposed patient is mentally ill; and

(2) as a result of that mental illness the proposed patient:

    (A) is likely to cause serious harm to himself;

    (B) is likely to cause serious harm to others; or

    (C) is:

        (i) suffering severe and abnormal mental, emotional, or physical distress;

        (ii) experiencing substantial mental or physical deterioration of the proposed patient's ability to function independently, which is exhibited by the proposed patient's inability, except for reasons of indigence, to provide for the proposed patient's basic needs, including food, clothing, health, or safety; and

        (iii) unable to make a rational and informed decision as to whether or not to submit to treatment.

(b) The judge may order a proposed patient to receive court-ordered temporary outpatient mental health services only if:

(1) the judge finds that appropriate mental health services are available to the patient; and

(2) the judge or jury finds, from clear and convincing evidence, that:

(A) the proposed patient is mentally ill;

(B) the nature of the mental illness is severe and persistent;

(C) as a result of the mental illness, the proposed patient will, if not treated, continue to:

(i) suffer severe and abnormal mental, emotional, or physical distress; and

(ii) experience deterioration of the ability to function independently to the extent that the proposed patient will be unable to live safely in the community without court-ordered outpatient mental health services; and

(D) the proposed patient has an inability to participate in outpatient treatment services effectively and voluntarily, demonstrated by:

(i) any of the proposed patient's actions occurring within the two-year period which immediately precedes the hearing; or

(ii) specific characteristics of the proposed patient's clinical condition that make impossible a rational and informed decision whether to submit to voluntary outpatient treatment.

(c) If the judge or jury finds that the proposed patient meets the commitment criteria prescribed by Subsection (a), the judge or jury must specify which criterion listed in Subsection (a)(2) forms the basis for the decision.

(d) To be clear and convincing under Subsection (a), the evidence must include expert testimony and, unless waived, evidence of a recent overt act or a continuing pattern of behavior that tends to confirm:

(1) the likelihood of serious harm to the proposed patient or others; or

(2) the proposed patient's distress and the deterioration of the proposed patient's ability to function.

(e) To be clear and convincing under Subdivision (b)(2), the evidence must include expert testimony and, unless waived, evidence of a recent overt act or a continuing pattern of behavior that tends to confirm:

(1) the proposed patient's distress;

(2) the deterioration of ability to function independently to the extent that the proposed patient will be unable to live safely in the community; and

(3) the proposed patient's inability to participate in outpatient treatment services effectively and voluntarily.

(f) The proposed patient and the proposed patient's attorney, by a written document filed with the court, may waive the right to cross-examine witnesses, and, if that right is waived, the court may admit, as evidence, the certificates of medical examination for mental illness. The certificates admitted under this subsection constitute competent medical or psychiatric testimony, and the court may make its findings solely from the certificates. If the proposed patient and the proposed patient's attorney do not waive in writing the right to cross-examine witnesses, the court shall proceed to hear testimony. The testimony must include competent medical or psychiatric testimony. In addition, the court may consider the testimony of a nonphysician mental health professional as provided by Section 574.031(f).

(g) An order for temporary inpatient or outpatient mental health services shall state that treatment is authorized for not longer than 90 days. The order may not specify a shorter period.

(h) A judge may not issue an order for temporary inpatient or outpatient mental health services for a proposed patient who is charged with a criminal offense that involves an act, attempt, or threat of serious bodily injury to another person.

(i) A judge may advise, but may not compel, the proposed patient to:

(1) receive treatment with psychoactive medication as specified by the outpatient mental health services treatment plan;

(2) participate in counseling; and

(3) refrain from the use of alcohol or illicit drugs.

§574.035. Order for Extended Mental Health Services

(a) The judge may order a proposed patient to receive court-ordered extended inpatient mental health services only if the jury, or the judge if the right to a jury is waived, finds, from clear and convincing evidence, that:

(1) the proposed patient is mentally ill;

(2) as a result of that mental illness the proposed patient:

(A) is likely to cause serious harm to himself;

(B) is likely to cause serious harm to others; or

(C) is:

(i) suffering severe and abnormal mental, emotional, or physical distress;

(ii) experiencing substantial mental or physical deterioration of the proposed patient's ability to function independently, which is exhibited by the proposed patient's inability, except for reasons of indigence, to provide for the proposed patient's basic needs, including food, clothing, health, or safety; and

(iii) unable to make a rational and informed decision as to whether or not to submit to treatment;

(3) the proposed patient's condition is expected to continue for more than 90 days; and

(4) the proposed patient has received court-ordered inpatient mental health services under this subtitle or under Article 46.02, Code of Criminal Procedure, for at least 60 consecutive days during the preceding 12 months.

(b) The judge may order a proposed patient to receive court-ordered extended outpatient mental health services only if:

(1) the judge finds that appropriate mental health services are available to the patient; and

(2) the jury, or the judge if the right to a jury is waived, finds from clear and convincing evidence that:

(A) the proposed patient is mentally ill;

(B) the nature of the mental illness is severe and persistent;

(C) as a result of the mental illness, the proposed patient will, if not treated, continue to:

(i) suffer severe and abnormal mental, emotional, or physical distress; and

(ii) experience deterioration of the ability to function independently to the extent that the proposed patient will be unable to live safely in the community without court-ordered outpatient mental health services;

(D) the proposed patient has an inability to participate in outpatient treatment services effectively and voluntarily, demonstrated by:

(i) any of the proposed patient's actions occurring within the two-year period which immediately precedes the hearing; or

(ii) specific characteristics of the proposed patient's clinical condition that make impossible a rational and informed decision whether to submit to voluntary outpatient treatment;

(E) the proposed patient's condition is expected to continue for more than 90 days; and

(F) the proposed patient has received court-ordered inpatient mental health services under this subtitle or under Section 5, Article 46.02, Code of Criminal Procedure, for at least 60 consecutive days during the preceding 12 months.

(c) If the jury or judge finds that the proposed patient meets the commitment criteria prescribed by Subsection (a), the jury or judge must specify which criterion listed in Subsection (a)(2) forms the basis for the decision.

(d) The jury or judge is not required to make the finding under Subsection (a)(4) or (b)(2)(F) if the proposed patient has already been subject to an order for extended mental health services.

(e) To be clear and convincing under Subsection (a), the evidence must include expert testimony and evidence of a recent overt act or a continuing pattern of behavior that tends to confirm:

(1) the likelihood of serious harm to the proposed patient or others; or

(2) the proposed patient's distress and the deterioration of the proposed patient's ability to function.

(f) To be clear and convincing under Subdivision (b)(2), the evidence must include expert testimony and evidence of a recent overt act or a continuing pattern of behavior that tends to confirm:

(1) the proposed patient's distress;

(2) the deterioration of ability to function independently to the extent that the proposed patient will be unable to live safely in the community; and

(3) the proposed patient's inability to participate in outpatient treatment services effectively and voluntarily.

(g) The court may not make its findings solely from the certificates of medical examination for mental illness but shall hear testimony. The court may not enter an order for extended mental health services unless appropriate findings are made and are supported by testimony taken at the hearing. The testimony must include competent medical or psychiatric testimony.

(h) An order for extended inpatient or outpatient mental health services shall state that treatment is authorized for not longer than 12 months. The order may not specify a shorter period.

(i) A judge may not issue an order for extended inpatient or outpatient mental health services for a proposed patient who is charged with a criminal offense that involves an act, attempt, or threat of serious bodily injury to another person.

(j) A judge may advise, but may not compel, the proposed patient to:

(1) receive treatment with psychoactive medication as specified by the outpatient mental health services treatment plan;

(2) participate in counseling; and

(3) refrain from the use of alcohol or illicit drugs.

§574.036. Order of Care or Commitment

(a) The judge shall dismiss the jury, if any, after a hearing in which a person is found to be mentally ill and to meet the criteria for court-ordered temporary or extended mental health services.

(b) The judge may hear additional evidence relating to alternative settings for care before entering an order relating to the setting for the care the person will receive.

(c) The judge shall consider in determining the setting for care the recommendation for the most appropriate treatment alternative filed under Section 574.012.

(d) The judge shall order the mental health services provided in the least restrictive appropriate setting available.

(e) The judge may enter an order:

(1) committing the person to a mental health facility for inpatient care if the trier of fact finds that the person meets the commitment criteria prescribed by Section 574.034(a) or 574.035(a); or

(2) committing the person to outpatient mental health services if the trier of fact finds that the person meets the commitment criteria prescribed by Section 574.034(b) or 574.035(b).

§574.037. Court-Ordered Outpatient Services

(a) The court, in an order that directs a patient to participate in outpatient mental health services, shall identify a person who is responsible for those services. The person identified must be the facility administrator or an individual involved in providing court-ordered outpatient services. A person may not be designated as responsible for the ordered services without the person's consent unless the person is the facility administrator of a department facility or the facility administrator of a community center that provides mental health services in the region in which the committing court is located.

(b) The person responsible for the services shall submit to the court within two weeks after the court enters the order a general program of the treatment to be provided. The program must be incorporated into the court order.

(c) The person responsible for the services shall inform the court of:

(1) the patient's failure to comply with the court order; and

(2) any substantial change in the general program of treatment that occurs before the order expires.

(d) A facility must comply with this section to the extent that the commissioner determines that the designated mental health facility has sufficient resources to perform the necessary services.

(e) A patient may not be detained in a private mental health facility without the consent of the facility administrator.

§574.0415. Information on Medications

(a) A mental health facility shall provide to a patient in the patient's primary language, if possible, and in accordance with board rules information relating to prescription medication ordered by the patient's treating physician.

(b) The facility shall also provide the information to the patient's family on request, but only to the extent not otherwise prohibited by state or federal confidentiality laws.

§574.042. Commitment to Private Facility

The court may order a patient committed to a private mental hospital at no expense to the state if the court receives:

(1) an application signed by the patient or the patient's guardian or next friend requesting that the patient be placed in a designated private mental hospital at the patient's or applicant's expense; and

(2) written agreement from the hospital administrator of the private mental hospital to admit the patient and to accept responsibility for the patient in accordance with this subtitle.

Rights of Patients—§574.105

§574.105. Rights of Patient

A patient for whom an application for an order to authorize the administration of a psychoactive medication is filed is entitled to:

(1) representation by a court-appointed attorney who is knowledgeable about issues to be adjudicated at the hearing;

(2) meet with that attorney as soon as is practicable to prepare for the hearing and to discuss any of the patient's questions or concerns;

(3) receive, immediately after the time of the hearing is set, a copy of the application and written notice of the time, place, and date of the hearing;

(4) be told, at the time personal notice of the hearing is given, of the patient's right to a hearing and right to the assistance of an attorney to prepare for the hearing and to answer any questions or concerns;

(5) be present at the hearing;

(6) request from the court an independent expert; and

(7) oral notification, at the conclusion of the hearing, of the court's determinations of the patient's capacity and best interests.

§574.106. Hearing on Patient's Capacity and Order Authorizing Psychoactive Medication

(a) The court may issue an order authorizing the administration of one or more classes of psychoactive medication only if the court finds by clear and convincing evidence after the hearing that:

(1) the patient is under an order for temporary or extended mental health services under Section 574.034 or 574.035;

(2) the patient lacks the capacity to make a decision regarding the administration of the proposed medication; and

(3) treatment with the proposed medication is in the best interest of the patient.

(b) In making its findings, the court shall consider:

(1) the patient's expressed preferences regarding treatment with psychoactive medication;

(2) the patient's religious beliefs;

(3) the risks and benefits, from the perspective of the patient, of taking psychoactive medication;

(4) the consequences to the patient if the psychoactive medication is not administered;

(5) the prognosis for the patient if the patient is treated with psychoactive medication; and

(6) alternatives to treatment with psychoactive medication.

(c) A hearing under this subchapter shall be conducted on the record by the probate judge or judge with probate jurisdiction, except as provided by Subsection (d).

(d) A judge may refer a hearing to a magistrate or court-appointed master who has training regarding psychoactive medications. The magistrate or master may effectuate the notice, set hearing dates, and appoint attorneys as required in this subchapter. A record is not required if the hearing is held by a magistrate or court-appointed master.

(e) A party is entitled to a hearing de novo by the judge if an appeal of the magistrate's or master's report is filed with the court within three days after the report is issued. The hearing de novo shall be held within 30 days of the filing of the application for an order to authorize psychoactive medication.

(f) If a hearing or an appeal of a master's or magistrate's report is to be held in a county court in which the judge is not a licensed attorney, the proposed patient or the proposed patient's attorney may request that the proceeding be transferred to a court with a judge who is licensed to practice law in this state. The county judge shall transfer the case after receiving the request, and the receiving court shall hear the case as if it had been originally filed in that court.

(g) As soon as practicable after the conclusion of the hearing, the patient is entitled to have provided to the patient and the patient's attorney written notification of the court's determinations under this section. The notification shall include a statement of the evidence on which the court relied and the reasons for the court's determinations.

(h) An order entered under this section shall authorize the administration to a patient, regardless of the patient's refusal, of one or more classes of psychoactive medications specified in the application and consistent with the patient's diagnosis. The order shall permit an increase or decrease in a medication's dosage, restitution of medication authorized but discontinued during the period the order is valid, or the substitution of a medication within the same class.

(i) The classes of psychoactive medications in the order must conform to classes determined by the department.

(j) An order issued under this section may be reauthorized or modified on the petition of a party. The order remains in effect pending action on a petition for reauthorization or modification. For the purpose of this subsection, "modification" means a change of a class of medication authorized in the order.

§574.109. Effect of Order

(a) A person's consent to take a psychoactive medication is not valid and may not be relied on if the person is subject to an order issued under Section 574.106.

(b) The issuance of an order under Section 574.106 is not a determination or adjudication of mental incompetency and does not limit in any other respect that person's rights as a citizen or the person's property rights or legal capacity.

VOLUNTARY ADMISSION FOR COURT-ORDERED SERVICES—§574.151

Voluntary Admission for Certain Persons for Whom Motion for Court-Ordered Services Has Been Filed

§574.151. Applicability

This subchapter applies only to a person for whom a motion for court-ordered mental health services is filed under Section 574.001, for whom a final order on that motion has not been entered under Section 574.034 or 574.035, and who requests voluntary admission to an inpatient mental health facility:

(1) while the person is receiving at that facility involuntary inpatient services under Subchapter B or under Chapter 573; or

(2) before the 31st day after the date the person was released from that facility under Section 573.023 or 574.028.

§574.152. Capacity to Consent to Voluntary Admission

A person described by Section 574.151 is rebuttably presumed to have the capacity to consent to admission to the inpatient mental health facility for voluntary inpatient mental health services.

§574.153. Rights of Person Admitted to Voluntary Inpatient Treatment

(a) A person described by Section 574.151 who is admitted to the inpatient mental health facility for voluntary inpatient mental health services has all of the rights provided by Chapter 576 for a person receiving voluntary or involuntary inpatient mental health services.

(b) A right assured by Section 576.021 may not be waived by the patient, the patient's attorney or guardian, or any other person acting on behalf of the patient.

§574.154. Participation in Research Program

Notwithstanding any other law, a person described by Section 574.151 may not participate in a research program in the inpatient mental health facility unless:

(1) the patient provides written consent to participate in the research program under a protocol that has been approved by the facility's institutional review board; and

(2) the institutional review board specifically reviews the patient's consent under the approved protocol.

§576.001. Rights Under Constitution and Law

(a) A person with mental illness in this state has the rights, benefits, responsibilities, and privileges guaranteed by the constitution and laws of the United States and this state.

(b) Unless a specific law limits a right under a special procedure, a patient has:

(1) the right to register and vote at an election;

(2) the right to acquire, use, and dispose of property, including contractual rights;

(3) the right to sue and be sued;

(4) all rights relating to the grant, use, and revocation of a license, permit, privilege, or benefit under law;

(5) the right to religious freedom; and

(6) all rights relating to domestic relations.

§576.002. Presumption of Competency

(a) The provision of court-ordered, emergency, or voluntary mental health services to a person is not a determination or adjudication of mental incompetency and does not limit the person's rights as a citizen, or the person's property rights or legal capacity.

(b) There is a rebuttable presumption that a person is mentally competent unless a judicial finding to the contrary is made under the Texas Probate Code.

§576.005. Confidentiality of Records

Records of a mental health facility that directly or indirectly identify a present, former, or proposed patient are confidential unless disclosure is permitted by other state law.

§576.006. Rights Subject to Limitation

(a) A patient in an inpatient mental health facility has the right to:

(1) receive visitors;

(2) communicate with a person outside the facility by telephone and by uncensored and sealed mail; and

(3) communicate by telephone and by uncensored and sealed mail with legal counsel, the department, the courts, and the state attorney general.

(b) The rights provided in Subsection (a) are subject to the general rules of the facility. The physician ultimately responsible for the patient's treatment may also restrict a right only to the extent that the restriction is necessary to the patient's welfare or to protect another person but may not restrict the right to communicate with legal counsel, the department, the courts, or the state attorney general.

(c) If a restriction is imposed under this section, the physician ultimately responsible for the patient's treatment shall document the clinical reasons for the restriction and the duration of the restriction in the patient's clinical record. That physician shall inform the patient and, if appropriate, the patient's parent, managing conservator, or guardian of the clinical reasons for the restriction and the duration of the restriction.

§576.007. Notification of Release

(a) The department or facility shall make a reasonable effort to notify an adult patient's family before the patient is discharged or released from a facility providing voluntary or involuntary mental health services if the patient grants permission for the notification.

(b) The department shall notify each adult patient of the patient's right to have his family notified under this section.

§576.008. Notification of Protection / Advocacy System

A patient shall be informed in writing, at the time of admission and discharge, of the existence, purpose, telephone number, and address of the protection and advocacy system established in this state under the federal Protection and Advocacy for Mentally Ill Individuals Act of 1986 (42 U.S.C. Sec. 10801, et seq.).

§576.009. Notification of Rights

A patient receiving involuntary inpatient mental health services shall be informed of the rights provided by this subtitle:

(1) orally, in simple, nontechnical terms, and in writing that, if possible, is in the person's primary language; or

(2) through the use of a means reasonably calculated to communicate with a hearing impaired or visually impaired person, if applicable.

§576.021. General Rights Relating to Treatment

(a) A patient receiving mental health services under this subtitle has the right to:

(1) appropriate treatment for the patient's mental illness in the least restrictive appropriate setting available;

(2) not receive unnecessary or excessive medication;

(3) refuse to participate in a research program;

(4) an individualized treatment plan and to participate in developing the plan; and

(5) a humane treatment environment that provides reasonable protection from harm and appropriate privacy for personal needs.

(b)participation in a research program does not affect a right provided by this chapter.

(c) A right provided by this section may not be waived by the patient, the patient's attorney or guardian, or any other person behalf of the patient.

§576.022. Adequacy of Treatment

(a) The facility administrator of an inpatient mental health facility shall provide adequate medical and psychiatric care and treatment to every patient in accordance with the highest standards accepted in medical practice.

(b) The facility administrator of an inpatient mental health facility may give the patient accepted psychiatric treatment and therapy.

§576.023. Periodic Examination

The facility administrator is responsible for the examination of each patient of the facility at least once every six months and more frequently as practicable.

§576.024. Use of Physical Restraint

(a) A physical restraint may not be applied to a patient unless a physician prescribes the restraint.

(b) A physical restraint shall be removed as soon as possible.

(c) Each use of a physical restraint and the reason for the use shall be made a part of the patient's clinical record. The physician who prescribed the restraint shall sign the record.

§576.025. Administration of Psychoactive Medication

(a) A person may not administer a psychoactive medication to a patient receiving voluntary or involuntary mental health services who refuses the administration unless:

(1) the patient is having a medication-related emergency;

(2) the patient is younger than 16 years of age and the patient's parent, managing conservator, or guardian consents to the administration on behalf of the patient;

(3) the refusing patient's representative authorized by law to consent on behalf of the patient has consented to the administration;

(4) the administration of the medication regardless of the patient's refusal is authorized by an order issued under Section 574.106; or

(5) the patient is receiving court-ordered mental health services authorized by an order issued under:

(A) Article 46.02 or 46.03, Code of Criminal Procedure; or

(B) Chapter 55, Family Code.

(b) Consent to the administration of psychoactive medication given by a patient or by a person authorized by law to consent on behalf of the patient is valid only if:

(1) the consent is given voluntarily and without coercive or undue influence;

(2) the treating physician or a person designated by the physician provided the following information, in a standard format approved by the department, to the patient and, if applicable, to the patient's representative authorized by law to consent on behalf of the patient:

(A) the specific condition to be treated;

(B) the beneficial effects on that condition expected from the medication;

(C) the probable health and mental health consequences of not consenting to the medication;

(D) the probable clinically significant side effects and risks associated with the medication;

(E) the generally accepted alternatives to the medication, if any, and why the physician recommends that they be rejected; and

(F) the proposed course of the medication;

(3) the patient and, if appropriate, the patient's representative authorized by law to consent on behalf of the patient is informed in writing that consent may be revoked; and

(4) the consent is evidenced in the patient's clinical record by a signed form prescribed by the facility or by a statement of the treating physician or a person designated by the physician that documents that consent was given by the appropriate person and the circumstances under which the consent was obtained.

(c) If the treating physician designates another person to provide the information under Subsection (b), then, not later than two working days after that person provides the information, excluding weekends and legal holidays, the physician shall meet with the patient and, if appropriate, the patient's representative who provided the consent, to review the information and answer any questions.

(d) A patient's refusal or attempt to refuse to receive psychoactive medication, whether given verbally or by other indications or means, shall be documented in the patient's clinical record.

(e) In prescribing psychoactive medication, a treating physician shall:

(1) prescribe, consistent with clinically appropriate medical care, the medication that has the fewest side effects or the least potential for adverse side effects, unless the class of medication has been demonstrated or justified not to be effective clinically; and

(2) administer the smallest therapeutically acceptable dosages of medication for the patient's condition.

(f) If a physician issues an order to administer psychoactive medication to a patient without the patient's consent because the patient is having a medication-related emergency:

(1) the physician shall document in the patient's clinical record in specific medical or behavioral terms the necessity of the order and that the physician has evaluated but rejected other generally accepted, less intrusive forms of treatment, if any; and

(2) treatment of the patient with the psychoactive medication shall be provided in the manner, consistent with clinically appropriate medical care, least restrictive of the patient's personal liberty.

(g) In this section, "medication-related emergency" and "psychoactive medication" have the meanings assigned by Section 574.101.

§576.026. Independent Evaluation

(a) A patient receiving inpatient mental health services under this subtitle is entitled to obtain at the patient's cost an independent psychiatric, psychological, or medical examination or evaluation by a psychiatrist, physician, or nonphysician mental health professional chosen by the patient. The facility administrator shall allow the patient to obtain the examination or evaluation at any reasonable time.

(b) If the patient is a minor, the minor and the minor's parent, legal guardian, or managing or possessory conservator is entitled to obtain the examination or evaluation. The cost of the examination or evaluation shall be billed by the professional who performed the examination or evaluation to the person responsible for payment of the minor's treatment as a cost of treatment.

§576.027. List of Medications

(a) The facility administrator of an inpatient mental health facility shall provide to a patient, a person designated by the patient, and the patient's legal guardian or managing conservator, if any, a list of the medications prescribed for administration to the patient while the patient is in the facility. The list must include for each medication:

(1) the name of the medication;

(2) the dosage and schedule prescribed for the administration of the medication; and

(3) the name of the physician who prescribed the medication.

(b) The list must be provided within four hours after the facility administrator receives a written request for the list from the patient, a person designated by the patient, or the patient's legal guardian or managing conservator and on the discharge of the patient. If sufficient time to prepare the list before discharge is not available, the list may be mailed within 24 hours after discharge to the patient, a person designated by the patient, and the patient's legal guardian or managing conservator.

(c) A patient or the patient's legal guardian or managing conservator, if any, may waive the right of any person to receive the list of medications while the patient is participating in a research project if release of the list would jeopardize the results of the project.

LEGALLY ADEQUATE CONSENT—§591

§591.006. Consent

(a) Consent given by a person is legally adequate if the person:

(1) is not a minor and has not been adjudicated incompetent to manage the person's personal affairs by an appropriate court of law;

(2) understands the information; and

(3) consents voluntarily, free from coercion or undue influence.

(b) The person giving the consent must be informed of and understand:

(1) the nature, purpose, consequences, risks, and benefits of and alternatives to the procedure;

(2) that the withdrawal or refusal of consent will not prejudice the future provision of care and services; and

(3) the method used in the proposed procedure if the person is to receive unusual or hazardous treatment procedures, experimental research, organ transplantation, or nontherapeutic surgery.

MENTAL RETARDATION—§592

§592.001. Purpose

The purpose of this chapter is to recognize and protect the individual dignity and worth of each person with mental retardation.

§592.002. Rules

The board by rule shall ensure the implementation of the rights guaranteed in this chapter.

§592.011. Rights Guaranteed

(a) Each person with mental retardation in this state has the rights, benefits, and privileges guaranteed by the constitution and laws of the United States and this state.

(b) The rights specifically listed in this subtitle are in addition to all other rights that persons with mental retardation have and are not exclusive or intended to limit the rights guaranteed by the constitution and laws of the United States and this state.

§592.012. Protection from Exploitation and Abuse

Each person with mental retardation has the right to protection from exploitation and abuse because of the person's mental retardation.

§592.013. Least Restrictive Living Environment

Each person with mental retardation has the right to live in the least restrictive setting appropriate to the person's individual needs and abilities and in a variety of living situations, including living:

(1) alone;

(2) in a group home;

(3) with a family; or

(4) in a supervised, protective environment.

§592.014. Education

Each person with mental retardation has the right to receive publicly supported educational services, including those services provided under the Education Code, that are appropriate to the person's individual needs regardless of the person's:

(1) chronological age;

(2) degree of retardation;

(3) accompanying disabilities or handicaps; or

(4) admission or commitment to mental retardation services.

§592.015. Employment

An employer, employment agency, or labor organization may not deny a person equal opportunities in employment because of the person's mental retardation, unless:

(1) the person's mental retardation significantly impairs the person's ability to perform the duties and tasks of the position for which the person has

applied; or

(2) the denial is based on a bona fide occupational qualification reasonably necessary to the normal operation of the particular business or enterprise.

§592.016. Housing

An owner, lessee, sublessee, assignee, or managing agent or other person having the right to sell, rent, or lease real property, or an agent or employee of any of these, may not refuse to sell, rent, or lease to any person or group of persons solely because the person is a person with mental retardation or a group that includes one or more persons with mental retardation.

§592.017. Treatment and Services

Each person with mental retardation has the right to receive for mental retardation adequate treatment and habilitative services that:

(1) are suited to the person's individual needs;

(2) maximize the person's capabilities;

(3) enhance the person's ability to cope with the person's environment; and

(4) are administered skillfully, safely, and humanely with full respect for the dignity and personal integrity of the person.

§592.018. Determination of Mental Retardation

A person thought to be a person with mental retardation has the right promptly to receive a determination of mental retardation using diagnostic techniques that are adapted to that person's cultural background, language, and ethnic origin to determine if the person is in need of mental retardation services as provided by Subchapter A, Chapter 593.

§592.019. Administrative Hearing

A person who files an application for a determination of mental retardation has the right to request and promptly receive an administrative hearing under Subchapter A, Chapter 593, to contest the findings of the determination of mental retardation.

§592.020. Independent Determination of Mental Retardation

A person for whom a determination of mental retardation is performed or a person who files an application for a determination of mental retardation under Section 593.004 and who questions the validity or results of the determination of mental retardation has the right to an additional, independent determination of mental retardation performed at the person's own expense.

§592.021. Additional Rights

Each person with mental retardation has the right to:

(1) presumption of competency;

(2) due process in guardianship proceedings; and

(3) fair compensation for the person's labor for the economic benefit of another, regardless of any direct or incidental therapeutic value to the person.

§592.031. Rights in General

(a) Each client has the same rights as other citizens of the United States and this state unless the client's rights have been lawfully restricted.

(b) Each client has the rights listed in this subchapter in addition to the rights guaranteed by Subchapter B.

§592.032. Least Restrictive Alternative

Each client has the right to live in the least restrictive habilitation setting and to be treated and served in the least intrusive manner appropriate to the client's individual needs.

§592.033. Individualized Plan

(a) Each client has the right to a written, individualized habilitation plan developed by appropriate specialists.

(b) The client, and the parent of a client who is a minor or the guardian of the person, shall participate in the development of the plan.

(c) The plan shall be implemented as soon as possible but not later than the 30th day after the date on which the client is admitted or committed to mental retardation services.

(d) The content of an individualized habilitation plan is as required by the department.

§592.034. Review and Reevaluation

(a) Each client has the right to have the individualized habilitation plan reviewed at least:

(1) once a year if the client is in a residential care facility; or

(2) quarterly if the client has been admitted for other services.

(b) The purpose of the review is to:

(1) measure progress;

(2) modify objectives and programs if necessary; and

(3) provide guidance and remediation techniques.

(c) Each client has the right to a periodic reassessment.

§592.035. Participation in Planning

(a) Each client, and parent of a client who is a minor or the guardian of the person, have the right to:

(1) participate in planning the client's treatment and habilitation; and

(2) be informed in writing at reasonable intervals of the client's progress.

(b) If possible, the client, parent, or guardian of the person shall be given the opportunity to choose from several appropriate alternative services available to the client from a service provider.

§592.036. Withdrawal from Voluntary Services

(a) Except as provided by Section 593.030, a client, the parent if the client is a minor, or a guardian of the person may withdraw the client from mental retardation services.

(b) This section does not apply to a person who was committed to a residential care facility as provided by Subchapter C, Chapter 593.

§592.037. Freedom from Mistreatment

Each client has the right not to be mistreated, neglected, or abused by a service provider.

§592.038. Freedom from Unnecessary Medication

(a) Each client has the right to not receive unnecessary or excessive medication.

(b) Medication may not be used:

(1) as punishment;

(2) for the convenience of the staff;

(3) as a substitute for a habilitation program; or

(4) in quantities that interfere with the client's habilitation program.

(c) Medication for each client may be authorized only by prescription of a physician and a physician shall closely supervise its use.

§592.039. Grievances

A client, or a person acting on behalf of a person with mental retardation or a group of persons with mental retardation, has the right to submit complaints or grievances regarding the infringement of the rights of a person with mental retardation or the delivery of mental retardation services against a person, group of persons, organization, or business to the appropriate public responsibility committee for investigation and appropriate action.

§592.040. Information About Rights

(a) On admission for mental retardation services, each client, and the parent if the client is a minor or the guardian of the person of the client, shall be given written notice of the rights guaranteed by this subtitle. The notice shall be in plain and simple language.

(b) Each client shall be orally informed of these rights in plain and simple language.

(c) Notice given solely to the parent or guardian of the person is sufficient if the client is manifestly unable to comprehend the rights.

§592.051. General Rights of Residents

Each resident has the right to:

(1) a normal residential environment;

(2) a humane physical environment;

(3) communication and visits; and

(4) possess personal property.

§592.052. Medical and Dental Care and Treatment

Each resident has the right to prompt, adequate, and necessary medical and dental care and treatment for physical and mental ailments and to prevent an illness or disability.

§592.053. Standards of Care

Medical and dental care and treatment shall be performed under the appropriate supervision of a licensed physician or dentist and shall be consistent with accepted standards of medical and dental practice in the community.

§592.054. Duties of Superintendent or Director

(a) Except as limited by this subtitle, the superintendent or director shall provide without further consent necessary care and treatment to each court-committed resident and make available necessary care and treatment to each voluntary resident.

(b) Notwithstanding Subsection (a), consent is required for all surgical procedures.

§592.055. Unusual or Hazardous Treatment

This subtitle does not permit the department to perform unusual or hazardous treatment procedures, experimental research, organ transplantation, or nontherapeutic surgery for experimental research.

MENTAL RETARDATION RECORDS—§595

§595.001. Confidentiality of Records

Records of the identity, diagnosis, evaluation, or treatment of a person that are maintained in connection with the performance of a program or activity relating to mental retardation are confidential and may be disclosed only for the purposes and under the circumstances authorized under Sections 595.003 and 595.004.

§595.002. Rules

The board shall adopt rules to carry out this chapter that the department considers necessary or proper to:

(1) prevent circumvention or evasion of the chapter; or

(2) facilitate compliance with the chapter.

§595.003. Consent to Disclosure

(a) The content of a confidential record may be disclosed in accordance with the prior written consent of:

(1) the person about whom the record is maintained;

(2) the person's parent if the person is a minor;

(3) the guardian if the person has been adjudicated incompetent to manage the person's personal affairs; or

(4) if the person is dead:

  (A) the executor or administrator of the deceased's estate; or

  (B) if an executor or administrator has not been appointed, the deceased's spouse or, if the deceased was not married, an adult related to the deceased within the first degree of consanguinity.

(b) Disclosure is permitted only to the extent, under the circumstances, and for the purposes allowed under department rules.

§595.004. Right to Personal Record

(a) The content of a confidential record shall be made available on the request of the person about whom the record was made unless:

(1) the person is a client; and

(2) the qualified professional responsible for supervising the client's habilitation states in a signed written statement that having access to the record is not in the client's best interest.

(b) The parent of a minor or the guardian of the person shall be given access to the contents of any record about the minor or person.

§595.005. Exceptions

(a) The content of a confidential record may be disclosed without the consent required under Section 595.003 to:

(1) medical personnel to the extent necessary to meet a medical emergency;

(2) qualified personnel for management audits, financial audits, program evaluations, or research approved by the department; or

(3) personnel legally authorized to conduct investigations concerning complaints of abuse or denial of rights of persons with mental retardation.

(b) A person who receives confidential information under Subsection (a)(2) may not directly or indirectly identify a person receiving services in a report of the audit, evaluation, or research, or otherwise disclose any identities.

(c) The department may disclose without the consent required under Section 595.003 a person's educational records to a school district that provides or will provide educational services to the person.

(d) If authorized by an appropriate order of a court of competent jurisdiction granted after application showing good cause, the content of a record may be disclosed without the consent required under Section 595.003. In determining whether there is good cause, a court shall weigh the public interest and need for disclosure against the injury to the person receiving services. On granting the order, the court, in determining the extent to which any disclosure of all or any part of a record is necessary, shall impose appropriate safeguards against unauthorized disclosure.

§595.006. Use of Record in Criminal Proceedings

Except as authorized by a court order under Section 595.005, a confidential record may not be used to:

(1) initiate or substantiate a criminal charge against a person receiving services; or

(2) conduct an investigation of a person receiving services.

§595.007. Confidentiality of Past Services

The prohibition against disclosing information in a confidential record applies regardless of when the person received services.

§595.008. Exchange of Records

The prohibitions against disclosure apply to an exchange of records between government agencies or persons, except for exchanges of information necessary for:

(1) delivery of services to clients; or

(2) payment for mental retardation services as defined in this subtitle.

§595.009. Receipt of Information by Persons Other Than Client or Patient

(a) A person who receives information that is confidential under this chapter may not disclose the information except to the extent that disclosure is consistent with the authorized purposes for which the information was obtained.

(b) This section does not apply to the person about whom the record is made, or the parent, if the person is a minor, or the guardian of the person.

§595.010. Disclosure of Physical or Mental Condition

This chapter does not prohibit a qualified professional from disclosing the current physical and mental condition of a person with mental retardation to the person's parent, guardian, relative, or friend.

MENTAL HEALTH RECORDS—§611

§611.001. Definitions

In this chapter:

(1) *"Patient"* means a person who consults or is interviewed by a professional for diagnosis, evaluation, or treatment of any mental or emotional condition or disorder, including alcoholism or drug addiction.

(2) *"Professional"* means:

    (A) a person authorized to practice medicine in any state or nation;

    (B) a person licensed or certified by this state to diagnose, evaluate, or treat any mental or emotional condition or disorder; or

    (C) a person the patient reasonably believes is authorized, licensed, or certified as provided by this subsection.

§611.002. Confidentiality of Information and Prohibition Against Disclosure

(a) Communications between a patient and a professional, and records of the identity, diagnosis, evaluation, or treatment of a patient that are created or maintained by a professional, are confidential.

(b) Confidential communications or records may not be disclosed except as provided by Section 611.004 or 611.0045.

(c) This section applies regardless of when the patient received services from a professional.

§611.003. Persons Who May Claim Privilege of Confidentiality

(a) The privilege of confidentiality may be claimed by:

(1) the patient;

(2) a person listed in Section 611.004(a)(4) or (a)(5) who is acting on the patient's behalf; or

(3) the professional, but only on behalf of the patient.

(b) The authority of a professional to claim the privilege of confidentiality on behalf of the patient is presumed in the absence of evidence to the contrary.

§611.004. Authorized Disclosure of Confidential Information Other than in Judicial or Administrative Proceeding

(a) A professional may disclose confidential information only:

(1) to a governmental agency if the disclosure is required or authorized by law;

(2) to medical or law enforcement personnel if the professional determines that there is a probability of imminent physical injury by the patient to the

patient or others or there is a probability of immediate mental or emotional injury to the patient;

(3) to qualified personnel for management audits, financial audits, program evaluations, or research, in accordance with Subsection (b);

(4) to a person who has the written consent of the patient, or a parent if the patient is a minor, or a guardian if the patient has been adjudicated as incompetent to manage the patient's personal affairs;

(5) to the patient's personal representative if the patient is deceased;

(6) to individuals, corporations, or governmental agencies involved in paying or collecting fees for mental or emotional health services provided by a professional;

(7) to other professionals and personnel under the professionals' direction who participate in the diagnosis, evaluation, or treatment of the patient;

(8) in an official legislative inquiry relating to a state hospital or state school as provided by Subsection (c);

(9) to designated persons or personnel of a correctional facility in which a person is detained if the disclosure is for the sole purpose of providing treatment and health care to the person in custody;

(10) to an employee or agent of the professional who requires mental health care information to provide mental health care services or in complying with statutory, licensing, or accreditation requirements, if the professional has taken appropriate action to ensure that the employee or agent:

(A) will not use or disclose the information for any other purposes; and

(B) will take appropriate steps to protect the information; or

(11) to satisfy a request for medical records of a deceased or incompetent person pursuant to Section 4.01(e), Medical Liability and Insurance Improvement Act of Texas (Article 4590i, Vernon's Texas Civil Statutes).

(b) Personnel who receive confidential information under Subsection (a)(3) may not directly or indirectly identify or otherwise disclose the identity of a patient in a report or in any other manner.

(c) The exception in Subsection (a)(8) applies only to records created by the state hospital or state school or by the employees of the hospital or school. Information or records that identify a patient may be released only with the patient's proper consent.

(d) A person who receives information from confidential communications or records may not disclose the information except to the extent that disclosure is consistent with the authorized purposes for which the person first obtained the information. This subsection does not apply to a person listed in Subsection (a)(4) or (a)(5) who is acting on the patient's behalf.

§611.0045. Right to Mental Health Record

(a) Except as otherwise provided by this section, a patient is entitled to have access to the content of a confidential record made about the patient.

(b) The professional may deny access to any portion of a record if the professional determines that release of that portion would be harmful to the patient's physical, mental, or emotional health.

(c) If the professional denies access to any portion of a record, the professional shall give the patient a signed and dated written statement that having access to the record would be harmful to the patient's physical, mental, or emotional health and shall include a copy of the written statement in the patient's records. The statement must specify the portion of the record to which access is denied, the reason for denial, and the duration of the denial.

(d) The professional who denies access to a portion of a record under this section shall redetermine the necessity for the denial at each time a request for the denied portion is made. If the professional again denies access, the professional shall notify the patient of the denial and document the denial as prescribed by Subsection (c).

(e) If a professional denies access to a portion of a confidential record, the professional shall allow examination and copying of the record by another professional if the patient selects the professional to treat the patient for the same or a related condition as the professional denying access.

(f) The content of a confidential record shall be made available to a person listed by Section 611.004(a)(4) or (5) who is acting on the patient's behalf.

(g) A professional shall delete confidential information about another person who has not consented to the release, but may not delete information relating to the patient that another person has provided, the identity of the person responsible for that information, or the identity of any person who provided information that resulted in the patient's commitment.

(h) If a summary or narrative of a confidential record is requested by the patient or other person requesting release under this section, the professional shall prepare the summary or narrative.

(i) The professional or other entity that has possession or control of the record shall grant access to any portion of the record to which access is not specifically denied under this section within a reasonable time and may charge a reasonable fee.

(j) Notwithstanding Section 5.08, Medical Practice Act (Article 4495b, Vernon's Texas Civil Statutes), this section applies to the release of a confidential record created or maintained by a professional, including a physician, that relates to the diagnosis, evaluation, or treatment of a mental or emotional condition or disorder, including alcoholism or drug addiction.

(k) The denial of a patient's access to any portion of a record by the professional or other entity that has possession or control of the record suspends, until the release of that portion of the record, the running of an applicable statute of limitations on a cause of action in which evidence relevant to the cause of action is in that portion of the record.

§611.005. Legal Remedies for Improper Disclosure or Failure to Disclose

(a) A person aggrieved by the improper disclosure of or failure to disclose confidential communications or records in violation of this chapter may petition the district court of the county in which the person resides for appropriate relief, including injunctive relief. The person may petition a district court of Travis County if the person is not a resident of this state.

(b) In a suit contesting the denial of access under Section 611.0045, the burden of proving that the denial was proper is on the professional who denied the access.

(c) The aggrieved person also has a civil cause of action for damages.

§611.006. Authorized Disclosure of Confidential Information in Judicial or Administrative Proceeding

(a) A professional may disclose confidential information in:

(1) a judicial or administrative proceeding brought by the patient or the patient's legally authorized representative against a professional, including malpractice proceedings;

(2) a license revocation proceeding in which the patient is a complaining witness and in which disclosure is relevant to the claim or defense of a professional;

(3) a judicial or administrative proceeding in which the patient waives the patient's right in writing to the privilege of confidentiality of information or when a representative of the patient acting on the patient's behalf submits a written waiver to the confidentiality privilege;

(4) a judicial or administrative proceeding to substantiate and collect on a claim for mental or emotional health services rendered to the patient;

(5) a judicial proceeding if the judge finds that the patient, after having been informed that communications would not be privileged, has made communications to a professional in the course of a court-ordered examination relating to the patient's mental or emotional condition or disorder, except that those communications may be disclosed only with respect to issues involving the patient's mental or emotional health;

(6) a judicial proceeding affecting the parent-child relationship;

(7) any criminal proceeding, as otherwise provided by law;

(8) a judicial or administrative proceeding regarding the abuse or neglect, or the cause of abuse or neglect, of a resident of an institution, as that term is

defined by Chapter 242;

(9) a judicial proceeding relating to a will if the patient's physical or mental condition is relevant to the execution of the will;

(10) an involuntary commitment proceeding for court-ordered treatment or for a probable cause hearing under:

(A) Chapter 462;

(B) Chapter 574; or

(C) Chapter 593; or

(11) a judicial or administrative proceeding where the court or agency has issued an order or subpoena.

(b) On granting an order under Subsection (a)(5), the court, in determining the extent to which disclosure of all or any part of a communication is necessary, shall impose appropriate safeguards against unauthorized disclosure.

§611.007. Revocation of Consent

(a) Except as provided by Subsection (b), a patient or a patient's legally authorized representative may revoke a disclosure consent to a professional at any time. A revocation is valid only if it is written, dated, and signed by the patient or legally authorized representative.

(b) A patient may not revoke a disclosure that is required for purposes of making payment to the professional for mental health care services provided to the patient.

(c) A patient may not maintain an action against a professional for a disclosure made by the professional in good faith reliance on an authorization if the professional did not have notice of the revocation of the consent.

§611.008. Request by Patient

(a) On receipt of a written request from a patient to examine or copy all or part of the patient's recorded mental health care information, a professional, as promptly as required under the circumstances but not later than the 15th day after the date of receiving the request, shall:

(1) make the information available for examination during regular business hours and provide a copy to the patient, if requested; or

(2) inform the patient if the information does not exist or cannot be found.

(b) Unless provided for by other state law, the professional may charge a reasonable fee for retrieving or copying mental health care information and is not required to permit examination or copying until the fee is paid unless there is a medical emergency.

(c) A professional may not charge a fee for copying mental health care information under Subsection (b) to the extent the fee is prohibited under Subchapter M, Chapter 161.

HUMAN RESOURCES CODE

ELDER ABUSE—§48

§48.001. Purpose

The purpose of this chapter is to provide for the authority to investigate the abuse, neglect, or exploitation of an elderly or disabled person and to provide protective services to that person.

§48.002. Definitions

(a) Except as otherwise provided under Section 48.251, in this chapter:

(1) " *Elderly person*" means a person 65 years of age or older.

(2) " *Abuse*" means:

    (A) the negligent or willful infliction of injury, unreasonable confinement, intimidation, or cruel punishment with resulting physical or emotional harm or pain to an elderly or disabled person by the person's caretaker, family member, or other individual who has an ongoing relationship with the person; or

    (B) sexual abuse of an elderly or disabled person, including any involuntary or nonconsensual sexual conduct that would constitute an offense under Section 21.08, Penal Code (indecent exposure) or Chapter 22, Penal Code (assaultive offenses), committed by the person's caretaker, family member, or other individual who has an ongoing relationship with the person.

(3) " *Exploitation*" means the illegal or improper act or process of a caretaker, family member, or other individual who has an ongoing relationship with the elderly or disabled person using the resources of an elderly or disabled person for monetary or personal benefit, profit, or gain without the informed consent of the elderly or disabled person.

(4) *"Neglect"* means the failure to provide for one's self the goods or services, including medical services, which are necessary to avoid physical or emotional harm or pain or the failure of a caretaker to provide such goods or services.

(5) *"Protective services"* means the services furnished by the department or by a protective services agency to an elderly or disabled person who has been determined to be in a state of abuse, neglect, or exploitation. These services may include social casework, case management, and arranging for psychiatric and health evaluation, home care, day care, social services, health care, and other services consistent with this chapter.

(6) *"Protective services agency"* means a public or private agency, corporation, board, or organization that provides protective services to elderly or disabled persons in the state of abuse, neglect, or exploitation.

(7) *"Department"* means the Department of Protective and Regulatory Services.

(8) *"Disabled person"* means a person with a mental, physical, or developmental disability that substantially impairs the person's ability to provide adequately for the person's care or protection and who is:

(A) 18 years of age or older; or

(B) under 18 years of age and who has had the disabilities of minority removed.

(9) *"Legal holiday"* means a state holiday listed in Subchapter B, Chapter 662, Government Code, or an officially declared county holiday.

(10) *"Volunteer"* means a person who:

(A) performs services for or on behalf of the department under the supervision of a department employee; and

(B) does not receive compensation that exceeds the authorized expenses the person incurs in performing those services.

(b) The definitions of "abuse," "neglect," and "exploitation" adopted by the department as prescribed by Section 48.251 apply to an investigation of abuse, neglect, or exploitation in a facility subject to Subchapters F and H.

§48.051. Report

(a) Except as prescribed by Subsection (b), a person having cause to believe that an elderly or disabled person is in the state of abuse, neglect, or exploitation shall report the information required by Subsection (d) immediately to the department.

(b) If a person has cause to believe that an elderly or disabled person has been abused, neglected, or exploited in a facility operated, licensed, certified, or registered by a state agency other than the Texas Department of Mental Health and Mental Retardation, the person shall report the information to the state agency that operates, licenses, certifies, or registers the facility for investigation by that agency.

(c) The duty imposed by Subsections (a) and (b) applies without exception to a person whose professional communications are generally confidential, including an attorney, clergy member, medical practitioner, social worker, and mental health professional.

(d) The report may be made orally or in writing. It shall include:

(1) the name, age, and address of the elderly or disabled person;

(2) the name and address of any person responsible for the elderly or disabled person's care;

(3) the nature and extent of the elderly or disabled person's condition;

(4) the basis of the reporter's knowledge; and

(5) any other relevant information.

§48.052. Failure to Report; Penalty

(a) A person commits an offense if the person has cause to believe that an elderly or disabled person has been abused, neglected, or exploited or is in the state of abuse, neglect, or exploitation and knowingly fails to report in accordance with this chapter. An offense under this subsection is a Class A misdemeanor.

(b) This section does not apply if the alleged abuse, neglect, or exploitation occurred in a facility licensed under Chapter 242, Health and Safety Code. Failure to report abuse, neglect, or exploitation that occurs in a facility licensed under that chapter is governed by that chapter.

§48.053. False Report; Penalty

A person commits an offense if the person knowingly or intentionally reports information as provided in this chapter that the person knows is false or lacks factual foundation. An offense under this section is a Class B misdemeanor.

§48.054. Immunity

(a) A person filing a report under this chapter or testifying or otherwise participating in any judicial proceeding arising from a petition, report, or investigation is immune from civil or criminal liability on account of his or her petition, report, testimony, or participation, unless the person acted in bad faith or with a malicious purpose.

(b) A person, including an authorized department volunteer, medical personnel, or law enforcement officer, who at the request of the department participates in an investigation required by this chapter or in an action that results from that investigation is immune from civil or criminal liability for any act or omission relating to that participation if the person acted in good faith and, if applicable, in the course and scope of the person's assigned responsibilities or duties.

(c) A person who reports the person's own abuse, neglect, or exploitation of another person or who acts in bad faith or with malicious purpose in reporting alleged abuse, neglect, or exploitation is not immune from civil or criminal liability.

§48.203. Voluntary Protective Services

(a) An elderly or disabled person may receive voluntary protective services if the person requests or consents to receive those services.

(b) The elderly or disabled person who receives protective services shall participate in all decisions regarding his or her welfare, if able to do so.

(c) The least restrictive alternatives should be made available to the elderly or disabled person who receives protective services.

(d) If an elderly or disabled person withdraws or refuses consent, the services may not be provided.

OCCUPATIONS CODE

GENERAL REGULATORY AUTHORITY REGARDING HEALTH CARE
PRACTITIONERS USE OF INTERNET

§106.001. Effect of internet activity.

(a) In this section:

(1) "Licensing authority" means a department, commission, board, office, or other agency of the state or a political subdivision of the state that regulates activities and persons under this title.

(2) "Internet" has the meaning assigned by Section 2002.001, Government Code.

(b) The fact that an activity occurs through the use of the Internet does not affect a licensing authority's power to regulate an activity or person that would otherwise be regulated under this title.

§107.001. Definitions.

In this chapter:

(1) 'Health professional' and 'physician' have the meanings assigned by Section 1455.001, Insurance Code.

(2) 'Telehealth service' and 'telemedicine medical service' have the meanings assigned by Section 57.042, Utilities Code.

§107.002. Informed consent.

A treating physician or health professional who provides or facilitates the use of telemedicine medical services or telehealth services shall ensure that the informed consent of the patient, or another appropriate individual authorized to make health care treatment decisions for the patient, is obtained before telemedicine medical services or telehealth services are provided.

§107.003. Confidentiality.

A treating physician or health professional who provides or facilitates the use of telemedicine medical services or telehealth services shall ensure that the confidentiality of the patient's medical information is maintained as required by...applicable law.

§107.004. Rules.

The Texas State Board of Medical Examiners, in consultation with the commissioner of insurance, as appropriate, may adopt rules necessary to:

(1) ensure that patients using telemedicine medical services receive appropriate, quality care;

(2) prevent abuse and fraud in the use of telemedicine medical services, including rules relating to the filing of claims and records required to be maintained in connection with telemedicine medical services;

(3) ensure adequate supervision of health professionals who are not physicians and who provide telemedicine medical services;

(4) establish the maximum number of health professionals who are not physicians that a physician may supervise through a telemedicine medical service; and

(5) require a face-to-face consultation between a patient and a physician providing a telemedicine medical service within a certain number of days following an initial telemedicine medical service only if the physician has never seen the patient.

Penal Code

Insanity—§8

§8.01. Insanity

(a) It is an affirmative defense to prosecution that, at the time of the conduct charged, the actor, as a result of severe mental disease or defect, did not know that his conduct was wrong.

(b) The term "mental disease or defect" does not include an abnormality manifested only by repeated criminal or otherwise antisocial conduct.

Use of force on child, student, or incompetent—§9

§9.61. Parent — Child

(a) The use of force, but not deadly force, against a child younger than 18 years is justified:

(1) if the actor is the child's parent or stepparent or is acting in loco parentis to the child; and

(2) when and to the degree the actor reasonably believes the force is necessary to discipline the child or to safeguard or promote his welfare.

(b) For purposes of this section, "in loco parentis" includes grandparent and guardian, any person acting by, through, or under the direction of a court with jurisdiction over the child, and anyone who has express or implied consent of the parent or parents.

§9.62. Educator — Student

The use of force, but not deadly force, against a person is justified:

(1) if the actor is entrusted with the care, supervision, or administration of the person for a special purpose; and

(2) when and to the degree the actor reasonably believes the force is necessary to further the special purpose or to maintain discipline in a group.

§9.63. Guardian — Incompetent

The use of force, but not deadly force, against a mental incompetent is justified:

(1) if the actor is the incompetent's guardian or someone similarly responsible for the general care and supervision of the incompetent; and

(2) when and to the degree the actor reasonably believes the force is necessary:

(A) to safeguard and promote the incompetent's welfare; or

(B) if the incompetent is in an institution for his care and custody, to maintain discipline in the institution.

DEVIATE SEXUAL ACTIVITY—§21

§21.01. Definitions

In this chapter:

(1) " *Deviate sexual intercourse* " means:

(A) any contact between any part of the genitals of one person and the mouth or anus of another person; or

(B) the penetration of the genitals or the anus of another person with an object.

(2) *"Sexual contact"* means any touching of the anus, breast, or any part of the genitals of another person with intent to arouse or gratify the sexual desire of any person.

(3) *"Sexual intercourse"* means any penetration of the female sex organ by the male sex organ.

§21.06. Homosexual Conduct

(a) A person commits an offense if he engages in deviate sexual intercourse with another individual of the same sex.

(b) An offense under this section is a Class C misdemeanor.

§21.07. Public Lewdness

(a) A person commits an offense if he knowingly engages in any of the following acts in a public place or, if not in a public place, he is reckless about whether another is present who will be offended or alarmed by his:

(1) act of sexual intercourse;

(2) act of deviate sexual intercourse;

(3) act of sexual contact; or

(4) act involving contact between the person's mouth or genitals and the anus or genitals of an animal or fowl.

(b) An offense under this section is a Class A misdemeanor.

§21.08. Indecent Exposure

(a) A person commits an offense if he exposes his anus or any part of his genitals with intent to arouse or gratify the sexual desire of any person, and he is reckless about whether another is present who will be offended or alarmed by his act.

(b) An offense under this section is a Class B misdemeanor.

§21.11. Indecency With a Child

(a) A person commits an offense if, with a child younger than 17 years and not his spouse, whether the child is of the same or opposite sex, he:

(1) engages in sexual contact with the child; or

(2) exposes his anus or any part of his genitals, knowing the child is present, with intent to arouse or gratify the sexual desire of any person.

(b) It is an affirmative defense to prosecution under this section that the actor:

(1) was not more than three years older than the victim and of the opposite sex;

(2) did not use duress, force, or a threat against the victim at the time of the offense; and

(3) at the time of the offense:

(A) was not required under Chapter 62, Code of Criminal Procedure, as added by Chapter 668, Acts of the 75th Legislature, Regular Session, 1997, to register for life as a sex offender; or

(B) was not a person who under Chapter 62 had a reportable conviction or adjudication for an offense under this section.

(c) An offense under Subsection (a)(1) is a felony of the second degree and an offense under Subsection (a)(2) is a felony of the third degree.

INTERFERENCE WITH CHILD CUSTODY—§25

§25.03. Interference With Child Custody

(a) A person commits an offense if he takes or retains a child younger than 18 years when he:

(1) knows that his taking or retention violates the express terms of a judgment or order of a court disposing of the child's custody; or

(2) has not been awarded custody of the child by a court of competent

jurisdiction, knows that a suit for divorce or a civil suit or application for habeas corpus to dispose of the child's custody has been filed, and takes the child out of the geographic area of the counties composing the judicial district if the court is a district court or the county if the court is a statutory county court, without the permission of the court and with the intent to deprive the court of authority over the child.

(b) A noncustodial parent commits an offense if, with the intent to interfere with the lawful custody of a child younger than 18 years, he knowingly entices or persuades the child to leave the custody of the custodial parent, guardian, or person standing in the stead of the custodial parent or guardian of the child.

(c) It is a defense to prosecution under Subsection (a)(2) that the actor returned the child to the geographic area of the counties composing the judicial district if the court is a district court or the county if the court is a statutory county court, within three days after the date of the commission of the offense.

(d) An offense under this section is a state jail felony.

SUNSET REVIEW

A Summary of the TSBEP 2005 Sunset Review

In 1969 the Texas legislature established a six-member Texas State Board of Examiners of Psychologists (TSBEP) that governed state certifications and licensure related to the practice of psychology, with the first license issued in 1970. Since then there have been numerous changes to the licensing statute, including an expansion of the TSBEP to nine members, addition of the regulation of the Licensed Specialists in School Psychology (LSSP) to the scope of the Board, and a number of other procedural and administrative changes designed to serve the public interest by determining who may use the title "Psychologist" and/or engage in the supervised or independent practice of psychology. In addition, in accordance to state law governing all legislatively authorized licensing agencies, the TSBEP has undergone three comprehensive "Sunset Reviews" leading to a reauthorization of the licensing act by the Texas legislature. In 2005, the Texas Legislature completed its most recent Sunset Review and approved continuation of the agency for 12 years.

There were few noteworthy changes arising with this most recent legislation that may directly affect current licensees of the TSBEP. The oral examination for licensure remains, but the TSBEP was directed to form a working group to review and make recommendations regarding the procedural aspects of the oral examination. Other changes in the statute included authority for the Board to: (1) grant a temporary license to appropriately licensed psychologists seeking to practice temporarily in Texas, (2) conduct Department of Safety criminal record investigations on prospective applicants and licensees on a quarterly basis, and (3) approve continuing education offerings by state and national psychological associations, and institutes of higher education. The revised statute eliminated the Psychological Association Advisory Committee (PAAC).

An extensive review of the Psychology licensing act is not included in this publication because all licensees receive a copy of the Act and board rules annually. In addition, the TSBEP website *http://www.tsbep.state.tx.us* provides a complete and current documentation of all Board rule changes and actions.

CASE LAW

Two legal decisions are included in this Section:

Thapar v. Zezulka provides an excellent discussion of the duty to warn and duty to protect doctrine in Texas. We waited over 20 years in Texas to know the status of these duties. The Texas Supreme Court has now given practitioners guidance when a patient threatens another person. In this case, the Texas Supreme Court takes the position that courts should not second-guess the decision by a practitioner to tell law enforcement personnel or medical personnel about the danger presented by a patient. This gives a good deal of discretion to practitioners who are faced with a difficult situation and the decision is certainly pro-therapist.

Abrams v. Jones concerns the privacy of information between a therapist, a child client, and the child's parents and provides a remedy for parents who request but are denied access to a child's records. Practitioners can draw guidance from this case about record keeping and the duty to parents and child clients.

DUTY TO WARN/PROTECT

(THAPAR VS. ZEZULKA)[1]

Background

The primary issue in this case is whether a mental-health professional can be liable in negligence for failing to warn the appropriate third parties when a patient makes specific threats of harm toward a readily identifiable person. In reversing the trial court's summary judgment, the court of appeals recognized such a cause of action.[2] Because the Legislature has established a policy against such a common-law cause of action, we refrain from imposing on mental-health professionals a duty to warn third parties of a patient's threats. Accordingly, we reverse the court of appeals' judgment and render judgment that Zezulka take nothing.

Because this is an appeal from summary judgment, we take as true evidence favorable to Lyndall Zezulka, the nonmovant.[3] Freddy Ray Lilly had a history of mental-health problems and psychiatric treatment. Dr. Renu K. Thapar, a psychiatrist, first treated Lilly in 1985, when Lilly was brought to Southwest Memorial Hospital's emergency room. Thapar diagnosed Lilly as suffering from moderate to severe post-traumatic stress disorder, alcohol abuse, and paranoid and delusional beliefs concerning his stepfather, Henry Zezulka, and people of certain ethnic backgrounds. Thapar treated Lilly with a combination of psychotherapy and drug therapy over the next three years.

For the majority of their relationship, Thapar treated Lilly on an outpatient basis. But on at least six occasions Lilly was admitted to Southwest Memorial Hospital, or another facility, in response to urgent treatment needs.

Often the urgency involved Lilly's problems in maintaining amicable

---

1 Thapar vs. Zezulka, 994 S.W.2d 635 (Tex. 1999)
2 961 S.W.2d 506.
3 See Science Spectrum, Inc. v. Martinez, 941 S.W.2d 910, 911 (Tex. 1997).

relationships with those with whom he lived. Lilly was also admitted on one occasion after threatening to kill himself. In August 1988, Lilly agreed to be admitted to Southwest Memorial Hospital. Thapar's notes from August 23, 1988, state that Lilly "feels like killing" Henry Zezulka. These records also state, however, that Lilly "has decided not to do it but that is how he feels." After hospitalization and treatment for seven days, Lilly was discharged. Within a month Lilly shot and killed Henry Zezulka.

Despite the fact that Lilly's treatment records indicate that he sometimes felt homicidal, Thapar never warned any family member or any law enforcement agency of Lilly's threats against his stepfather. Nor did Thapar inform any family member or any law enforcement agency of Lilly's discharge from Southwest Memorial Hospital.

Lyndall Zezulka, Henry's wife and Lilly's mother, sued Thapar for negligence resulting in her husband's wrongful death. Zezulka alleged that Thapar was negligent in diagnosing and treating Lilly and negligent in failing to warn of Lilly's threats toward Henry Zezulka. It is undisputed that Thapar had no physician-patient relationship with either Lyndall or Henry Zezulka. Based on this fact, Thapar moved for summary judgment on the ground that Zezulka had not stated a claim for medical negligence because Thapar owed no duty to Zezulka in the absence of a doctor-patient relationship. The trial court overruled Thapar's motion.

Thapar filed a motion for rehearing of her summary judgment motion based largely on our decision in Bird v. W.C.W, in which we held that no duty runs from a psychologist to a third party to not negligently misdiagnose a patient's condition.[4] In light of Bird, the trial court reconsidered and granted summary judgment for Thapar. Zezulka appealed.

After concluding that Zezulka was not stopped from complaining about the trial court's judgment by her agreement to resolve the duty question through summary judgment, a conclusion with which we agree, the court of appeals reversed the trial court's judgment.[5] The court of appeals held that the no-duty ground asserted in Thapar's motion for summary judgment was not a defense to the cause of action pleaded by Zezulka.[6]

To decide this case we must determine the duties a mental-health professional owes to a nonpatient third party. Zezulka stated her claims against Thapar in negligence. Liability in negligence is premised on duty, a breach of which proximately causes injuries, and damages resulting from that breach.[7] Whether a legal duty exists is a threshold question of law for the court to decide from the facts surrounding the occurrence in question.[8] If there is no duty, there

4   868 S.W.2d 767 (Tex. 1994).
5   See 961 S.W.2d at 510-11.
6   See id. at 511.
7   See Bird, 868 S.W.2d at 769 (citing Greater Houston Transp. Co. v. Phillips, 801 S.W.2d 523, 525 (Tex. 1990)).
8   See St. John v. Pope, 901 S.W.2d 420, 424 (Tex. 1995); Bird, 868 S.W.2d at 769.

cannot be negligence liability.[9]

In her second amended petition Zezulka lists seventeen particulars by which she alleges Thapar was negligent. But each allegation is based on one of two proposed underlying duties: *(1) a duty to not negligently diagnose or treat a patient that runs from a psychiatrist to nonpatient third parties; or (2) a duty to warn third parties of a patient's threats.* In her motion for summary judgment Thapar asserted that she owed Zezulka no duty. Thus, we must determine if Thapar owed Zezulka either of these proposed duties.

Negligent Diagnosis And Treatment

First, we consider Zezulka's allegations that Thapar was negligent in her diagnosis and treatment of Lilly's psychiatric problems. Among other claims, Zezulka alleged that Thapar was negligent in releasing Lilly from the hospital in August 1988, in failing to take steps to have Lilly involuntarily committed, and in failing to monitor Lilly after his release to ensure that he was taking his medication. All of these claims are based on Thapar's medical diagnosis of Lilly's condition, which dictated the treatment Lilly should have received and the corresponding actions Thapar should have taken.[10] The underlying duty question here is whether the absence of a doctor-patient relationship precludes Zezulka from maintaining medical negligence claims against Thapar based on her diagnosis and treatment of Lilly.

In Bird we held that no duty runs from a psychologist to a third party to not negligently misdiagnose a patient's condition.[11] Since Bird, we have had occasion to consider several permutations of this same duty question.[12] Bird and our post-Bird writings answer definitively the first duty question presented by the facts before us: Thapar owes no duty to Zezulka, a third party nonpatient, for negligent misdiagnosis or negligent treatment of Lilly.[13] Accordingly, Thapar was entitled to summary judgment on all of the claims premised on Zezulka's first duty theory.

Failure to Warn

Second, we consider Zezulka's allegations that Thapar was negligent for failing to warn either the Zezulkas or law enforcement personnel of Lilly's

9 See Van Horn v. Chambers, 970 S.W.2d 542, 544 (Tex. 1998); St. John, 901 S.W.2d at 424; Graff v. Beard, 858 S.W.2d 918, 919 (Tex. 1993).

10 See, e.g., Van Horn, 970 S.W.2d at 545.

11 Bird, 868 S.W.2d at 769-70 (citing Vineyard v. Kraft, 828 S.W.2d 248, 251 (Tex. App._Houston [14th Dist.] 1992, writ denied); Wilson v. Winsett, 828 S.W.2d 231, 232-33 (Tex. App._Amarillo 1992, writ denied); Fought v. Solce, 821 S.W.2d 218, 220 (Tex. App._Houston [1st Dist.] 1991, writ denied); Dominguez v. Kelly, 786 S.W.2d 749 (Tex. App._El Paso 1990, writ denied)).

12 See Van Horn, 970 S.W.2d at 543; Edinburg Hosp. Auth. v. Trevino, 941 S.W.2d 76, 77-79 (Tex. 1997); Krishnan v. Sepulveda, 916 S.W.2d 478, 482 (Tex. 1995); see also Praesel v. Johnson, 967 S.W.2d 391, 392 (Tex. 1998); Cathey v. Booth, 900 S.W.2d 339, 342 (Tex. 1995).

13 See Van Horn, 970 S.W.2d at 545; Trevino, 941 S.W.2d at 79; Krishnan, 916 S.W.2d at 482; Bird, 868 S.W.2d at 770.

threats. We are not faced here with the question of whether a doctor owes a duty to third parties to warn a patient of risks from treatment which may endanger third parties.[14] Instead, we are asked whether a mental-health professional owes a duty to directly warn third parties of a patient's threats.

The California Supreme Court first recognized a mental-health professional's duty to warn third parties of a patient's threats in the seminal case Tarasoff v. Regents of University of California.[15] The court of appeals here cited Tarasoff in recognizing a cause of action for Thapar's failure to warn of her patient's threats.[16] But we have never recognized the only underlying duty upon which such a cause of action could be based -- a mental-health professional's duty to warn third parties of a patient's threats. Without considering the effect of differences in the development of California and Texas jurisprudence on the outcome of this issue, we decline to adopt a duty to warn now because the confidentiality statute governing mental-health professionals in Texas makes it unwise to recognize such common-law duty.

The Legislature has chosen to closely guard a patient's communications with a mental-health professional. In 1979, three years after Tarasoff issued, the Legislature enacted a statute governing the disclosure of communications during the course of mental-health treatment.[17] The statute classifies communications between mental-health "professional[s]" and their "patient[s]/client[s]" as confidential and prohibits mental-health professionals from disclosing them to third parties unless an exception applies.[18]

Zezulka complains that Thapar was negligent in not warning members of the Zezulka family about Lilly's threats. But a disclosure by Thapar to one of the Zezulkas would have violated the confidentiality statute because no exception in the statute provides for disclosure to third parties threatened by the patient.[19]

14 See Gooden v. Tips, 651 S.W.2d 364, 365-66 (Tex. App._Tyler 1983, no writ) (holding doctor owed duty to third party to warn patient not to drive after prescribing the drug Quaalude to patient); see also Flynn v. Houston Emergicare, Inc., 869 S.W.2d 403, 405-06 (Tex. App._Houston [1st Dist.] 1994, writ denied) (holding doctor owed no duty to third party to warn patient not to drive after patient was treated for cocaine use because doctor did not create impairment that resulted in injury).

15 551 P.2d 334, 345-47 (Cal. 1976).

16 961 S.W.2d at 511 n.2. The court of appeals also cited four Texas cases that considered whether to adopt a Tarasoff duty but did not. See 916 S.W.2d at 511 n.2 (citing Limon v. Gonzaba, 940 S.W.2d 236, 238-41 (Tex. App._San Antonio 1997, writ denied); Kehler v. Eudaly, 933 S.W.2d 321, 329-32 (Tex. App._Fort Worth 1996, writ denied); Kerrville State Hosp. v. Clark, 900 S.W.2d 425, 435-36 (Tex. App._Austin 1995), rev'd on other grounds, 923 S.W.2d 582 (Tex. 1996);Williams v. Sun Valley Hosp., 723 S.W.2d 783, 785-86 (Tex. App._El Paso 1987, writ ref'd n.r.e.)).

17 See Act of May 9, 1979, 66th Leg., R.S., ch. 239, 1979 Tex. Gen. Laws 512 (amended 1991) (current version at Tex. Health & Safety Code § 611.002 (1996)).

18 See § 2(a), 1979 Tex. Gen. Laws at 513.

19 See § 4, 1979 Tex. Gen. Laws at 514.

We considered a similar situation in Santa Rosa Health Care Corp. v. Garcia,[20] in which we concluded there is no duty to disclose confidential information when disclosure would violate the confidentiality statute.[21] The same reasoning applies here. Under the applicable statute, Thapar was prohibited from warning one of his patient's potential victims and therefore had no duty to warn the Zezulka family of Lilly's threats.

Zezulka also complains that Thapar was negligent in not disclosing Lilly's threats to any law enforcement agency. There is an exception in the confidentiality statute that provides for disclosure to law enforcement personnel in certain circumstances.[22] The statute, however, permits these disclosures but does not require them:

(b) Exceptions to the privilege of confidentiality, in other than court proceedings, allowing disclosure of confidential information by a professional, exist only to the following:...

(2) to medical or law enforcement personnel where the professional determines that there is a probability of imminent physical injury by the patient/client to himself or to others, or where there is a probability of immediate mental or emotional injury to the patient/client....[23]

The term "allowing" in section 4(b), quoted above, makes clear that disclosure of confidential information under any of the statute's exceptions is permissive but not mandatory. Imposing a legal duty to warn third parties of patient's threats would conflict with the scheme adopted by the Legislature by making disclosure of such threats mandatory.

We consider legislative enactments that evidence the adoption of a particular public policy significant in determining whether to recognize a new common-law duty.[24] For example, in recognizing the existence of a common-law duty to guard children from sexual abuse, we found persuasive the Legislature's strongly avowed policy to protect children from abuse.[25] The statute expressing this policy, however, makes the reporting of sexual abuse mandatory[26] and makes

---

20 964 S.W.2d 940, 941 (Tex. 1998) (involving disclosure of HIV test under Tex. Rev. Civ. Stat. art. 4419b-1, § 9.03).

21 Id. at 944.

22 See § 4(b), 1979 Tex. Gen. Laws at 514.

23 See § 4, 1979 Tex. Gen. Laws at 514 (emphasis added). Current Tex. Health & Safety Code § 611.004(a)(2) adopts the same standard: (a) A professional may disclose confidential information only:... (2) to medical or law enforcement personnel if the professional determines that there is a probability of imminent physical injury by the patient to the patient or others or there is a probability of immediate mental or emotional injury to the patient...

24 See Gibbs v. Jackson, ___ S.W.2d ___, ___ (Tex. 1999); Smith v. Merritt, 940 S.W.2d 602, 604-05 (Tex. 1997) (citing Graff, 858 S.W.2d at 919).

25 See Golden Spread Council, Inc. v. Akins, 926 S.W.2d 287, 291 (Tex. 1996).

26 Tex. Fam. Code § 261.101(a) states: "A person having cause to believe that a child's physical or mental health or welfare has been adversely affected by abuse or neglect by any person shall immediately make a report as provided by this subchapter."

failure to report child abuse a crime.[27] Further, under the statute, those who report child abuse in good faith are immune from civil and criminal liability.[28] Thus, imposing a common law duty to report was consistent with the legislative scheme governing child abuse.

The same is not true here. The confidentiality statute here does not make disclosure of threats mandatory nor does it penalize mental-health professionals for not disclosing threats. And, perhaps most significantly, the statute does not shield mental-health professionals from civil liability for disclosing threats in good faith. On the contrary, mental-health professionals make disclosures at their peril.[29] Thus, if a common-law duty to warn is imposed, mental-health professionals face a Catch-22. They either disclose a confidential communication that later proves to be an idle threat and incur liability to the patient, or they fail to disclose a confidential communication that later proves to be a truthful threat and incur liability to the victim and the victim's family.

The confidentiality statute here evidences an intent to leave the decision of whether to disclose confidential information in the hands of the mental-health professional. In the past, we have declined to impose a common-law duty to disclose when disclosing confidential information by a physician has been made permissible by statute but not mandatory.[30] We have also declined to impose a common-law duty after determining that such a duty would conflict with the Legislature's policy and enactments concerning the employment-at-will doctrine.[31] Our analysis today is consistent with the approach in those cases.

Because of the Legislature's stated policy, we decline to impose a common law duty on mental-health professionals to warn third parties of their patient's threats. Accordingly, we conclude that Thapar was entitled to summary judgment because she owed no duty to Zezulka, a third-party nonpatient. We reverse the court of appeals' judgment and render judgment that Zezulka take nothing.

---

27 See Tex. Fam. Code § 261.109.

28 See Tex. Fam. Code § 261.106.

29 See § 5, 1979 Tex. Gen. Laws at 514.

30 See Praesel, 967 S.W.2d at 396-98.

31 See Austin v. HealthTrust, Inc._The Hosp. Co., 967 S.W.2d 400, 403 (Tex. 1998); see also Winters v. Houston Chronicle Pub. Co., 795 S.W.2d 723, 724-25 (Tex. 1990).

CONFIDENTIALITY OF A CHILD'S MENTAL HEALTH RECORDS

(ABRAMS VS. JONES)[1]

This case presents issues of statutory construction. We are called upon to determine if either section 153.072 of the Family Code or section 611.0045 of the Health and Safety Code allows a parent to demand access to detailed notes of his or her child's conversations with a mental health professional when that parent is not acting on behalf of the child or when the mental health professional believes that releasing the information would be harmful to the child's physical, mental, or emotional health. The Legislature has balanced a child's need for effective treatment and a parent's rights and has imposed some limits on a parent's right of access to confidential mental health records. Accordingly, we reverse the judgment of the court of appeals and render judgment that Jones take nothing.

Background

The child whose records are at issue is Karissa Jones. Her parents, Donald and Rosemary Jones, divorced when she was about seven years old. Both parents remarried sometime before the present controversy erupted, and Rosemary Jones is now Rosemary Droxler. In the original decree, Karissa's parents were appointed joint managing conservators of her and her younger sister. Two years after the divorce, her father initiated further court proceedings to become the sole managing conservator of his daughters. Litigation ensued for two more years. Karissa's parents ultimately agreed to a modification of the original order, but both parents were retained as joint managing conservators. The modified decree gave Jones certain rights of access to his children's psychological records.

---

1 Abrams vs. Jones, 35 S.W.3d 620 (Tex. 2000)

Several months after the modification proceedings were concluded, Rosemary Droxler sought the professional services of a psychologist, Dr. Laurence Abrams, for Karissa. The uncontroverted evidence is that Karissa, who by this time was eleven years old, was agitated and showed signs of sleeplessness and worry. At the time the trial court heard this case, Abrams had seen Karissa six times for about fifty minutes on each occasion.

At the beginning of Abrams's first consultation with Karissa, she was reluctant to talk to him. When Abrams explored that reluctance with her, she told him that she was concerned that he would relate what she had to say to her parents. Abrams responded that he would have to provide a report to her parents, but that he could give them a general description of what was discussed without all the specifics. Abrams and Karissa reached an understanding about what he would and would not tell her parents, and he was thereafter able to establish a rapport with her.

Shortly after Karissa began seeing Abrams, her father (Jones) and his legal counsel met with Abrams and requested that he release all of her records. Abrams gave Jones and his counsel a verbal summary of information, sharing with them the basic subject matter of his consultations with Karissa. Abrams related that Karissa had told him that Jones's new wife (who formerly was Karissa's nanny) had said to Karissa that when she turned twelve, she would have to choose where she lived. Karissa told Abrams that she was afraid there would be more conflict in court between her parents because of this choice. Abrams described Karissa as in a "panic" when he first saw her over what she believed to be her impending decision and an ensuing battle between her parents. Abrams also told Jones that Karissa had said that she leaned toward choosing to live with her father and that she was at times unhappy living with her mother because her mother was away from home more than Karissa liked.

After Abrams had related this information about his sessions with Karissa, Jones told Abrams that no conversations of the nature Abrams had described had occurred between Jones and Karissa or between Karissa and her stepmother. At some point in the dialogue among Abrams, Jones, and Jones's attorney, Abrams either agreed with Jones's counsel or said in response to a question from counsel that Karissa's mother had taken Karissa to see Abrams "to get a leg up on" Jones in court.

A few days after the meeting among Jones, his counsel, and Abrams, Jones's counsel again pressed for Abrams's records in two letters to Abrams. Abrams responded verbally and in writing that releasing the detailed notes about his conversations with Karissa would not be in her best interest. Abrams offered to give his notes to any other psychologist that Jones might choose to replace Abrams as Karissa's counselor, and Abrams explained that Karissa's new psychologist could then determine whether it was in Karissa's best interest to give Abrams's notes to Jones. Jones did not seek another counselor for Karissa, and Abrams did not release his notes to Jones. Abrams continued to treat Karissa until this suit was filed by Jones to compel Abrams to release his notes. The record is silent as to whether Abrams was to continue treatment after this suit was resolved.

Droxler, Karissa's mother, entered an appearance in the suit against Abrams, and she agreed with Abrams that neither parent should have access to his notes of conversations with Karissa. A hearing was held before the trial court. Abrams testified that a sense of protection and closeness is an integral part of psychotherapy and that without some expectation of confidentiality, Karissa would not have opened up to him. He said that Karissa had several discussions with him about the confidentiality of their sessions. Abrams testified that in his opinion the release to either parent of his detailed notes of what Karissa had said was not in her best interest.

Jones took the position in the trial court that as a parent, he was unconditionally entitled to see all of Abrams's records regarding his daughter. He further represented to the trial court that based on his conversations with Karissa, he was of the opinion that she did not object to the release of her records. Abrams testified, however, that Karissa had asked him not to reveal the details of their conversations, and that during the week before the hearing, her mother delivered a note which Karissa had written to Abrams again asking that he maintain the confidentiality of their discussions.

Abrams's detailed notes about what Karissa had told him during his professional consultations with her were provided to the trial court. The court, however, stated on the record at the conclusion of the hearing that it had not reviewed them and did not intend to. There is no indication that it ever did so.

The trial court held that Jones was entitled to Abrams's notes. Abrams appealed, and Karissa's mother (Droxler) filed briefing in the court of appeals in support of Abrams's position. The court of appeals affirmed the trial court's judgment with one justice dissenting. Abrams v. Jones, 983 S.W.2d 377 (Tex. App.-Houston [14th Dist.] 1999). We granted Abrams's petition for review, which was supported by Karissa's mother.

There are three questions of statutory construction that we must decide. They are (1) whether section 153.073 of the Family Code gives a divorced parent greater rights of access to mental health records than parents in general have under chapter 611 of the Texas Health and Safety Code, (2) whether section 611.0045(b) of the Health and Safety Code allows a professional to deny a parent access to portions of mental health records if the professional concludes that their release would harm the child, and (3) whether a parent is always deemed to be acting on behalf of his or her child when requesting mental health records.

Rights of Divorced Parents for Access to Records

Do divorced parents have greater rights of access to records than parents in general? As indicated above, the first question that we must resolve is whether section 153.073 of the Family Code or chapter 611 of the Health and Safety Code governs this matter. TEX. FAM. CODE § 153.073; TEX. HEALTH & SAFETY CODE §§611.001 to 611.008. We conclude that chapter 611 provides the framework within which this case must be decided.

Section 153.073 of the Family Code addresses parental rights upon dissolution of the parents' marriage to one another. It provides that unless a court orders otherwise, a parent who is appointed a conservator "has at all times the right... as specified by court order... of access to medical, dental, psychological, and educational records of the child." TEX. FAM. CODE §153.073(a)(2). Jones contends that this section of the Family Code mandates that a parent who is appointed a conservator has access at all times to all psychological records of the child. We disagree.

We interpret section 153.073 to ensure that a court may grant a parent who is divorced and who has been named a conservator the same rights of access to his or her child's psychological records as a parent who is not divorced. We do not interpret section 153.073 to override the provisions of chapter 611 of the Health and Safety Code that specifically address parents' rights to the mental health records of their children. The legislative history of section 153.073 indicates that it was enacted to equalize the rights of nonmanaging-conservator parents in comparison to managing-conservator parents. See HOUSE COMM. ON JUDICIAL AFFAIRS, BILL ANALYSIS, Tex. H.B. 1630, 73d Leg., R.S. (1993) (explaining that this provision was needed to remedy (1) previous limitations on nonmanaging conservators during periods of possession, when the child might need health care, and (2) the fact that managing conservators were not required to consult with the other parent about important decisions affecting the child's health, education, or welfare). The Legislature did not intend in section 153.073 to give greater rights to divorced parents than to parents who are not divorced. We turn to chapter 611 of the Health and Safety Code.

Denying Parental Access to Records

Can a professional deny parents access to a child's mental health records if such access is harmful? The Legislature has determined that a patient's right of access to his or her own mental health records is not absolute. Section 611.0045 of the Health and Safety Code says that a "professional may deny access to any portion of a record if the professional determines that release of that portion would be harmful to the patient's physical, mental, or emotional health." TEX. HEALTH & SAFETY CODE § 611.0045(b).

There are, however, checks and balances on a professional's decision not to disclose portions of a mental health record to a patient. A patient may select another professional for treatment of the same or related condition, and the professional denying access must allow the newly retained professional to examine and copy the records that have not been released to the patient. Id. § 611.0045(e). The newly retained professional may then decide whether to release the records to the patient.

There are provisions in chapter 611 of the Health and Safety Code that deal specifically with the mental health records of a minor. Section 611.0045(f) provides that the "content of a confidential record shall be made available to a [parent] who is acting on the patient's behalf." Id. § 611.0045(f). n1 Jones contends that a parent necessarily acts on behalf of his or her child when seeking access to a child's mental health records under section 611.0045(f). The court of appeals agreed. It held that "by requesting that Abrams turn over Karissa's mental health records, Jones was necessarily 'acting on behalf' of Karissa as contemplated by section 611.0045(f) of the Code." Abrams v. Jones, 983 S.W.2d 377, 381 (Tex. App.-Houston [14th Dist.] 1999).

In construing a statute, we must attempt to give effect to every word and phrase if it is reasonable to do so. See City of Amarillo v. Martin, 971 S.W.2d 426, 430 (Tex. 1998); see also TEX. GOV'T CODE § 311.021(2) (stating that in enacting a statute, it is presumed that the entire statute is intended to be effective). If the Legislature had intended for a parent to have access to all aspects of a child's mental health records by simply proving that he or she is indeed the child's parent, the Legislature would not have needed to add the phrase "who is acting on the patient's behalf" in section 611.0045(f).

We agree with the dissent in the court of appeals that, unfortunately, parents cannot always be deemed to be acting on the child's behalf. See Abrams, 983 S.W.2d at 382 (Edelman, J., dissenting). An obvious example is when a parent has sexually molested a child and later demands access to the child's mental health treatment records. A court would not presume that the parent is acting on the child's behalf in such circumstances. Similarly, parents embroiled in a divorce or other suit affecting the parent/child relationship may have motives of their own for seeking the mental health records of the child and may not be acting "on the patient's [child's] behalf." TEX. HEALTH & SAFETY CODE § 611.0045(f). We therefore conclude that a mental health professional is not required to provide access to a child's confidential records if a parent who requests them is not acting "on behalf of" the child.

Request for Records and "Acting on Behalf of the Child"

Is a parent always deemed to be acting on behalf of his or her child when requesting mental health records? When a parent is acting on behalf of his or her child, the question that then arises is whether, under section 611.0045(b), a professional may nevertheless deny access to a portion of a child's records if their release would be harmful to the patient's physical, mental, or emotional health. TEX. HEALTH & SAFETY CODE § 611.0045(b). Jones contends that subsection (b) only applies when "the patient" seeks his or her own records and not when a parent seeks a child's records. We disagree.

Section 611.0045(f) contemplates that when a parent seeks a child's mental health records "on the patient's behalf," the parent steps into the shoes of the patient. Id. § 611.0045(f). Subsection (f) affords third parties, including a parent, no greater rights than those of the patient. This is evident when section

611.0045(f) is considered in its entirety. It applies not only to parents, but to "a person who has the written consent of the patient." Id. §§ 611.004(a)(4), 611.0045(f). It would be unreasonable to construe subsection (f) to allow a patient to obtain through a third person a record that a mental health professional has determined under subsection (b) would be harmful if released to the patient. Because subsection (b) may limit a patient's rights to his or her own records, subsection (b) can also limit a parent's or third party's right to a patient's records when the third party or parent stands in the patient's stead.

In construing a statute or code provision, a court may consider, among other matters, the (1) object sought to be attained by the statute, (2) circumstances under which the statute was enacted, (3) legislative history, (4) consequences of a particular construction, and (5) laws on similar subjects. See Tex. Gov't Code § 311.023. This Court has recently recognized that, through Chapter 611, "the Legislature has chosen to closely guard a patient's communications with a mental-health professional." Thapar v. Zezulka, 994 S.W.2d 635, 638 (Tex. 1999). One purpose of confidentiality is to ensure that individuals receive therapy when they need it. See R.K. v. Ramirez, 887 S.W.2d 836, 840 (Tex. 1994) (describing the purposes of the physician-patient privilege under the Texas Rules of Evidence). Although a parent's responsibilities with respect to his or her child necessitate access to information about the child, if the absence of confidentiality prevents communications between a therapist and the patient because the patient fears that such communications may be revealed to their detriment, neither the purposes of confidentiality nor the needs of the parent are served.

If a professional does deny a parent access to part of a child's records, the parent has recourse under section 611.0045(e).Tex. Health & Safety Code §611.0045(e). First, the professional denying access must allow examination and copying of the record by another professional selected by the parent acting on behalf of the patient to treat the patient for the same or a related condition. Id. Second, a parent denied access to a child's records has judicial recourse. See id. § 611.005(a). We therefore conclude that the court of appeals erred in construing sections 611.0045(b) and (f) of the Health and Safety Code as giving a parent totally unfettered access to a child's mental health records irrespective of the child's circumstances or the parent's motivation.

We turn to the facts of this case and the interplay between section 611.045 and section 611.005 of the Health and Safety Code, which provides a remedy to a parent if a child's mental health records have been improperly withheld.

Recourse When a Child's Records Improperly Withheld

What recourse is there for a parent when a child's mental health records have been improperly withheld? As already indicated above, a person who is aggrieved by a professional's improper "failure to disclose confidential communications or records" may petition a district court for appropriate relief.

TEX. HEALTH & SAFETY CODE §611.005(a). A professional who denies access has "the burden of proving that the denial was proper." Id. § 611.005(b). Accordingly, Abrams bore the burden of proving in these proceedings that he properly denied access to his notes about his conversations with Karissa.

The trial court ruled against Abrams. Abrams did not request and the trial court did not make any findings of fact or conclusions of law. But because the reporter's record is part of the record on appeal, the legal sufficiency of the trial court's implied finding in support of the judgment, which was that Abrams failed to meet his burden of proof, may be challenged in the same manner as jury findings. See Roberson v. Robinson, 768 S.W.2d 280, 281 (Tex. 1989). We must examine the entire record to determine whether Abrams established as a matter of law that his denial of access was proper either because Abrams established that (1) Jones was not acting on Karissa's behalf, or (2) access to the notes would be harmful to Karissa's mental or emotional health.

Jones never indicated that he was seeking the notes on behalf of Karissa, as distinguished from his own behalf. At the hearing, Jones testified that his motivation for obtaining Abrams's notes was in part the indication that Karissa's mother had hired Abrams "to get a leg up on me in court." Although this is some evidence that Jones was not acting on behalf of Karissa but was acting in his own interest, it is not conclusive. Jones's testimony that he was "partially" motivated by what he perceived to be his former wife's custody tactics indicated that there were additional reasons for seeking Karissa's records. Abrams did not prove conclusively that Jones was not acting on behalf of Karissa.

But even if Jones were acting on behalf of Karissa, Abrams testified that in his professional opinion it would be harmful to her to release his notes detailing their conversations. When Abrams first saw Karissa, she would not talk to him. He was unable to establish a rapport with her until they discussed confidentiality. Abrams asked her "what it would take to get her to talk," and he explained at the hearing that "it came down to, she needed protection.... She needed protection against anyone knowing what she said. She simply couldn't talk if there was a chance either parent would know what she said." Abrams made the decision during the first session with Karissa not to give his notes to either of her parents. He testified, "I had to in order to be able to treat the girl." He told Karissa at that session that he would not disclose his notes to her parents unless required to do so by a court. Karissa thereafter opened up to Abrams. Abrams explained at the hearing that an integral part of psychotherapy is that the patient have a sense of protection and security and that she drop defensive mechanisms. Abrams continued to treat Karissa after he had denied her father access to the notes, and she responded positively to treatment after Abrams assured her that the details of her conversations would be confidential. Treatment continued until this suit was filed. None of this testimony was contradicted or even challenged. See Allright, Inc. v. Strawder, 679 S.W.2d 81, 82 (Tex. App.-Houston [14 Dist.] 1984, writ ref'd n.r.e.) (observing that "uncontroverted testimony, even from a witness categorized as an expert, may be taken as true as a matter of law if it is clear, direct and positive, and is free from contradictions, inconsistencies, inaccuracies and circumstances tending to cast suspicion thereon"). This testimony, in the absence of contrary evidence, is sufficient to establish as a matter of law that release of Karissa's records would have been harmful to her.

Jones's testimony that in his opinion, Karissa did not object to the release of Abrams's notes does not raise a fact question of whether their release would be harmful to her. Karissa was a layperson--an eleven-year-old layperson. She was not qualified to make a determination of whether release of her records would be harmful to her physical, mental, or emotional health. See TEX. HEALTH & SAFETY CODE § 611.0045(b). The uncontradicted evidence established as a matter of law that Abrams's denial of access to his detailed notes was proper.

Conclusion and Dissenting Opinions

The trial court erred in holding that Jones was entitled to the detailed notes about his daughter's conversations with her mental health professional under the facts of this case. Accordingly, we reverse the judgment of the court of appeals and render judgment that Jones take nothing.

—*Priscilla R. Owen, Justice*

DISSENT: JUSTICE BAKER, dissenting.

I believe that the court of appeals majority correctly construed the statutory scheme and properly applied the law to the facts to reach the result it reached. Accordingly, I respectfully dissent from the Court's decision in this case.

—*James A. Baker, Justice*

JUSTICE HECHT, dissenting.

In this Term's decisions construing the Parental Notification Act,[2] the Court has exhibited a disturbing lack of regard for the rights of parents to raise and care for their children;[3] This case continues in that vein, holding that under chapter 611 of the Texas Health and Safety Code, mental health care professionals — who, as defined by statute,[4] include everyone from physicians to pretenders — have broad discretion to deny parents access to their children's mental health records, broader discretion than even a district judge has to order

2 TEX. FAM. CODE §§ 33.001-.011.

3 In re Doe 1(I), 19 S.W.3d 249, 2000 Tex. LEXIS 21 (Tex. 2000); In re Doe 2, 19 S.W.3d 278, 2000 Tex. LEXIS 25 (Tex. 2000); In re Doe 3, 19 S.W.3d 300, 2000 Tex. LEXIS 26 (Tex. 2000); In re Doe 4(I), 19 S.W.3d 322, 2000 Tex. LEXIS 27 (Tex. 2000); In re Doe 4(II), 19 S.W.3d 337, 2000 Tex. LEXIS 34 (Tex. 2000); In re Doe 1(II), 19 S.W.3d 346, 2000 Tex. LEXIS 67 (Tex. 2000).

4 TEX. HEALTH & SAFETY CODE § 611.001(2) ("'Professional' means: (A) a person authorized to practice medicine in any state or nation; (B) a person licensed or certified by this state to diagnose, evaluate, or treat any mental or emotional condition or disorder; or (C) a person the patient reasonably believes is authorized, licensed, or certified as provided by this subsection.").

disclosure. As eager as the Court has been to find justification for allowing a child to have an abortion without telling her parents, contrary to a trial court's view of the evidence, it will come as no surprise that the Court has no difficulty keeping parents ignorant of their children's mental health records, contrary to the trial court's conclusion. As in the parental notification cases, the Court casts responsibility for its decision in this case on the Legislature. But this steady erosion of parental authority is judicial, not legislative; it results from the Court's view of statutory language through a prism of presumed diminution in parental authority. I respectfully dissent.

It should go without saying that parents generally need to know information contained in their children's health records in order to make decisions for their well-being. To remove any doubt that this is true, even after divorce, for any parent with custodial responsibility for a child, section 153.073(a)(2) of the Texas Family Code states that "unless limited by court order, a parent appointed as a conservator of a child has at all times the right... of access to medical, dental, psychological, and educational records of the child...." A parent's right to this information is not an insignificant matter and should not be restricted absent compelling reasons.

Section 611.0045 of the Texas Health and Safety Code, the pertinent parts of which are quoted in the margin,[5] permits a mental health care "professional", broadly defined as stated above, to deny a patient access to his own mental health records if disclosure would harm the patient's physical, mental, or emotional health. For the same reason, access may be denied to a patient's representative, including a parent if the patient is a child.[6] In a suit

---

5 Section 611.0045. Right to Mental Health Record:(a) Except as otherwise provided by this section, a patient is entitled to have access to the content of a confidential record made about the patient; (b) The professional may deny access to any portion of a record if the professional determines that release of that portion would be harmful to the patient's physical, mental, or emotional health; (c) If the professional denies access to any portion of a record, the professional shall give the patient a signed and dated written statement that having access to the record would be harmful to the patient's physical, mental, or emotional health and shall include a copy of the written statement in the patient's records. The statement must specify the portion of the record to which access is denied, the reason for denial, and the duration of the denial; (d) The professional who denies access to a portion of a record under this section shall redetermine the necessity for the denial at each time a request for the denied portion is made. If the professional again denies access, the professional shall notify the patient of the denial and document the denial as prescribed by Subsection (c); (e) If a professional denies access to a portion of a confidential record, the professional shall allow examination and copying of the record by another professional if the patient selects the professional to treat the patient for the same or a related condition as the professional denying access; (f) The content of a confidential record shall be made available to a person listed by Section 611.004(a)(4) or (5) who is acting on the patient's behalf; (h) If a summary or narrative of a confidential record is requested by the patient or other person requesting release under this section, the professional shall prepare the summary or narrative.
6 The persons referred to in section 611.0045(f) who can act on behalf of a patient

to obtain the records, the professional has the burden of proving that denial of access is proper.[7] Nothing in the statute suggests that this burden should be anything but substantial. Certainly, a patient should not be denied access to his own mental health records absent solid, credible evidence that disclosure will cause him real, demonstrable harm. A general concern that disclosure to the patient would not be in his best interest should not be enough to deny him access. The statute sets no different harm standard for denying a parent access to a child's records. Denial of access cannot be based on some general concern that the child may be displeased or discomfited, even severely, about the disclosure. Rather, denial must be grounded on evidence of actual impairment to the child's health.

As the parental notification cases recently demonstrate, the meaning the Court gives a statutory standard is best demonstrated not by the words used to describe it but by its application in specific circumstances. This case illustrates how little evidence the Court believes is necessary not simply to raise the issue of whether a parent should be denied a child's mental health records but to conclusively establish -- so that no court can rule otherwise -- that a parent is not entitled to the records. The Court's decision to deny access to the records in this case rests entirely on the testimony of Abrams, a licensed clinical psychologist, who stated at a hearing in the district court: that Jones's former wife brought their eleven-year-old daughter, Karissa, to him in February 1996 because Karissa was agitated and showed signs of worry and sleeplessness; that Karissa refused to open up to him until he promised her that he would not reveal the details of their conversations to her parents, even though she understood that a judge might later order disclosure; that Karissa then told him she was troubled that if when she turned twelve in October she had to express a preference for living with one parent or the other, as her stepmother (her former nanny) had suggested she might,[8] it would provoke more hostility between her parents; that after meeting with Karissa six times in five months, she seemed much better; that Karissa had reiterated her desire for confidentiality in their last

---

are "a person who has the written consent of the patient, or a parent if the patient is a minor, or a guardian if the patient has been adjudicated as incompetent to manage the patient's personal affairs", id. §611.004(a)(4), or "the patient's personal representative if the patient is deceased", id. §611.004(a)(5).

7   Id. § 611.005(b) ("In a suit contesting the denial of access under Section 611.0045, the burden of proving that the denial was proper is on the professional who denied the access.").

8   Cf. TEX. FAM. CODE § 153.134(a)(6) ("If a written agreement of the parents is not filed with the court, the court may render an order appointing the parents joint managing conservators only if the appointment is in the best interest of the child, considering the following factors:... (6) if the child is 12 years of age or older, the child's preference, if any, regarding the appointment of joint managing conservators...."); id. § 153.008 ("If the child is 10 years of age or older, the child may, by writing filed with the court, choose the managing conservator, subject to the approval of the court."); id. § 153.009(b) ("When the issue of managing conservatorship is contested, on the application of a party, the court shall interview a child 10 years of age or older and may interview a child under 10 years of age.").

meeting four months earlier in June 1996, and in a note her mother had brought to him a few days before the October 15 hearing; and that he had told Karissa's father, Jones, that his former wife had hired him to "get a leg up on" Jones in their continuing court proceedings. On the specific issue of whether disclosing Karissa's records to Jones would harm Karissa's health, Abrams's testimony in its entirety is as follows:

Q: Is it your opinion at this time that the release of those records would be physically or emotionally harmful to Karissa?

A: Yes, sir.

Q: And what is that opinion?

A: That would have harmed her, as a matter of fact. It would be the very essence, it would make her get better, to give her protection.

Q: As we sit here on October 15th of 1996, is it still your opinion that it would be harmful to her mental or emotional health if these records are released?

A: Yes, sir.

Q: And can you tell the Judge why you believe that?

A: I've had no communications from her to be otherwise. I asked her the last time I saw her, in June about it, she reaffirmed her need for it. I received a note from her last week asking for it again.

The Court holds that this testimony, which did not persuade the district judge, conclusively established that Karissa's health would be harmed by disclosing her records to her father. The Court not only denies the trial court any meaningful role in determining credibility and weighing evidence, it reaches a conclusion, as a matter of law, on evidence that is inconclusive. Assuming that Abrams's testimony established that Karissa's health would have been harmed in February 1996 if he could not have promised her a measure of confidentiality because she would not have opened up to him and he could not have counseled her, the only evidence that disclosure of the records would harm Karissa's health in October 1996, when Abrams was no longer seeing her, was that she continued to request confidentiality. Jones disputed whether Karissa still wanted Abrams's records kept from him, testifying that based on his conversations with his daughter, his opinion was that she wanted him to have the records.

The Court concludes that Jones's testimony is no evidence that disclosure would not harm Karissa because an eleven-year-old is not qualified to say what would be harmful to her health. But if that is true, as I agree it is, then Abrams's testimony that Karissa continued to request confidentiality must likewise be disregarded. Karissa is no more qualified to say that disclosure of her records to her father would harm her health than that it would not. If Abrams's opinion cannot be based on Karissa's wishes, then it has no basis at all. Asked why he believed that disclosure would harm Karissa's health, Abrams answered, "I've had no communications from her to be otherwise."

Surely the Court does not think that a need for confidentiality at one point in time precludes disclosure of information forever. Nothing in the evidence before us suggests that Abrams would ever see Karissa again. Her twelfth birthday was three days after the hearing, and her anxieties about any choices she would have to make at that point were soon to be resolved one way or the other. No reason that Abrams gave for denying Jones access to his daughter's records remained valid. Had the trial judge found from this evidence that there might yet be some lingering need for nondisclosure, I could understand this Court's deference to that finding. But I do not understand how this Court can conclude that no reasonable trial judge could find from this evidence that Karissa's health would not be harmed by allowing her father access to her records.

It is no answer to say, as the Court seems to, that section 611.0045 allows a parent to take a child to other professionals until one is found who will release the records. True, Jones could simply have taken his daughter to one professional or another until he found one willing to turn over her records, and the statute gives Abrams no way to object. But the statute is not a full-employment guarantee for mental health care professionals, and no parent should be forced to shop a child as a patient merely to obtain the child's records. More importantly, I see no justification for applying section 611.0045 to permit one professional to trump another, regardless of their relative qualifications, and yet let any professional trump a district judge.

The Court's determination to restrict parental access to mental health records despite and not because of the statute is further demonstrated by its conclusion that section 611.0045 authorizes nondisclosure not only when the child's health may be harmed but when a parent is not "acting on the patient's behalf" as provided in subsection (f) of the statute. These words cannot, in my view, be sensibly read to create a separate standard for access to records. One might think that a parent could easily meet such a standard by stating that his or her request for a child's records was motivated out of love and concern for the child, but the Court concludes that evidence that parents are hostile to one another is enough by itself to support an inference that they are selfishly motivated and therefore not acting on their child's behalf.

The evidence the Court points to in this case is especially problematic. Abrams told Jones — Jones did not merely have his suspicions — that he believed he had been hired by Karissa's mother to counsel Karissa in order to give the mother "a leg up" in her ongoing disputes with Jones over custody of Karissa and her sister. The Court is troubled by Jones's frank admission in the October hearing that Abrams's statement to him was part of his motivation for obtaining Karissa's records, even though it could not have been important to Jones when he first went to meet with Abrams the preceding February — which was before Abrams had expressed the view that he himself was being used by Karissa's mother. It is difficult to imagine any reasonable, candid parent who would not acknowledge a similar motivation under the circumstances; indeed, one might have been less inclined to believe Jones if he had denied any such motivation. To rest denial of access to a child's medical records merely on inferences drawn from disputes between the parents conflicts with their rights under section 153.073(a)(2) of the Texas Family Code.

By construing section 611.0045 as establishing an acting-on-behalf-of standard for gaining access to a child's mental health records, the Court requires inquiry into, and inevitable disputes over, a parent's subjective motivations, instead of focusing on the more objective harm-to-the-patient's-health standard. I do not read section 611.0045 to require such an inquiry, which will almost always exacerbate difficulties between divorced parents.

While Abrams appears to have been professional in his dealings with the parties, and the district court did not suggest the contrary, the court was not bound by Abrams's views. Today's decision, coming as it does four years after the events at issue, cannot be of much importance to these parties. Karissa will soon be sixteen. Its importance lies in the difficulties it will cause future parties and in its further deterioration of parents' rights to raise their children.

—*Justice Hecht*

HIPAA

TEXAS LAW AND THE FEDERAL HEALTH INSURANCE PORTABILITY AND ACCOUNTABILITY ACT

The Health Insurance Portability and Accountability Act (HIPAA) was signed into law in 1996 as a surviving vestige of the Clinton Administration effort to overhaul the health care system. HIPAA was intended to create a more cost efficient health care system by facilitating electronic communication of health information among health care providers, health plans (including employer-sponsored group plans, Medicaid, Medicare, etc.), health care clearinghouses, and a variety of business associates that are indirectly involved in the health care enterprise (accountants, billing services, attorney's, etc.). In order to encourage the use of electronic transmission of health care information, Congress approved the bill, acknowledged that patient privacy would be of paramount concern in the electronic era of health care, and shifted responsibility to the Department of Health and Human Services (HSS) for promulgating certain rules for protecting privacy and to assume ultimate regulatory authority for enforcement. HIPAA became effective in 2001, though compliance implementation did not begin until two years later.

As of this writing, actual enforcement of HIPAA in regards to an individual health care provider practice has been limited to one case involving Medicare fraud by a non-psychologist. It seems reasonable, on the short term, to assume HHS will likely engage in more educative rather than legal intervention with individual practitioners, with the exception of those cases involving egregious crimes or serious fraudulent events. Further, it is more likely that HHS will devote its policing activity to larger health care entities, such as insurance companies and managed care companies, where protected health care information may be compromised on a large scale. For the independent psychologist or small group practice, HIPAA will serve as the "standard of practice" in civil court actions initiated against service providers by disgruntled patients. Nevertheless, it is worth noting that violation of HIPAA carries civil penalties of not more than $100 for each violation, not to exceed $25,000 in a calendar year, fines of up to $250,000, and imprisonment for up to 10 years, or both.

There are three basic HIPAA rules germane to the typical Texas psychologist engaged in health care practice: the Privacy, Transaction, and Security Rules. Please note that HIPAA is not intended to address forensic or other forms of non-health service related psychological records or communications. Briefly, the HIPAA Privacy Rule describes in some considerable detail when and to whom individually identifiable health information can be disclosed. The electronic transmission of protected health information (PHI) triggers the Privacy Rule and requires that the psychologist's entire health care practice be in compliance with HIPAA regulations. Therefore, a psychologist may not segment or segregate certain patient files as being non-HIPAA compliant simply because there has been no electronic transmission of patient health care information.

There is little about the Privacy Rule that has dramatically changed the practice of psychology in Texas. With patient confidentiality serving as a cornerstone to the profession and firmly underscored in the APA ethics code, Texas law, and Texas licensure regulations, most psychologists are practicing well above the minimum standards established by the HIPAA Privacy Rule. One important provision of the Privacy Rule that has been of considerable importance and assistance to psychologists and their clients has been the federal mandate limiting the information that third party payers may require for payment of services. Specifically, the release of psychotherapy process notes may not be demanded as a condition for payment of services. However, psychologists are cautioned that a court ordered subpoena will likely open these records for review in a court of law and that patient access to their personal health care records was one of the specific aims of HIPAA. We strongly suggest adherence to the American Psychological Association's standards for record keeping. It is also important to note that HIPAA specifies that health care records be preserved for a period of six years, however, for psychological records Texas law specifies ten years, and for another ten years past age of majority for health care records for minors. As HIPAA was intended to establish a minimal floor for protected patient information, the federal act specifically indicates that when the various health care entities, including practitioners, determine a conflict or inconsistency exists between this federal law and state statue, adherence to the "higher standard" should be followed. In the case of maintenance of patient records, Texas law prevails.

The Transaction Rule with a compliance date of October 16, 2003, addresses more technical aspects of the electronic health care transaction process and requires the use of standardized formats relevant to health care claims when sent electronically. There appears to be two primary aspects of this HIPAA rule impacting psychological practice. First, HIPAA specifies use of a standard diagnostic code set, the IDC of Diseases, 9th edition (ICD-9 CM) Vol.

1 & 2. Hence, psychologists may have to use a billing service or clearinghouse to convert DSM codes to ICD codes. Second, as part of the transaction standards, the Current Procedural Terminology (CPT) must be used but will not otherwise require a conversion. Currently, there is no regulatory address of these "transaction" issues in Texas law.

The HIPAA Security Rule was the last of the three primary rules to be finalized, largely because it is the most complex due to the constantly changing world of technology. The reader should note that compliance with the HIPAA Privacy and Transaction Rules *does not* ensure compliance with the HIPAA Security Rule. The Security Rule requires assurance that confidential electronic patient health information (EPHI) is kept secure from inappropriate or incidental disclosure. The rule addresses administrative, physical, and technical procedures and processes regarding office space, files (hardcopy and electronic), computers and other electronic gadgetry (PDA'S , cell phones, electronic tablets). Compliance with the Security Rule requires a process called a "risk analysis." This risk analysis is painstaking, will likely involve at least several hours of time to complete by the typical private practitioner, and must be thoroughly documented. Essentially, a risk analysis requires psychologists to determine the physical, procedural, and administrative security risks inherent in their maintenance and communication of protected health information. We anticipate that the HIPAA Security Rule will effectively define the minimally acceptable standards of practice in this regard.

Finally, it is also important to underscore that the HIPAA Privacy, Transaction and Security Rules do not require psychologists to use electronic means for the communication of health care information, including billing. Indeed, some psychologists have made effort to arrange an electronic–free practice in order to dodge HIPAA regulatory authority. Unfortunately for these technologically defiant psychologists, they may soon find that most third party payers will require them to submit billings electronically. As well, as discussed earlier, the HIPAA security rule will likely define the appropriate standard of care regarding the protection of patient records, whether or not they are stored or communicated electronically. Psychologists are encouraged to become more familiar with these HIPAA rules with understanding that HIPAA may at least set standards for the security and accessibility of patient records.

Much of the material presented here was derived directly from materials provided by the American Psychological Association's Practice Directorate. A more thorough description of HIPAA rules and its implications for psychological practice, as well as helpful web-based products designed to facilitate compliance with HIPAA, may be found at *http://www.apapractice.org*.

OPINIONS
FROM THE
ATTORNEY
GENERAL

ATTORNEY GENERAL OPINION LETTERS

AND OPEN RECORD OPINIONS

This section contains selected letters from the archive of Attorney General Opinions and Open Records Opinions that are relevant to practice. These opinions are relatively difficult to research because of the way they are indexed on the website of the Texas Attorney General. We hope that this archive will assist practitioners who have questions related to these decisions, such as whether data and protocols are a part of a patient's file and thus open to the patient (LO 97-073) and the oversight of the TSBEP over employees in exempt agencies (JC-321).

Public Disclosure of Investigations

OFFICE OF THE ATTORNEY GENERAL

STATE OF TEXAS

GREG ABBOTT ATTORNEY GENERAL	September 24, 2003
Mr. Brett Norbraten General Counsel Texas State Board of Examiners of Psychologists 333 Guadalupe, Suite 2-450 Austin, Texas 78701	OR2003-6711 Re: Whether certain information about pending TSBEP investigations is subject to required public disclosure.

Dear Mr. Norbraten:

You ask whether certain information is subject to required public disclosure under chapter 552 of the Government Code. Your request was assigned ID# 189106.

The Texas State Board of Examiners of Psychologists (the "board") received a request for "the names, addresses and phone numbers of any and all individuals and/or practices that are now under investigation for any violation of their Occupations, Code or Act where the final decision to conduct an investigation of them has been made by your agency." You claim that the requested information is excepted from disclosure under section 552.101 of the Government Code. We have considered the exception you claim and reviewed the submitted information.

Section 552.101 of the Government Code excepts from required public disclosure "information considered to be confidential by law, either constitutional, statutory, or by judicial decision." This section encompasses information made confidential by statutes such as section 501.205 of the Occupations Code. Chapter 501 of the Occupations Code codifies the Psychologists' Licensing Act. *See* Occ. Code §§ 501.001, *et seq.* Section 501.205(a) provides, in relevant part, that "except as provided by Subsection (b), a complaint and investigation concerning a license holder and all information and materials compiled by the board in connection with the complaint and investigation are not subject to... disclosure under Chapter 552, Government Code[.]" Subsection (b) of section 501.205 provides as follows:

(b) A complaint or investigation subject to Subsection (a) and all information and materials compiled by the board in connection with the complaint may be disclosed to:

(1) the board and board employees or agents involved in license holder discipline;

(2) a party to a disciplinary action against the license holder or that party's designated representative;

(3) a law enforcement agency if required by law;

(4) a governmental agency, if:

(A) the disclosure is required or permitted by law; and

(B) the agency obtaining the disclosure protects the identity of any patient whose records are examined; or

(5) a legislative committee or committee staff directed to make an inquiry regarding state hospitals or schools, by either house of the legislature, the presiding officer of either house of the legislature, or the chairman of the legislative committee if the information or records that identify a patient or client are not released for any purpose unless the patient consents and the records are created by the state hospital or school or its employees.

From our review of the submitted information, we conclude that the information falls within the ambit of section 501.205 of the Occupations Code. We find that the requestor does not fall into any of the five exceptions enumerated in that statute. Therefore, the submitted information must be withheld under section 552.101 of the Government Code in conjunction with section 501.205 of the Occupations Code.

With regards to future requests to the State Board of Examiners of Psychologists for information compiled by the board in connection with a complaint and investigation of a license holder, where the requestor does not fall into any of the five exceptions enumerated in section 501.205(b) of the Occupations Code, you may consider this ruling to be a previous determination under section 552.301(a) of the Government Code. This previous determination applies only to the information described above. See Open Records Decision No. 673 at 7 (2001). Moreover, so long as the elements of law, facts and circumstances do not change so as to no longer support the findings set forth above, the board need not ask for a decision from this office again with respect to this type of information requested of the board.

This ruling triggers important deadlines regarding the rights and responsibilities of the governmental body and of the requestor. For example, governmental bodies are prohibited from asking the attorney general to reconsider this ruling. Gov't Code § 552.301(f). If the governmental body wants to challenge this ruling, the governmental body must appeal by filing suit in Travis County within 30 calendar days. Id. § 552.324(b). In order to get the full benefit of such an appeal, the governmental body must file suit within

10 calendar days. *Id.* § 552.353(b)(3), (c). If the governmental body does not appeal this ruling and the governmental body does not comply with it, then both the requestor and the attorney general have the right to file suit against the governmental body to enforce this ruling. *Id.* § 552.321(a).

If this ruling requires the governmental body to release all or part of the requested information, the governmental body is responsible for taking the next step. Based on the statute, the attorney general expects that, within 10 calendar days of this ruling, the governmental body will do one of the following three things: 1) release the public records; 2) notify the requestor of the exact day, time, and place that copies of the records will be provided or that the records can be inspected; or 3) notify the requestor of the governmental body's intent to challenge this letter ruling in court. If the governmental body fails to do one of these three things within 10 calendar days of this ruling, then the requestor should report that failure to the attorney general's Open Government Hotline, toll free, at (877) 673-6839. The requestor may also file a complaint with the district or county attorney. *Id.* § 552.3215(e).

If this ruling requires or permits the governmental body to withhold all or some of the requested information, the requestor can appeal that decision by suing the governmental body. *Id.* § 552.321(a); *Texas Dep't of Pub. Safety v. Gilbreath*, 842 S.W.2d 408, 411 (Tex. App.--Austin 1992, no writ).

Please remember that under the Act the release of information triggers certain procedures for costs and charges to the requestor. If records are released in compliance with this ruling, be sure that all charges for the information are at or below the legal amounts. Questions or complaints about over-charging must be directed to Hadassah Schloss at the Texas Building and Procurement Commission at (512) 475-2497.

If the governmental body, the requestor, or any other person has questions or comments about this ruling, they may contact our office. We note that a third party may challenge this ruling by filing suit seeking to withhold information from a requestor. Gov't Code § 552.325. Although there is no statutory deadline for contacting us, the attorney general prefers to receive any comments within 10 calendar days of the date of this ruling.

Sincerely,

Debbie K. Lee
Assistant Attorney General
Open Records Divisio

Recognized Member of the Clergy

OFFICE OF THE ATTORNEY GENERAL

STATE OF TEXAS

JOHN CORNYN ATTORNEY GENERAL	August 5, 2002

Ms. Sherry L. Lee, Executive Director
Texas State Board of Examiners of
    Psychologists
333 Guadalupe, Suite, 2-450
Austin, Texas 78701
	Opinion No. JC-0535
	
	Re: What constitutes a "recognized
	    member of the clergy" for
	    purposes of section 501.004(4)
	    of the Occupations Code from
	    the Psychologists Licensing Act

Dear Ms. Lee,

You have asked this office how the Texas State Board of Examiners of Psychologists (the "Board") may determine, for the purpose of section 501.004(4) of the Occupations Code (the "Code"), whether to accept particular claims that an individual is exempt from the licensing requirements of the Code on the ground that he or she is a "recognized member of the clergy" who is acting "within the person's ministerial capabilities."[1] Tex. Occ. Code Ann. § 501.004(4) (Vernon 2002). You ask what guidelines may exist in Texas law or regulation that would define such recognition. In particular, you ask whether a person who has been ordained "via the Internet or mail for a fee" is a recognized member of the clergy. Request Letter, *supra* note 1 at 1. *(Ed. note Footnote omitted).* We conclude that, in examining the question of whether a person who purposes to be exempt from licensing under the Code is a recognized member of the clergy, the Board may take into account, as one factor, the ordination of that person for a fee by Internet or mail. However, the Board should not conclusively presume that a person is not a recognized member of the clergy based on that factor alone, unless the person provides no other evidence of his or her ministerial activities and religious affiliation other than the Internet or mail order certificate.

Chapter 501 of the Occupations Code, the Psychologists' Licensing Act, establishes the Board and requires those who "engage in or represent that [they are] engaged in the practice of psychology" to be licensed by the Board unless they are "exempt under Section 501.004." Tex. Occ. Code Ann. 501.251 (Vernon 2000). Section 501.004 exempts "the activity or services of a recognized member of the clergy who is acting within the person's ministerial capabilities" if the clergy man does not describe him- or herself as a psychologist or the services as psychological. Id 5091.004(4). The Board has the power to commence an action for injunctive relief to prevent a violation of chapter 501. Id. § 501.501(a). Engaging in the unlicensed practice of psychology is a Class A misdemeanor. Id. § 501.503.

As we understand the situation giving rise to your inquiry, the Board, when seeking to enjoin the unlicensed practice of psychology, is faced with "persons who claim exemption using a ministerial certificate or other ordination procured without training via the mail or Internet." Request Letter, *supra* note 1, at 1. Recognizing the possibility that such claims may be made for the purpose of evading the strictures of the Code, but mindful of the free exercise rights embodied in the First Amendment to the United States Constitution, you inquire as to the criteria by which the Board can distinguish spurious claims of exemption from legitimate ones.

You ask "[w]hat guidelines exist in the laws or regulations of the State of Texas that define 'recognition' of a member of the clergy?" *Id.* We note that the statute governing licensed professional counselors also exempts "a recognized religious practitioner." *See* Tex. Occ. Code Ann. § 503.054(2) (Vernon 2002). The Texas State Board of Examiners of Professional Counselors has promulgated a rule further defining "[r]ecognized religious practitioner" as "[a] rabbi, member of the clergy, or person of similar status who is a member in good standing of and accountable to a legally recognized denomination, church, sect or religious organization legally recognized under the Internal Revenue Code § 501(c)(3) . . . . " 22 Tex. Admin. Code § 681.2(14) (2002). Such practitioners must be counseling "within the scope . . . of their regular or specialized ministerial duties . . . under the auspices of ... [their] organization," must be "accountable to [its] established authority," and must not hold themselves out as professional counselors. *Id. See also* Tex. R. Evid. 505 (defining member of clergy for purposes of privileged communications as "a minister, priest, rabbi, accredited Christian Science Practitioner, or other similar functionary of a religious organization or an individual reasonably believed so to be by the person consulting with such individual.").

In our view, the Texas State Board of Examiners of Professional Counselors' rule offers a model that may be of value to you, given its focus on a member of the clergy as a person who has an acknowledged place within some sort of religious organization. In both your statute and that of the licensed professional counselors, an exemption is in effect being offered for pastoral counseling, an activity that implies a relation within and accountability to a religious organization. Moreover, in both cases, the counseling is limited to the clergy member's ministry, in his or her ministerial capacity.

Determining what constitutes a legitimate claim for a religious exemption from generally applicable law and distinguishing such a claim from those asserted for the purpose of evading the effect of such law is a difficult task. In the necessarily factual investigation of whether a claim for religious exemption such as the one about which you have asked is valid or spurious, the Board may rely on a variety of inquiries. By way of example, and in light of the Board of Examiners of Professional Counselors' rule, we note that the Internal Revenue Service has historically relied in this context on a series of questions developed to investigate whether a religious organization may qualify as a church for tax exemption purposes, including, among other things, whether such an organization has a distinct legal existence, a recognized creed, a distinct ecclesiastical government, a formal code of doctrine and discipline, a distinct religious history, a literature of its own, ordained ministers selected after a prescribed course of study, and regular congregations and services. See Scialabba, Kurtzman, and Steinhart, *Mail-Order Ministries Under the Section 170 Charitable Contribution Deduction: The First Amendment Restrictions, the Minister's Burden of Proof; and the Effect of TRA '86*, 11 CAMPBELL L. Rev. 27 n.31 (Winter 1988) (citing Internal Revenue Manual); *see also* INTERNAL REVENUE SERVICE, FORM 1023: APPLICATION FOR RECOGNITION OF EXEMPTION, SCHEDULE A (revised 1998) (current Internal Revenue Service questions).

Your particular concern is what once was referred to as "Mail-Order Ministries." *See supra, Mail-Order Ministries*, 11 CAMPBELL L. REV. 1. Such enterprises permit any person, for a small fee or donation, to receive credentials asserting that they have been ordained as clergy. Some recipients have used such credentials in a variety of schemes to avoid the law, and in particular to attempt to evade payment of income taxes. *See, e.g., Church of World Peace, Inc. v. Commissioner,* 67 T.C.M. (CCH) 2282 (1994); *Stephenson v. Commissioner,* 79 T.C. 995 (1983) ("Life Science Church of Allegan"); *Davis v. Commissioner,* 81 T.C. 806 (1983) ("Universal Life Church"). One such ministry is the Universal Life Church of Modesto, California. As the district court notes in *Universal Life Church v. Utah:*

The ULC will ordain anyone free, for life, without questions of faith. Anyone can be *ordained a* ULC minister in a matter of minutes by clicking onto the ULC's website and by providing a name, address, and e-mail address. Anyone can also be ordained by mailing to the ULC a name and address. There is no oath, ceremony, or particular form required.

The ULC requires virtually nothing from its ministers: they are not required to perform any religious ceremonies, to oversee a congregation, to provide religious guidance or counseling, to report religious ceremonies to headquarters, to keep in contact with the ULC other than routine *address* changes, or to attend any worship services.

Universal Life Church v. Utah, 189 F. Supp.2d *1302,* 1307 (D. Utah 2002).

In Universal Life Church, the district court declared unconstitutional on equal protection

grounds a Utah statute that distinguished between ministers who applied for their ordination through the Internet or mail from those who had applied "via fax, telephone, or in person." *Id.* at 1317-18. The statute at issue forbade only ministers who had applied for their credentials through the Internet or mail, but not those who applied in another manner, from, solemnizing marriages. *See id.* at 1307. While the court dismissed the Universal Life Church's substantive due process claim on the ground that the Utah legislature could reasonably decide that "one who so cavalierly becomes a minister might not appreciate the gravity of solemnizing a marriage," *id.* at 1315-16, it held that a distinction based solely on the method of application for ordination was "a classification whose relationship to a goal is so attenuated as to render the distinction arbitrary and irrational." *Id.* at 1317-18.

While *Universal Life Church* is not controlling law in Texas, it demonstrates that the Board is better advised not to distinguish between applicants for exemption from the strictures of chapter 501 solely on the basis of the *means* by which they obtained ordination. The Board may, however, require more information from a person claiming such exemption than the mere production of a ministerial certificate granted by mail or Internet

Accordingly, while mere Internet ordination, which would appear to be the cyberspace equivalent of mail-order ministry, is a factor which the Board may consider in seeking to enjoin a purported minister from practicing psychology without a license, that factor alone may not be dispositive in every case. The Board should inquire further in seeking to establish whether the person in question has a legitimate claim for exemption as a member of the clergy. If, for example, the facts show that the *sole "religious" activity* of the person in question is the provision of counseling otherwise indistinguishable from the *practice of* psychology, or that such counseling is independent of any relationship or *accountability to* a religious organization of some sort, we believe that the Board would be justified in seeking to enjoin such activity.

SUMMARY

In examining whether a person is a "recognized member of the clergy" acting within the person's ministerial capabilities" for the purpose of exemption from the licensing requirements of chapter 501 of the Occupations Code, the Texas State Board of Examiners of Psychologists may consider, as one factor, the ordination of that person for a fee by Internet or mail. However, the Board should not conclusively presume that the person may not make a claim for exemption based on that factor alone. The Board should inquire further in seeking to establish whether the person in question has a legitimate claim for exemption as a member of the clergy, and may require more information from a person making such a claim for exemption than the mere production of a ministerial certificate granted by mail or Internet.

Yours very Truly,

JOHN CORNYN,
Attorney General of Texas

TSBEP Oversight of Licensees in Exempt Agencies

OFFICE OF THE ATTORNEY GENERAL - STATE OF TEXAS

JOHN CORNYN

January 5, 2001

Ms. Sherry L. Lee   Opinion No. JC-0321
Executive Director
Texas State Board of Examiners of   Re: Whether, under the Psychologists'
   Psychologists   Licensing Act, chapter 501 of the
333 Guadalupe, Suite 2-450   Occupations Code, the Board of Examiners
Austin, Texas 78701   of Psychologists may investigate the activity
                                         or service of a person who is licensed by the
                                         Board if the activity or service is performed
                                         within the scope of the person's employment
                                         by an "exempt facility," and related
                                         questions; reconsidering Attorney General
                                         Opinion JM-1247 (1990) (RQ-0213-JC)

Dear Ms. Lee

    The Psychologists' Licensing Act (the "Act"), chapter 501 of the Occupations Code, see TEX. OCC. CODE ANN. §501.001 (Vernon 2000), does not apply to the "activity or service of a person who is employed as a psychologist or psychological associate by a governmental agency or regionally accredited institution of higher education" if the activity or service is among the "duties the person is employed to perform within the confines of the agency or institution." Id. § 501.004(a)(1). Attorney General Opinion JM-1247 concludes that a person who is employed to practice psychology for a governmental agency or regionally accredited institution of higher education (together, an "exempt facility"), but who has chosen to obtain a license under the Act is subject to the Act even with respect to duties the licensee is employed to perform and performs "within the confines of" the employing exempt facility. See Tex. Att'y Gen. Op. No. JM-1247 (1990) at 3. You ask whether Attorney General Opinion JM-1247 correctly construes the Act to permit the State Board of Examiners of Psychologists (the "Board") to investigate misconduct by a voluntarily licensed psychologist or psychological associate committed "within the confines of" an exempt facility.[1] It does not. Section 501.004(a)(1) of the Act expressly exempts the activity or service of a licensee who is employed at an exempt facility if the activity or service is within the "duties the person is employed by the" exempt

---

1 Letter from Ms. Sherry L. Lee, Executive Director, Texas State Board of Examiners
   of Psychologists, to Honorable John Cornyn, Texas Attorney General (Mar. 30,
   2000) (on file with Opinion Committee) [hereinafter Request Letter].

facility "to perform within the confines of the agency or institution." TEX. OCC. CODE ANN. §501.001 (Vernon 2000). Thus, the Board has no jurisdiction of duties a voluntarily licensed person is employed by an exempt facility "to perform within the confines of the" exempt facility. *See id.* We further interpret the statutory phrase "within the confines of" to refer to duties within the scope of employment, whether or not the duties are performed within the geographic bounds of the exempt facility.

You ask five specific questions regarding the Board's jurisdiction to investigate a complaint against a licensed psychologist or psychological associate who is employed by an exempt facility. *See id.*

1. Is Attorney General Opinion Number JM-1247 still a valid opinion?

2. By forwarding complaints to an exempt facility for investigation, does the Board violate its duty to investigate complaints filed against its licensees?

3. Is it necessary to obtain a formal written agreement, such as a memorandum of understanding, between the Board and the exempt agency or institution before a complaint can be referred for investigation at the agency level?

4. What, if any, is the Board's recourse if an exempt agency or facility is unwilling to permit the Board to investigate an alleged violation and is unwilling to conduct [its] own investigation on behalf of the Board?

5. If a complaint must be dismissed due to the Board's inability to investigate the matter, has the Board violated Section 501.204(a)(2) of the Act, which requires the Board to ensure that a complaint is not dismissed without appropriate consideration?

Id. at 1-2. Questions 2-5 appear to assume that the Board has jurisdiction to investigate complaints regarding the activity or service of a licensee who is employed by an exempt facility, even though the activity or service is within the scope of employment. Because we conclude that Attorney General Opinion JM-1247 is incorrect and that the Board has jurisdiction to investigate complaints concerning a licensee's activity or service performed at an exempt facility only if the activity or service is beyond the scope of employment at the exempt facility, we do not answer these questions.

You also ask us to evaluate a Board policy statement. *See id.* at 1. Under the "Policy Statement on Licensees Who Work in Exempt Facilities" (the "Policy Statement"),

> persons who are employed in exempt facilities as psychologists or psychological associates are not required to be licensed.... However, ...persons who are [so] employed... and who provide services to the public for added compensation above their salary from the exempt agency [must] be licensed....

Therefore, any "activities and services" regarding the practice of psychology and licensure with this Board outside the context of the exempt setting are subject to the requirements of the Act and the rules and to the discipline of the Board.....

Complaints received by the Board concerning the "activities and services" of a licensee in an exempt setting are referred to the appropriate exempt agency so that the matter can be resolved in the most expedient and proper manner. Complaints pertaining to the "activities and services" occurring outside of the exempt setting by a licensee who is employed by an exempt agency will be investigated and resolved by the Board.

Policy Statement attached to Request Letter, *supra* note 1. We conclude that, to be completely consistent with our interpretation, the Policy Statement should make clear that a licensee's activity or service, performed at an exempt facility but beyond the scope of the licensee's employment with the exempt facility, is subject to the Act and may be investigated by the Board.

Your questions arise from two types of situations. *See* Telephone conversation with Amy Swann, General Counsel, Board (June 29, 2000). In the first, the employer, an exempt facility, asks the Board to investigate the conduct of a person who is employed by the facility to practice psychology there and who has voluntarily obtained a license. *See id.* You do not indicate whether the conduct in question was performed within the scope of the licensee's employment. In the second scenario, the Board learns of alleged misconduct by a licensee who is employed to practice psychology by an exempt facility, but when the Board informs the exempt facility of the allegations or attempts to investigate the allegations, the exempt facility does not cooperate. *See id.* Presumably, some of the exempt facilities about which you ask are governmental agencies, but others are private entities, such as private colleges and universities.

Several portions of the Act relate to the issues you raise. Under the Act, a person "engaged in the practice of psychology" generally must be licensed by the Board. TEX. OCC. CODE ANN. §§501.003(a), .251 (Vernon 2000); *see also id.* § 501.003(b), (c) (defining when person "is engaged in the practice of psychology" and "practice of psychology"). A psychologist may obtain a license under section 501.252 of the Occupations Code, while a psychological associate may obtain a license under section 501.259. *See id.* §§ 501.002(4), (5), .252, .259.

Among the Board's duties is that of receiving and investigating complaints about a licensee's conduct. The Board is required to regulate the investigation and disposition of complaints:

(a) The board shall adopt rules concerning the investigation of a complaint filed with the board. The rules adopted under this subsection must:

(1) distinguish between categories of complaints;

(2) ensure that a complaint is not dismissed without appropriate consideration;

(3) require that the board be advised of a complaint that is dismissed and that a letter be sent to the person who filed the complaint explaining the action taken on the dismissed complaint;

(4) ensure that the person who filed the complaint has an opportunity to explain the allegations made in the complaint; and

(5) prescribe guidelines concerning the categories of complaints that require the use of a private investigator and the procedures for the board to obtain the services of a private investigator.

(b) The board shall:

(1) dispose of each complaint in a timely manner; and

(2) establish a schedule for conducting each phase of a complaint that is under the control of the board not later than the 30th day after the date the complaint is received by the board.

Id. §501.204(a), (b). The board may discipline a licensee who violates the Act or who commits certain other acts. *See id.* §§501.402, .451.

Section 501.004(a)(1) of the Act exempts from the Act's application the activity or service of a person who is employed by an exempt facility to practice psychology if the activity or service is among the employee's duties performed "within the confines of" the exempt facility:

(a) This chapter does not apply to:

(1) the activity or service of a person, or the use of an official title by the person, who is employed as a psychologist or psychological associate by a governmental agency or regionally accredited institution of higher education if the person performs duties the person is employed by the agency or institution to perform within the confines of the agency or institution.

Board. TEX. OCC. CODE ANN. §§501.004(a)(1) (Vernon 2000). The Board may assist an agency to formulate voluntary guidelines for persons who perform psychological services:

(a) The board may cooperate with an agency that is not subject to this chapter to formulate voluntary guidelines to be observed in the training, activities, and supervision of persons who perform psychological services.

(b) Except as provided by Subsection (a), the board may not adopt a rule that relates to the administration of an agency that is not subject to this chapter.

Id. Sec.501.155.

Attorney General Opinion JM-1247, issued in 1990, concludes that a person who practices psychology at an exempt facility and who has voluntarily obtained a license is "subject to" the Act's provisions. *See* Tex. Att'y Gen. Op. No. JM-1247 (1990) at 3. (For the sake of clarity and except where noted, we refer to the statutory provisions discussed in Attorney General Opinion JM-1247 as they are codified now, and not to the pre-codified version actually cited in the opinion. See Act of May 13, 1999, 76th Leg., R.S., ch. 388, § 1, ch. 501, 1999 Tex. Gen. Laws 1431, 1853-74 (codifying chapter 501, Occupations Code); *id.* § 6, 1999 Tex. Gen. Laws 1431, 2439-40 (repealing article 4512c, Revised Civil Statutes).) The opinion construes section 501.004(a), which provided that "'[n]othing in this Act shall be construed to apply to... the activities, services and use of official title on the part of a person employed as a psychologist'" by an exempt facility. See Tex. Att'y Gen. Op. No. JM-1247 (1990) at 1 (quoting TEX. REV. CIV. STAT. ANN. art. 4512c, § 21). "If the phrase '[n]othing in this Act shall be construed to apply' is taken absolutely literally," the opinion reasons, "persons described in the exemptions... would be ineligible for... licensure[, and w]e do not think... that the purpose of section [501.004(a)] is to make certain individuals ineligible for... licensure. Rather, the plain purpose of the exemption... is to allow persons to engage in certain types of employment without a... license." *Id.* at 2. Consequently, the opinion determines, a person who voluntarily chooses to be licensed is subject to the board's rules "to the extent that [the rules] are qualifications for... licensure." *Id.* at 3. Finally, the opinion states that the Board may "cancel, revoke, suspend, or refuse to renew [the].... license [of a voluntary licensee] for any of the reasons the board may take such action in regard to... licenses generally.... Similarly, ... any person who chooses to seek licensure... is subject to the fees imposed by" section 501.152. Id.

Since Attorney General Opinion JM-1247 was issued, the Board "has attempted to conduct investigations and resolve consumer complaints relating to violations that have occurred while [a] licensee was providing psychological services in an exempt setting." Request Letter, supra note 1, at 2. Investigation and enforcement have, at times, been difficult:

> [T]he [B]oard has experienced mixed results with regard to the amount of cooperation it has received from other agencies and institutions during the Board's direct investigation into alleged violations. For example, [B]oard investigators have experienced difficulties obtaining requested documents, mental health records, or other information needed to substantiate the complainant's alleged violations. The Board's difficulty in investigating the complaints first hand has necessitated the forwarding of complaints to the exempt facility for investigation at the agency level. Once an investigation has been completed and the results received, the Board [is] able to determine the appropriate disciplinary action to be taken against the licensee. Unfortunately, in the majority of cases the Board does not receive a response of any kind from the exempt facilities. Without the ability to ascertain whether... a violation has been committed, the Board is compelled to dismiss the complaint.

Id.

We believe Attorney General Opinion JM-1247 incorrectly interprets section 501.004's plain language, and so we overrule it. Subsection (a)(1) states that chapter 501 does not apply to the activity or service of a person who practices psychology at an exempt facility if the activity or service is among the duties the person is employed by the exempt facility to perform and is performed "within the confines of the" exempt facility. *See* TEX. OCC. CODE ANN. § 501.004(a)(1) (Vernon 2000). Under subsection (a)(1), it is not the *practitioner* who is exempt from the Act; rather, it is certain *activities* or *services* performed by a person who is employed by an exempt facility as a psychologist or psychological associate. Whether or not the employee of an exempt facility is licensed is irrelevant. Attorney General Opinion JM-1247, by contrast, construes subsection (a)(1) to exempt the practitioner unless the practitioner is licensed, and if the practitioner is licensed, then all of his or her activities and services performed as a psychologist or psychological associate are subject to the Act. *See* Tex. Att'y Gen. Op. No. JM-1247 (1990) at 3.

The activity or service of a person, licensed or not, who is employed by an exempt facility as a psychologist or psychological associate is not subject to the Act only if the activity or service is among the "duties the person is employed... to perform within the confines of the" exempt facility. TEX. OCC. CODE ANN. § 501.004(a)(1) (Vernon 2000). But a licensed psychologist's or psychological associate's activity or service is subject to the Act despite the licensee's employment by an exempt facility if the activity or service is not among the duties the person is employed to perform "within the confines of the" exempt facility. *Id.* The Board has a duty to investigate allegations regarding an activity or service that is not among the duties a licensee is employed to perform "within the confines of" an exempt facility.

While section 501.004(a)(1) facially limits its application to activities or services that are among the duties a person is employed by an exempt facility to perform "within the confines of" the exempt facility, *id.*, we are uncertain what the phrase "within the confines of" means. The Act does not define it. The term "confines" often has geographic connotations. *See* III OXFORD ENGLISH DICTIONARY 708-09 (2d ed. 1989) (defining "confine"). Practically speaking, though, we cannot imagine that the legislature intended that a person, employed by an exempt facility to practice psychology, who commits some misconduct outside of the geographic boundaries of an exempt facility but within the scope of his or her employment--for, example, on a home visit--should be treated differently than an identical person who commits the misconduct within the walls of the exempt facility. Based on our presumption that the legislature intends the law to achieve "a just and reasonable result," TEX. GOV'T CODE ANN. § 311.021(3) (Vernon 1998), we conclude that the Board lacks jurisdiction to investigate alleged misconduct committed within the scope of a person's employment by an exempt facility, regardless of the geographic location at which the alleged misconduct occurred.

Whether a particular activity or service is beyond the scope of a licensee's employment is a question to be determined in the first instance by the employing exempt facility. It is, after all, the employing exempt facility that has established any particular employee's scope of employment. By contrast, the Board is unable to make that determination.

Where, as we understand sometimes happens, an employing exempt facility asks the Board to investigate the conduct of a licensed employee, *see supra* at 3 (citing Telephone Conversation with Amy Swann), we believe the Board may presume that the exempt facility has determined that the activity or service is beyond the scope of employment. Accordingly, the Board has jurisdiction to investigate the allegations.

On the other hand, where an exempt facility refuses to inform the Board whether a particular activity or service is within the scope of an employee's employment, the Board may assume that the activity or service complained of is within the scope of the licensee's employment and that the Board does not have jurisdiction to investigate. While this assumption is not explicitly stated in the Act, it is the interpretation most consistent with the "hands-off" policy that appears to underlie section 501.004. Our goal is to effect the legislative intent. *See National Liab. & Fire Ins. Co. v. Allen,* 15 S.W.3d 525, 527 (Tex. 2000) (stating that court's objective is to determine and effect legislature's intent). By exempting from the Act's application the activity or service of an employee of an exempt facility, where the activity or service is within the scope of employment, the Act suggests that the Board is not to interfere in the workings of an exempt facility.

Our conclusion that the Board may investigate a complaint regarding the activity or service of a licensee employed by an exempt facility only if the activity or service is beyond the scope of employment, does not mean that the Board may not take notice of a past complaint in an investigation against the same licensee, where the investigation is within the Board's jurisdiction. If the Board does so, it must provide a process that protects the licensee's due-process rights.

Likewise, although the Board has no duty to investigate a complaint regarding an activity or service within the scope of a licensee's employment at an exempt facility, nothing in the Act explicitly forbids the Board to forward a complaint to the exempt facility, so long as the Board complies with any applicable confidentiality provisions. See, e.g., Tex. Occ. Code Ann. _ 501.205 (Vernon 2000) (directing that complaint information is not subject to disclosure except to certain entities).

Because your questions 2-5 appear to assume that the Board has jurisdiction to investigate any licensee activity or service performed at an exempt facility, we do not answer them.

Finally, the Policy Statement does not reflect completely our conclusion today: that the activity or service of a licensee performed at an exempt facility but beyond the scope of the licensee's employment with the exempt facility is subject to the Act and to Board regulation. As the Policy Statement makes clear, "'activities and services' regarding the practice of psychology" of a licensee "outside the context of [an] exempt setting are subject to" Board oversight. See Policy Statement attached to Request Letter, supra note 1. But the Policy Statement suggests that all of a licensee's activities and services that are performed within "the context of the exempt setting" are beyond the Act and the Board's concomitant authority to investigate. Id. Consistently with our conclusions here, the Policy Statement should make clear that a licensee's activity or service, performed at an exempt facility but beyond the scope of the licensee's employment with the exempt facility, is subject to the Act and to investigation by the Board.

SUMMARY

Attorney General Opinion JM-1247 (1990), which concluded that the Psychologists' Licensing Act, chapter 501 of the Occupations Code, applies to a person who is employed to practice psychology for a governmental agency or regionally accredited institution of higher education (together, an "exempt facility") if the person has voluntarily obtained a license under the Act, is overruled. Rather, the Board of Examiners of Psychologists has jurisdiction of a licensee's activity or service only if the activity or service is beyond the scope of the licensee's employment by the exempt facility. SEE TEX. OCC. CODE ANN. _ 501.004(a) (Vernon 2000) ("Applicability"). The Board has no jurisdiction to investigate a complaint regarding the activity or service of a licensee employed by an exempt facility if the activity or service is within the scope of employment. Board policy should make clear that a licensee's activity or service, performed at an exempt facility but beyond the scope of the licensee's employment with the exempt facility, is subject to the Act and to investigation by the Board.

Yours very truly,

JOHN CORNYN
Attorney General of Texas

ANDY TAYLOR
First Assistant Attorney General

CLARK KENT ERVIN
Deputy Attorney General - General Counsel

SUSAN D. GUSKY
Chair, Opinion Committee

Kymberly K. Oltrogge
Assistant Attorney General - Opinion Committee

TSBEP Disclosures of Complaint Information

OFFICE OF THE ATTORNEY GENERAL

STATE OF TEXAS

JAMES W. MORRIS, III   May 11, 2000
ASSISTANT ATTORNEY GENERAL

Ms. Amy F. Swann   OR 2000-1850
General Counsel
Texas State Board of Examiners of
     Psychologists
333 Guadalupe, Suite 2-450
Austin, Texas 78701

Ms. Amy F. Swann
General Counsel
Texas State Board of Examiners of Psychologists
333 Guadalupe, Suite 2-450
Austin, Texas 78701

OR 2000-1850

Dear Ms. Swann:

You ask whether certain information is subject to required public disclosure under the Public Information Act (the "Act"), chapter 552 of the Government Code. Your request was assigned ID# 135880.

The Texas State Board of Examiners of Psychologists (the "board") received a request for information relating to a named psychologist, including any and all complaints filed against that individual and reprimands, probations, or suspensions of her license to practice. You inform us that the board has released responsive information relating to disciplinary actions and board orders. You have submitted and seek to withhold responsive complaints filed with the board and information and materials compiled by the board in connection with its investigations of those complaints. You claim that the submitted information is excepted from disclosure under section 552.101 of the Government Code. We have considered the exception you claim and have reviewed the information you submitted.

You claim that the submitted information is protected from disclosure under section 552.101 in conjunction with section 501.205 of the Occupations Code.[1] Chapter 501 of the Occupations Code codifies the Psychologists' Licensing Act. *See* Occ. Code § 501.001. Section 501.205(a) provides, in relevant part, that "except as provided by Subsection (b), a complaint and investigation concerning a license holder and all information and materials compiled by the board in connection with the complaint and investigation are not subject to... disclosure under Chapter 552, Government Code[.]" Occ. Code § 501.205(a)(1). Subsection (b) of section 501.205 provides as follows:

A complaint or investigation subject to Subsection (a) and all information and materials compiled by the board in connection with the complaint *may* be disclosed to:

(1) the board and board employees or agents involved in license holder discipline;

(2) a party to a disciplinary action against the license holder or that party's designated representative;

(3) a law enforcement agency if required by law;

(4) a governmental agency, if:

(A) the disclosure is required or permitted by law; and

(B) the agency obtaining the disclosure protects the identity of any patient whose records are examined; or

(5) a legislative committee or committee staff directed to make an inquiry regarding state hospitals or schools, by either house of the legislature, the presiding officer of either house of the legislature, or the chairman of the legislative committee if the information or records that identify a patient or client are not released for any purpose unless the patient consents and the records are created by the state hospital or school or its employees.

Occ. Code § 501.205(b) (emphasis added).

In this instance, you inform us that the requestor is an attorney who is not a party, or the legal representative of a party, to any complaint. You assert that, "[b]ecause the requestor does not appear to fall into one of the five exceptions... the information contained in a complaint investigation file cannot be released as a matter of law." You seek clarification concerning disclosure of the submitted information under section 501.205(b) to a non-party to a disciplinary complaint. We believe that section 501.205(a) clearly protects from public disclosure information and materials that the board compiles in connection with complaints lodged against license holders and the board's investigations of such complaints. We further believe that section 501.205 permits the board to release

---

1 Section 552.101 of the Act excepts from required public disclosure "information considered to be confidential by law, either constitutional, statutory, or by judicial decision." Gov't Code § 552.101. Statutory confidentiality under section 552.101 requires express language making certain information confidential or providing that it shall not be released to the public. See Open Records Decision No. 478 at 2 (1987)

such information only to the persons and entities and under the circumstances that are delineated by section 501.205(b). Based on your representation that the requestor is not within the ambit of section 501.205(b) and our review of the submitted information, we conclude that the submitted information is excepted from public disclosure under section 552.101 of the Government Code in conjunction with section 501.205 of the Occupations Code. Therefore, the requested information must not be released.

Limits of Ruling

This letter ruling is limited to the particular records at issue in this request and limited to the facts as presented to us; therefore, this ruling must not be relied upon as a previous determination regarding any other records or any other circumstances.

This ruling triggers important deadlines regarding the rights and responsibilities of the governmental body and of the requestor. For example, governmental bodies are prohibited from asking the attorney general to reconsider this ruling. Gov't Code §552.301(f). If the governmental body wants to challenge this ruling, the governmental body must appeal by filing suit in Travis County within 30 calendar days. *Id.* §552.324(b). In order to get the full benefit of such an appeal, the governmental body must file suit within 10 calendar days. *Id.* § 552.353(b)(3), (c). If the governmental body does not appeal this ruling and the governmental body does not comply with it, then both the requestor and the attorney general have the right to file suit against the governmental body to enforce this ruling. *Id.* § 552.321(a).

If this ruling requires the governmental body to release all or part of the requested information, the governmental body is responsible for taking the next step. Based on the statute, the attorney general expects that, within 10 calendar days of this ruling, the governmental body will do one of the following three things: *1) release the public records; 2) notify the requestor of the exact day, time, and place that copies of the records will be provided or that the records can be inspected; or 3) notify the requestor of the governmental body's intent to challenge this letter ruling in court.* If the governmental body fails to do one of these three things within 10 calendar days of this ruling, then the requestor should report that failure to the attorney general's Open Government Hotline, toll free, at 877/673-6839. The requestor may also file a complaint with the district or county attorney. *Id.* § 552.3215(e).

If this ruling requires or permits the governmental body to withhold all or some of the requested information, the requestor can appeal that decision by suing the governmental body. *Id.* § 552.321(a); *Texas Department of Public Safety v. Gilbreath*, 842 S.W.2d 408, 411 (Tex. App.--Austin 1992, no writ).

If the governmental body, the requestor, or any other person has questions or comments about this ruling, they may contact our office. Although there is no statutory deadline for contacting us, the attorney general prefers to receive any comments within 10 calendar days of the date of this ruling.

Sincerely,

James W. Morris, III
Assistant Attorney General
Open Records Division

Keeping Test Data Private from Patients

OFFICE OF THE ATTORNEY GENERAL

STATE OF TEXAS

DAN MORALES   August 20, 1997
ATTORNEY GENERAL

The Honorable Sherry L. Lee   Letter Opinion No. 97-073
Executive Director
Texas State Board of Examiners of   Re: Whether board rule that excludes
    Psychologists   testing materials and data from
333 Guadalupe, Suite 2-450   patient's psychological record is
Austin, Texas 78701   consistent with requirements of
                                         chapter 611, Health and Safety
                                         Code, granting patients access
                                         to their mental health records
                                         (ID#39134)

Dear Ms. Lee:

You ask whether certain provisions of a rule promulgated by the Texas State Board of Examiners of Psychologists ("the board") are consistent with the requirements of chapter 611 of the Health and Safety Code. The board, as the agency responsible for certifying and licensing psychologists,[1] is authorized by section 8 of article 4512c, V.T.C.S., to "make all rules, not inconsistent with the Constitution and laws of this state, which are reasonably necessary for the proper performance of its duties." The board is also required to adopt and publish a code of ethics.[2] The board's rules must be consistent with state laws. We are asked to determine whether the board's rule that excludes "test data and protocols" from the definition of patient records is consistent with chapter 611 of the Health and Safety Code.

Chapter 611 of the Health and Safety Code provides confidentiality for "[c]ommunications between a patient and a professional, and records of the identity, diagnosis, evaluation, or treatment of a patient that are created or maintained by a professional."[3] A " professional" within this provision includes

---

1   No one may be licensed as a psychologist unless the person is certified as a
    psychologist and has had at least two years of supervised experience in the field of
    psychological servies. V.T.C.S art. 4512c,§ 21; see also id. §11 (requirements for
    certification as a psychologist).
2   Id. § 8(a).
3   Health & Safety Code § 611.002(a).

a psychologist licensed or certified by the board.[4] Pursuant to section 611.0045 of the Health and Safety Code, "a patient is entitled to have access to the content of a confidential record made about the patient," with certain exceptions set out in the provision. "On receipt of a written request from a patient to examine or copy all or part of the patient's recorded mental health care information," a professional shall make the information available for examination during regular business hours and provide a copy to the patient, if requested.[5]

The rule that you inquire about governs confidentiality of and access to records of psychological services rendered by persons licensed and/or certified by the board. It is codified at title 22 of the Texas Administrative Code, section 465.22. For purposes of the rule, "psychological records include any information that can be used to document the delivery, progress, or results of any psychological services; including, but not limited to... any assessment, plan for intervention, consultation, handwritten notes, summary reports and/or testing reports."[6]

Section 465.22(d)(5), which concerns releasing information about a patient, provides that "[t]est data and protocols belong to the psychologist," and that "[t]est data and protocols shall be made available only to another qualified mental health professional and only upon receipt of proper written authorization from the patient/client or other individual legally authorized to release psychological records on behalf of a patient or client."

Thus, as you explain, the rule distinguishes "test data" from test reports. "Test data" refers only to the testing materials, test booklets, and protocols[7](8) used in the testing to generate test results. The rule treats test data as records of the psychologist and not as patient records, so that these materials are not available to the patient. Test reports and test results are defined as part of the patient's records and are available to the patient.

You indicate various policy reasons for the limitations on the disclosure of test data found in section 465.22(d)(5). You state that "inappropriate disclosure [of psychological test material] may seriously impair the security and threaten the validity of the test and its validity as a measurement tool,"[8] for

---

4 *Tumlinson v. State*, 663 S.W. 2d 539, 542 (Tex. App. --Dallas 1983, pet. ref'd).
5 Health & Safety Code § 611.008.
6 TEX. STATE BD. OF EXAM'RS OF PSYCHOLOGISTS, 21 Tex Reg. 9599-9600 (1996), adopted 22 Tex. Reg. 47 (1997).
7 A medical dictionary defines "protocol" as a "written plan specifying the procedures to be followed in giving a particular examination, in conducting research, or in providing care for a particular condition." MOSBY'S MEDICAL, NURSING, AND ALLIED HEALTH DICTIONARY 1290 (4th ed. 1994). We assume the protocols you refer to consist of a set of instructions to be followed in giving and evaluating certain psychiatric exam.s
8 Request letter from Sherry L. Lee, Executive Director, *Texas State Board of Examiners of Psychologists*, to Sarah J. Shirley, Divion Chief, *Attorney General Opinion Committee* (Sept. 23, 1996) on file with *Attorney General Opinion Committee*.

example, if an individual obtains prior knowledge of test items.[9] In addition, you discuss the interests of companies that own test data used by psychologists and inform us that some test data is copyrighted or subject to other protections for intellectual property. You also state that the rule prevents the release of test data to individuals not qualified to interpret it, to protect such patients from potentially harmful effects that might arise from misunderstanding the test data. Psychologists are required by board rule to "ensure that an explanation of the results [of an assessment] is provided using language that is reasonably understandable to the person assessed or to another legally authorized person on behalf of the client."[10]

While chapter 611 of the Health and Safety Code does not define patient records, it does refer to records relating to the "diagnosis, evaluation, or treatment of a mental or emotional condition or disorder, including alcoholism or drug addiction."[11] We have no difficulty in concluding that psychological tests relate to the diagnosis and evaluation of a mental or emotional condition, but we are unable in the opinion process to determine whether patient records within chapter 611 necessarily include "test data" as you have described it. The answer to this question requires the investigation and resolution of factual matters as to the content of test data, its relevance to patients, expert opinion as to the content of patient records, and other matters that cannot be determined in a legal opinion.[12] Although we question whether this rule is valid, administrative rules are entitled to a presumption of validity.[13] Accordingly, we cannot say that it is invalid as a matter of law.

We would like to point out a possible effect of this rule on records of a psychologist that are subject to the Open Records Act.[14] Under the Open Records Act, all information maintained by governmental bodies is available to the public unless specifically excepted from disclosure. Chapter 611 of the Health and Safety Code excepts patient records created or maintained by a psychologist from disclosure to the public, but to the extent that test data are

---

9   See AMERICAN PSYCHOLOGIST, COMMITTEE ON PSYCHOLOGICAL TESTS AND ASSESSMENT, AMERICAN PSYCHOLOGICAL ASSOCIATION, STATEMENT OF THE DISCLOSURE OF TEST DATA, at 644-46 (June 1996) discussing various issues of test security

10 22 T.A.C. § 465.36(c)(2)(I).

11 Health & Safety Code § 611.0045(j)

12 Before section 465.22 was amended in 1996, the definition of psychological records included "testing reports *and relevant supporting data.*" See 22 T.A.C. § 465.22(b)(1)(E) at 21 Tex. Reg. 9599-9600. The amendment was adopted "to clarify the requirements for retention and release of test data and protocols to ensure test security and validity of the test for other consumers of psychological services." 21 Tex Reg. 9599.

13 *See Texas Railroad Com'n v. Shell Oil Col, Inc.,* 161 S.W.2d 1022, 1026 (Tex. 1942); *McCarty v. Texas Parks and Wildlife Dept.,* 919 S.W. 2d 853 (Tex. App. - Austin 1996).

14 Gov't Code ch. 552. Records of a mental health professional sometimes become part of a public employee's personnel file. *See generally* Open Records Decisions Nos. 565 (1990) (psychological records of former police officer); 314 (1982) (psychiatric evaluation of teacher included in personnel file).

in fact not patient records, they will not be within the chapter 611 exception. However, depending on the nature of particular items of test data, other statutes or legal doctrines may be relevant to questions of disclosure under the Open Records Act.[15]

SUMMARY

Pursuant to chapter 611 of the Health and Safety Code, which gives patients access to their patient records created or maintained by mental health professionals, the Texas State Board of Examiners of Psychologists has promulgated a rule that defines test results as patient records and excludes testing materials, test booklets, and protocols used in generating test results from the definition of patient records. We will accord the rule the presumption of validity that attaches to administrative rules.

Where records of a psychologist are subject to the Open Records Act, the confidentiality provisions of chapter 611 will exempt "patient records" from disclosure to the public, but will not exempt the testing materials excluded from the definition of patient records. However, other provisions of law may be relevant.

Yours very truly,

Susan Garrison
Assistant Attorney General
Opinion Committee

---

15 For example, you state that items of "test data" are often copyrighted. The Open Records Act does not require the custodian of public records to furnish copies of copyrighted records to members of the public. Attorney General Opinions JM-672 (1987), MW-307 (1981). Such records are available for public inspection, and the person who requests them may make copies unassisted by the state. *Id.*

Prohibition on Use of "Extenders"

OFFICE OF THE ATTORNEY GENERAL

STATE OF TEXAS

DAN MORALES
ATTORNEY GENERAL

December 19, 1996

Sherry Lee
Executive Director Texas State Board
　of Examiners of Psychologists
333 Guadalupe, Suite 2-450
Austin, Texas 78701

Letter Opinion No. 96-147

Re: Whether the Board of Examiners of
　Psychologists may authorize the use
　of "psychological extenders" acting
　under the supervision of a licensed
　psychologist (ID# 38948)

Dear Ms. Lee:

Your predecessor in office asked for an opinion regarding the legality of licensed psychologists using non-licensed individuals to provide psychological services as "psychological extenders" under the supervision of licensed psychologists. More specifically, she asked the question in terms of the authority of the State Board of Examiners of Psychologists (the "board") to enact a rule empowering licensed psychologists to permit unlicensed individuals to perform psychological services under the supervision of the licensed psychologists. We believe such a practice or rule would contravene the express terms of the Psychologists' Certification and Licensing Act (the "act").

The act prohibits anyone from engaging in the practice of psychology or representing himself as a psychologist or a psychological associate unless he is certified, licensed, or exempt under the act. V.T.C.S. art. 4512c, § 20; compare id. with V.T.C.S. art. 4495b, §§ 3.06(d), .061 (allowing physicians, while providing supervision, to delegate medical acts to non-physicians). Accordingly, the act also provides a criminal penalty for anyone who practices psychology in violation of the act. V.T.C.S. art. 4512c, § 25. Moreover, the act provides no exemption for persons merely acting under the direction of a licensed psychologist. See id. § 22 (exemptions); see also id. § 21(a)(2) (requirement of two years of supervised practice prior to licensing). Therefore, the act expressly prohibits a non-certified, non-licensed, and non-exempt individual from engaging in the practice of psychology or representing himself as a psychologist or psychological associate. Psychological associates, even though licensed under the act, must act under supervision of a licensed psychologist. Id. §§ 19A(l)(2) (Psychological Associate

Advisory Committee to recommend rules regarding supervision requirements for psychological associates practicing less than five years), 19A(l)(7) (same to recommend guidelines for practice with minimal supervision for psychological associates with five or more years experience); see also 22 T.A.C. § 465.18 (licensed psychologist responsible for supervision of certified psychologists and psychological associates).

Section 20 implicitly prohibits the board from enacting a rule that would allow licensed psychologists to permit unlicensed individuals to perform psychological services. Under Texas administrative law, agency rules are valid only if expressly or impliedly authorized by statute. State v. Jackson, 376 S.W.2d 341, 344-5 (Tex. 1964); Bexar County Bail Bond Bd. v. Deckard, 604 S.W.2d 214, 216 (Tex. Civ. App.-- San Antonio 1980, no writ); Attorney General Opinion JM-1017 (1989) at 3; see 2 TEX. JUR. 3D Administrative Law § 16 (1979) (and authorities cited) (agency rules must be within clear intent of statute). In this case, the board is authorized to enact rules that are "not inconsistent with the Constitution and laws of this state." V.T.C.S. art. 4512c § 8(a). Because the practice of licensed psychologists using non-licensed, non-certified, and non-exempt individuals to provide psychological services would violate the Psychologists' Certification and Licensing Act, the State Board of Examiners of Psychologists may not enact a rule allowing such a practice.

SUMMARY

Licensed psychologists may not use non-licensed, non-certified, and non-exempt individuals to provide psychological services. Such a practice would violate the Psychologists' Certification and Licensing Act. Consequently, the State Board of Examiners of Psychologists may not enact a rule authorizing such a practice.

Yours very truly,

Rick Gilpin
Deputy Chief
Opinion Committee

Disclosure under Subpoena

OFFICE OF THE ATTORNEY GENERAL

STATE OF TEXAS

DAN MORALES   September 23, 1996
ATTORNEY GENERAL

Ms. Rebecca E. Forkner   Letter Opinion No. 96-102
Executive Director
Texas State Board of Examiners of   Re: Effect of provision of chapter
    Psychologists   611, Health and Safety Code,
333 Guadalupe, Suite 2-450   authorizing mental health
Austin, Texas 78701   professional to disclose confidential
                                         information about a patient in
                                         response to a subpoena (ID# 38823)

Dear Ms. Forkner:

On behalf of the Texas State Board of Examiners of Psychologists ("the board"), you inquire about a recent amendment to chapter 611 of the Health and Safety Code, which establishes the confidentiality of the mental health records of a patient that are created or maintained by a psychologist[1] and sets out exceptions to the confidentiality provision. Senate Bill 667 of the 74th Legislature addressed the disclosure of health and mental health care information by hospitals, physicians, and mental health professionals.[2] Among other provisions, it adopted section 611.006 of the Health and Safety Code, which provides for disclosure of mental health information in judicial and administrative proceedings. Section 611.006 states as follows:

(a) A professional may disclose confidential information in:

(1) a judicial or administrative proceeding brought by the patient or the patient's legally authorized representative against a professional, including malpractice proceedings;

(2) a license revocation proceeding in which the patient is a complaining

---

1   Chapter 611 defines "professional" to include a licensed physician, "a person licensed or certified by this state to diagnose, evaluate, or treat any mental or emotional condition or disorder," or "a person the patient reasonably believes" to hold the required license or certificate. Health & Safety Code § 611.001(2).

2   Act of May 29, 1995, 74th Leg., R.S., ch. 856, 1995 Tex. Gen. Laws 4290.

witness and in which disclosure is relevant to the claim or defense of a professional;

(3) a judicial or administrative proceeding in which the patient waives the patient's right in writing to the privilege of confidentiality of information or when a representative of the patient acting on the patient's behalf submits a written waiver to the confidentiality privilege;

(4) a judicial or administrative proceeding to substantiate and collect on a claim for mental or emotional health services rendered to the patient;

(5) a judicial proceeding if the judge finds that the patient, after having been informed that communications would not be privileged, has made communications to a professional in the course of a court-ordered examination relating to the patient's mental or emotional condition or disorder,... [exception omitted];

(6) a judicial proceeding affecting the parent-child relationship;

(7) any criminal proceeding, as otherwise provided by law;

(8) a judicial or administrative proceeding regarding the abuse or neglect, or the cause of abuse or neglect, of a resident of an institution, as that term is defined by Chapter 242;

(9) a judicial proceeding relating to a will if the patient's physical or mental condition is relevant to the execution of the will;

(10) an involuntary commitment proceeding for court-ordered treatment or for a probable cause hearing...;

(11) a judicial or administrative proceeding where the court or agency has issued an order or subpoena.

(b) On granting an order under Subsection (a)(5), the court, in determining the extent to which disclosure of all or any part of a communication is necessary, *shall impose appropriate safeguards against unauthorized disclosure.* [Emphasis added.]

You state that psychologists typically receive numerous subpoena duces tecum[3] for psychological records of present and former patients, and you ask how a psychologist should respond to receiving such a subpoena. You believe that subsection 611.006(a)(11) conflicts with a board rule governing the release of patient records, 465.22(d)(3), which provides as follows:

An individual licensed and/or certified by this Board shall release information about a patient or client only upon written authorization by the patient, client, or appropriate legal guardian; pursuant to a proper court order, or as required by applicable state or federal law.

22 T.A.C. § 465.22(d)(3). The board interprets the quoted rule as

3 A subpoena duces tecum issued pursuant to rule 177a of the Texas Rules of Civil Procedure requires a witness to produce documentary evidence.

requiring a psychologist to refuse to honor a subpoena unless it is accompanied by an authorization for release signed by the client or his or her legal guardian.

Because the rules for issuing subpoenas in civil cases[4] are relevant to your question about the effect of subsection 611.006(a)(11) on the board's rule, we will review them before answering it. The Texas Rules of Civil Procedure authorize various forms of discovery, including requests and motions for production, examination, and copying of documents.[5] Rule 176 provides for issuing subpoenas to witnesses in civil suits:

> The clerk of the district or county court, or justice of the peace,[6] as the case may be, at the request of any party to a suit pending in his court, or of any agent or attorney, shall issue a subpoena for any witness or witnesses who may be represented to reside within one hundred miles of the courthouse of the county in which the suit is pending....

A subpoena may also command a witness to produce books, papers, and documents.[7]

A witness summoned in any suit "shall attend the court... until discharged by the court or party summoning such witness."[8] If a witness fails to attend after being summoned, the witness "may be fined by the court as for contempt of court, and an attachment may issue against the body of such witness to compel the attendance of such witness."[9] "Any witness refusing to give evidence may be committed to jail, there to remain without bail until such witness shall consent

---

4   We will not review rules for issuing subpoenas in administrative proceedings under the Administrative Procedure Act, Gov't Code ch. 2001, because discovery in a contested case under that act is governed by the Rules of Civil Procedure. Gov't Code § 2001.091; Attorney General Opinion JM-1075 (1989) at 2. See also Gov't Code § 2001.089 (state agency authorized to issue subpoenas for witnesses and records in contested case).

5   Tex. R. Civ. P. 166b.

6   Section 611.006(11) authorizes a professional to disclose confidential information in "a judicial or administrative proceeding where the court or agency has issued an order or subpoena." (Emphasis added.) You suggest that a "subpoena" within this provision means a subpoena issued only after a review by a court or agency as to whether the person requesting the records has a need for the information that overrides the patient's general right to confidentiality. It appears that you equate "court" with "judge" in reading this statute. Your argument is not consistent with procedures for issuing and contesting subpoenas established in the Rules of Civil Procedure. Moreover, the term "court" does not necessarily mean "judge." It has been defined more broadly, as "an instrumentality of sovereignty, the repository of its judicial power, with authority to adjudge as to the rights of person or property between adversaries." Armadillo Bail Bonds v. State, 772 S.W.2d 193, 195 (Tex. App.--Dallas 1989), aff'd 802 S.W.2d 237 (Tex. Crim. App. 1990). The phrase "court or agency" in section 611.006(a)(11) appears to refer to the legal entity that has jurisdiction of a matter, and not to the individual officers or employees who perform its functions.

7   Tex. R. Civ. P. 177a.

8   Tex. R. Civ. P. 179.

9   Id.

to give evidence."[10] Thus, the rules provide for enforcing a subpoena. They also provide a way for the witness to raise a claim of privilege. Rule 177a allows a witness to move to quash or modify a subpoena that is "unreasonable and oppressive." Rule 166b of the Rules of Civil Procedure authorizes a person from whom discovery is sought to seek a protective order limiting discovery.[11]

Rules of civil procedure are promulgated by the Texas Supreme Court pursuant to article V, section 31(b) of the Texas Constitution, which states in part that "[t]he Supreme Court shall promulgate rules of civil procedure for all courts not inconsistent with the laws of the state...." If a rule of civil procedure conflicts with a statute, the rule must yield.[12] However, we find no conflict between subsection 611.006(a)(11) and rules 176 and 177a. Subsection 611.006(a)(11) in fact makes it clear that a psychologist may comply with a subpoena.[13]

Subsection 611.006(a)(11) does not expressly condition a psychologist's compliance with a subpoena upon a written release signed by the patient or guardian. To read subsection 611.006(a)(11) as requiring a written release would render it superfluous, because subsection 611.006(a)(3) authorizes a psychologist to disclose confidential information about a patient in a judicial or administrative proceeding if a written waiver is provided by the patient or the patient's representative. It is presumed that the legislature intended the entire statute to be effective.[14] Moreover, the overall purpose of Senate Bill 667 was to "define the appropriate disclosure of patient health and mental health care information by hospitals, doctors, and mental health professionals."[15] Its legislative history states that it adopted provisions authorizing " professionals" to disclose mental health records in judicial or administrative proceedings.[16]

---

10 Tex. R. Civ. P. 180.

11 Tex. R. Civ. P. 166b.

12 Tex. Const. art. V, § 31(b); Few v. Charter Oak Fire Ins. Co., 463 S.W.2d 424, 425 (Tex. 1971); Drake v. Muse, Currie & Kohen, 532 S.W.2d 369, 372 (Tex. Civ. App.--Dallas 1975, writ ref'd n.r.e.); C. E. Duke's Wrecker Serv., Inc. v. Oakley, 526 S.W.2d 228, 232 (Tex. Civ. App.--Houston [1st Dist.] 1975, writ ref'd n.r.e.); Attorney General Opinion DM-308 (1994) at 2. See Gov't Code § 22.004(c) (rule adopted by supreme court repeals all conflicting laws and parts of laws governing practice and procedure in civil actions, but substantive law is not repealed).

13 Subsection 611.006(a) states that a professional "may disclose confidential information" in various circumstances, and you suggest that the use of the word "may" means that the psychologist has discretion to comply or not comply with the subpoena, so that he may refuse compliance unless it is accompanied by a written release. We disagree with your argument. The bill analysis to Senate Bill 667 states that section 611.006 "[s]ets forth conditions under which a professional is authorized to disclose confidential information in a judicial or administrative proceeding." House Public Health Committee, Bill Analysis, Tex. S.B. 667, 74th Leg., R.S. (1995) at 3 (emphasis added). Moreover, your suggested construction of section 611.006 ignores the mandatory nature of a subpoena.

14 Gov't Code § 311.021(2).

15 House Research Organization, Bill Analysis, Tex. S.B. 667, 74th Leg., R.S. (1995).

16 Id.; see also House Public Health Committee, Bill Analysis, Tex. S.B. 667, 74th Leg., R.S. (1995) at 1 ("Background" statement cites expense and delay involved in obtaining medical records for a court case). Senate Bill 667 also added to the provisions of article 4495b, V.T.C.S. that authorize a physician to disclose medical

To the extent that an administrative rule is inconsistent with a statute, the rule must yield.[17] This well-established standard is incorporated into the provision defining the board's rule-making power: the board "may make all rules not inconsistent with the Constitution and laws of this state, which are reasonably necessary for the proper performance of its duties...."[18] Rule 465.22(d)(3), as interpreted by the board, is inconsistent with subsection 611.006(a)(11) and is invalid to the extent of the inconsistency. Accordingly, a psychologist's duty to comply with a subpoena for patient records is not contingent on receiving a written waiver from the patient or patient's representative.[19]

You also suggest that section 611.006(a)(11) conflicts with rule 510 of the Texas Rules of Civil Evidence, which establishes the confidentiality of communications between a patient and a mental health professional, subject to exceptions permitting disclosure of such communications in court proceedings.[20] Several of the exceptions in rule 510 are similar to exceptions in section 611.006. For example, disclosure is authorized if the proceedings are brought by the patient against a professional, if the patient or his or her representative signs a waiver, or if the purpose of the proceeding is to collect on a claim for mental or emotional health services rendered to the patient.[21] Rule 510 also provides the following broad exception in court proceedings as to a communication or record relevant to an issue of the physical, mental or emotional condition of a patient in any proceeding in which any party relies upon the condition as a part of the party's claim or defense.[22] [footnote 22]

A psychologist may claim the rule 510 privilege on behalf of the patient, and the authority to do so is presumed in the absence of evidence to

records in court or administrative proceedings. See Act of May 29, 1995, 74th Leg., R.S., ch. 856, § 3, 1995 Tex. Gen. Laws 4290, 4293-94 (codified as V.T.C.S. art. 4495b, § 5.08 (g)(8), (9), (11), (12)).

17 Kelley v. Industrial Accident Board, 358 S.W.2d 874 (Tex. Civ. App.--Austin 1962, writ ref'd); see also Bexar Co. Bail Bond Bd. v. Deckard, 604 S.W.2d 214 (Tex. Civ. App.--San Antonio 1980, no writ).

18 V.T.C.S. art. 4512c, § 8(a).

19 We do not consider whether a psychologist was authorized to disregard a subpoena for patient records in the absence of a written waiver prior to the effective date of section 611.006(a)(11), Health and Safety Code.

20 On November 23, 1982, the Texas Supreme Court entered an order adopting the Texas Rules of Civil Evidence. See Order, 641-642 S.W.2d at XXXV (Sept. 1, 1983). Under this order, former article 5561h, V.T.C.S. (1925), now codified as Health and Safety Code, chapter 611, was deemed repealed with respect to civil actions and replaced by rule 510 of the Texas Rules of Evidence. Wimberly Resorts Property, Inc. v. Pfeuffer, 691 S.W.2d 27, 29 (Tex. App.--Austin 1985, no writ); see List of Repealed Statutes and Enumeration, 641-642 S.W.2d at LXVIII (Sept. 1, 1983); Health & Safety Code § 611.001 historical note (Vernon 1992) [Act of May 7, 1979, 66th Leg., R.S., ch. 239, § 1, 1979 Tex. Gen. Laws 512, 513]. Section 611.006 of the Health and Safety Code relates to a psychologist's authority to disclose otherwise confidential information in an administrative or judicial proceeding and thus appears to reflect provisions of the Rules of Civil Evidence.

21 Tex. R. Civ. Evid. 510(d)(1), (2), (3).

22 Tex. R. Civ. Evid. 510(d)(5).

the contrary.[23] The Rules of Civil Procedure provide methods for a witness to claim that records are privileged and to have the question resolved by the court. If a psychologist believes that he or she has received a subpoena for records that are privileged and not within an exception to rule 510, he or she should avail himself of the protections found in the Rules of Civil Procedure.[24] Thus, section 611.006(a)(11) and rule 510 of the Texas Rules of Civil Evidence may be construed in harmony.[25]

You also ask the following questions about the psychologist's obligation upon receiving a subpoena that is not accompanied by a signed release:

Must the psychologist contact the patient to give the patient the opportunity to file a motion to quash before releasing the records? If the psychologist fails to contact the patient or cannot locate the patient and it is later determined that the records were not subject to being subpoenaed, is the psychologist then liable under [chapter 611 of the] Health and Safety Code[26]... to the patient for releasing the records? Does the psychologist bear the responsibility of hiring an attorney to determine if the records are privileged from being subpoenaed? If the psychologist delays in producing the records while attempting to contact the patient, can the psychologist be sanctioned for the delay?

Section 611.006(11) authorizes a psychologist to provide confidential information in "a judicial or administrative proceeding where the court or agency has issued an order or subpoena." However, as we have already pointed out, a particular subpoena might seek records that are privileged and not within an exception to rule 510. You wish to know what the psychologist's responsibility would be in such a case. We are able to address these questions only in the most general way, by pointing out that courts of various states have found a mental health professional may be liable in tort to a patient for the unauthorized disclosure of confidential patient information,[27] but we have found no case

23 Tex. R. Civ. Evid. 510(c)(2).
24 Attorney General Opinion H-231 (1974).
25 You have asked us to consider the recent decision in Jaffee v. Redmond, 116 S. Ct. 1923 (1996), in which the United States Supreme Court, exercising its authority under Federal Rule of Evidence 501 to define new evidentiary privileges, recognized the existence of a psychotherapist-patient privilege. Jaffee v. Redmond is not relevant to the question before us, because a privilege for psychotherapist-patient communications already exists in Texas, see Rule of Civil Evidence 510, and because Texas courts, unlike federal courts, lack authority to establish new privileges, see Tex. R. Civ. Evid. 501.
26 Section 611.005 of the Health and Safety Code provides that "[a] person aggrieved by the improper disclosure of or failure to disclose confidential... records in violation of this chapter may petition the district court of the county in which the person resides for appropriate relief, including injunctive relief."
27 See generally 24 AM. JUR. Proof of Facts 3d, 123, Proof of Unauthorized Disclosure of Confidential Patient Information by a Psychotherapist (1994); Judy E. Zelin, J.D., Annotation, Physician's Tort Liability for Unauthorized Disclosure of Confidential Information About Patient, 48 A.L.R. 4th 668 (1986). These authorities relate to disclosures of confidential information in a wide variety of circumstances, not limited to disclosures in judicial proceedings.

addressing the psychologist's duty at the point of receiving a *subpoena duces tecum* for patient records that may or may not be privileged from disclosure in a judicial proceeding. Moreover, the question of liability must be decided on the basis of the relevant facts and circumstances of each case. Although it may be advisable for a psychologist to notify a patient that his records have been subpoenaed, we cannot determine that the action would be either necessary or sufficient to protect the psychologist from liability to the patient should privileged information from the patient's records be disclosed. We believe that the individual psychologist should consult a private attorney if such issues arise in connection with his or her practice.

SUMMARY

A psychologist is authorized to disclose confidential information about a patient in a judicial or administrative proceeding where the court or agency has issued an order or subpoena without receiving a written waiver of confidentiality from the patient or patient's representative. A rule of the Board of Examiners of Psychologists interpreted by the board as requiring such a waiver is invalid to the extent of inconsistency with the exception to the confidentiality requirement found in section 611.006(a)(11) of the Health and Safety Code. If a psychologist has received a subpoena for patient mental health records he or she believes are privileged by rule 510 of the Rules of Evidence, he or she may raise the claim of privilege under applicable provisions of the Rules of Civil Procedure. Although it may be advisable for a psychologist to notify a patient that his records have been subpoenaed, we cannot determine that the action would be either necessary or sufficient to protect the psychologist from liability in tort in the event that the patient's privileged mental health information is disclosed in a judicial proceeding.

Yours very truly,

Susan L. Garrison
Assistant Attorney General
Opinion Committee

Disclosure of Patient-Child Information

OFFICE OF THE ATTORNEY GENERAL

STATE OF TEXAS

DAN MORALES   August 20, 1992
ATTORNEY GENERAL

Ms. Patricia S. Tweedy, M.P.A.   Letter Opinion No. 92-039
Executive Director
Texas State Board of Examiners of   Re: Whether privileged information
    Psychologists   relevant to the parent-child
9101 Burnet Road, Suite 212   relationship that a psychologist
Austin, Texas 78758   gained during a voluntary
                                        psychological evaluation of a
                                        person involved in, or associated
                                        with, court proceedings involving
                                        the parent-child relationship are
                                        excepted from disclosure under
                                        Texas Rule of Civil Evidence
                                        510(d)(6) (RQ-349)

Dear Ms. Tweedy:

You have requested an opinion concerning rule 510(d)(6) of the Texas Rules of Civil Evidence. To place your question in context, you state that the Texas State Board of Examiners of Psychologists has pending before it a complaint involving a professional's alleged disclosure of privileged mental health information in a court proceeding involving "the parent-child relationship." The complainant, a non-party to the judicial proceedings but the step-mother of the children in question, voluntarily submitted to a psychological evaluation for purposes related to a child custody dispute. Pursuant to a court order, the evaluating psychologist subsequently submitted to the court a written report on her evaluation of the complainant. The complainant alleges that the evaluating psychologist, who is licensed as a psychologist in the State of Texas pursuant to V.T.C.S. article 4512c, disclosed privileged information in the proceedings without her consent. See TEX. R. CIV. EVID. 509(e).

Rule 510 pertains to the confidentiality of communication between a patient[1] and a professional[2] such as a medical physician. The general rule of privilege articulated in rule 510 states that communication between a patient and a professional is confidential as between the two parties and may not be disclosed to any third persons other than those present to further the interest of the patient in the diagnosis, examination, or treatment of the patient. Id. 510(a)(4), (b)(1). Records pertaining to the "identity, diagnosis, evaluation, or treatment of a patient" are confidential. Id. 510(b)(2). Section 510(d) lists several exceptions to the general rule of privilege. You ask specifically about the exception provided in rule 510(d)(6):

> *Exceptions to the privilege in court proceedings exist when the disclosure is relevant in any suit affecting the parent-child relationship.*

The Rules of Civil Evidence provide that the court shall determine the admissibility of evidence. See id. 104; see also id. 103. This office will not issue an opinion that is in effect an appeal of a judicial decision. Attorney General Opinions JM-287 (1984); H-905 (1976); O-1874 (1940).

Accordingly, we cannot answer your question.

SUMMARY

> *Pursuant to Texas Rule of Civil Evidence 510(d)(6), a licensed psychologist may disclose privileged information if the information is relevant in any suit affecting the parent-child relationship. The Opinion Committee will not issue an opinion that effectively overrules a judicial decision.*

Yours very truly,

Kymberly K. Oltrogge
Assistant Attorney General
Opinion Committee

---

1 Rule 510(a)(2) defines "patient" as any person who (A) consults, or is interviewed by, a professional for purposes of diagnosis, evaluation, or treatment of any mental or emotional condition or disorder, including alcoholism and drug addiction; or (B) is being treated voluntarily or being examined for admission to voluntary treatment for drug abuse

2 .Rule 510(a)(1) defines "professional" as any person (A) authorized to practice medicine in any state or nation; or (B) licensed or certified by the State of Texas in the diagnosis, evaluation or treatment of any mental or emotional disorder; or (C) involved in the treatment or examination of drub abusers; or (D) reasonably believed by the patient to be included in any of the preceding categories.

Public Access to Psychologists' Licensing Files

OFFICE OF THE ATTORNEY GENERAL

STATE OF TEXAS

MARK WHITE

ATTORNEY GENERAL

November 30, 1981

Ms. Patti Bizzell
Texas State Board of Examiners of
Psychologists
5555 N. Lamar, Suite H-126
Austin, Texas 78751

Open Records Decision No. 290
(ORD-290)

Re: Access under Open Records Act to
psychologists' licensing files

Dear Ms. Bizzell:

You have requested our decision under the Open Records Act, article 6252-17a, V.T.C.S., as to whether complaints, charges and actions taken in disciplinary hearings involving licensees of the Texas State Board of Examiners of Psychologists are available to the public. Section 23 of article 4512c, V.T.C.S., provides:

Sec. 23. (a)The Texas State Board of Examiners of Psychologists shall have the right to cancel, revoke, suspend, or refuse to renew the license or certification of any psychologist... upon proof that the psychologist:

(1)has been convicted of a felony or of a violation of the law involving moral turpitude by any court; the conviction of a felony shall be the conviction of any offense which if committed within this state would constitute a felony under the laws of this state; or

(2)used drugs or intoxicating liquors to an extent that affects his professional competency; or

(3)has been guilty of fraud or deceit in connection with his services rendered as a psychologist; or

(4)has aided or abetted a person, not a licensed psychologist, in representing himself as a psychologist within this state; or

(5)has been guilty of unprofessional conduct as defined by the rules established by the Board; or

(6)for any cause for which the Board shall be authorized to take that action by another section of this Act.

....

(e) The Board shall have the right and may, upon majority vote, rule that the order revoking, canceling, or suspending the psychologists' license or certification be probated so long as the probationer conforms to such orders and rules as the Board may set out as the terms of probation. The Board, at the time of probation, shall set out the period of time which shall constitute the probationary period. Provided further, that the Board may at any time while the probationer remains on probation hold a hearing, and upon majority vote, rescind the probation and enforce the Board's original action in revoking, canceling, or suspending the psychologists' license or certification, the said hearing to rescind the probation shall be called by the Chairman of the Texas State Board of Examiners of Psychologists who shall cause to be issued a notice setting a time and place for the hearing and containing the charges or complaints against the probationer, said notice to be served on the probationer or his counsel at least ten (10) days prior to the time set for the hearing. When personal service is impossible, or cannot be effected, the same provisions for service in lieu of personal service as heretofore set out in this Act shall apply. At said hearing the respondent shall have the right to appear either personally or by counsel or both, to produce witnesses or evidence in his behalf, to cross-examine witnesses, and to have subpoenas issued by the Board. The Board shall thereupon determine the charges upon their merits. *All charges, complaints, notices, orders, records, and publications authorized or required by the terms of this Act shall be privileged.* The order revoking or rescinding the probation shall not be subject to review or appeal. (Acts 1981, 67th Leg., ch. 766, at 2856-57.)

You have received requests for information regarding disciplinary proceedings affecting several licensees of the board. The requestors seek disclosure of the charges filed, the board's decision in the matter, and the present status of the licensee.

Section 3(a)(1) of the Open Records Act excepts from disclosure *information deemed confidential by law, either Constitutional, statutory, or by judicial decision.*

The following statement in article 4512c, section 23(e) would seem to create a category of "information deemed confidential by [statutory] law": *"All charges, complaints, notices, orders, records, and publications authorized or required by the terms of this Act shall be privileged."* The usual meaning of "privileged" is "confidential." Black's Law Dictionary 270 (5th ed. 1979). The term refers to communications which are, as a matter of public policy, excepted from disclosure. *Communist Party of the United States v. Subversive Activities*

Control Board, 254 F.2d 314, 321 (D.C. Cir. 1958). For reasons that will become apparent, however, we must conclude that, for purposes of section 23, "privileged" is not tantamount to "confidential."

In literal terms, the declaration of section 23 is applicable to charges, complaints, notices, orders, records and publications "authorized or required *by the terms of this Act.*" (Emphasis added). Thus, it would prohibit disclosure of the roster of licensed psychologists which the board is required to publish annually and which section 18 of the act specifically deems public information. It would except from disclosure the "standards for qualification" of sub-doctoral personnel which section 19 directs the board to set. It would even make confidential the board's annual report required by section 10.

Because of these absurd results, we believe it is clear that the declaration of section 23 was not intended to prohibit disclosure of all board records. It might be argued that, since the declaration appears in section 23, which is concerned exclusively with disciplinary proceedings, its effect should be limited to records which relate to such proceedings. Even if so restricted, however, the declaration conflicts both with specific portions of section 23 and with other law.

Although the declaration deems "notices" to be "privileged," section 23 itself provides that "[p]roceedings for the refusal, suspension, or revocation of a license or certificate or for the reprimand of a person are governed by the Administrative Procedure and Texas Register Act," article 6252-13a, V.T.C.S., as is every "appeal of an action of the Board." "Judicial review of an action of the Board shall be conducted under the substantial evidence rule," with the result that the entire record considered by the court will become public. V.T.C.S. art. 4512c, §23(c), (d). Furthermore, the Open Meetings Act, article 6252-17, V.T.C.S., is applicable to the original disciplinary proceedings before the board. V.T.C.S. art. 6252-17, §2(a). It has frequently been said that the Open Records Act should be construed in harmony with the Open Meetings Act. Attorney General Opinion H-484 (1974); Open Records Decision Nos. 159 (1977); 68 (1975). Thus, to construe "privileged" in section 23 to mean "confidential" would result in conflicts within section 23 and between section 23 and other statutes. We must conclude that, whatever the legislature intended the term "privileged" to mean, it did not intend that it should be construed to mean "confidential." We note that "privileged" has been used in Texas to refer to those communications which require proof of malice in a libel action. *International & Great Northern Railroad Company v. Edmundson*, 222 S.W. 181, 183-84 (Tex. Comm'n App. 1920).

Thus, although complaints, charges and actions taken in disciplinary hearings involving board licensees are not excepted from disclosure as "information deemed confidential by [statutory] law," some of the information contained in the files you have submitted to us is excepted as "information deemed confidential by [judicial decision]." V.T.C.S. art. 6252-17a, §3(a)(1). Previous open records decisions have recognized that particular material in a licensing file may be excepted from disclosure by a constitutional or common law right of privacy. Open Records Decision Nos. 215 (1978); 157 (1977). *See Industrial Foundation of the South v. Texas Industrial Accident Board*, 540 S.W.2d 668, 685-87 (Tex. 1976). After examining the files you have submitted to us, it is our opinion that only the following material is excepted from disclosure by a constitutional or common law right of privacy: a portion of the statement of complainant from file number two and the affidavits of the two complainants from file number four. With these exceptions, none of the information in these files is excepted from disclosure under section 3(a)(1).

Very truly yours,

Mark White
Attorney General of Texas

John W. Fainter, JR.
First Assistant Attorney General

Richard E. Gray III
Executive Assistant Attorney General

Prepared by Rick Gilpin
Assistant Attorney General

OPINIONS
FROM THE
TSBEP

Synopses of TSBEP Opinion Letters

Texas State Board of Examiners of Psychologists

This section contains paraphrased excerpts of letters received and answered by the Texas State Board of Examiners of Psychologists (TSBEP) since the publication of the last edition of this book. The portions of the letters contained herein represent material of general interest to psychology licensees, and are thus provided here for reader review. The material has been abbreviated to allow the reader to receive the essential material in executive summary format. The letters and responses may be viewed in their entirety in the Board's Opinion Letter File, available under the Public Information Act. The number code following each question references the date of the opinion letter in the Board's file. Readers are cautioned that responses may be invalidated by later changes in Board rules or policies. Additionally, as part of its record retention policy, the Board does not rely on opinions that are more than 3 years old and destroys opinion letters after 5 years. Since the responses below refer to specific facts outlined in the original letters, readers are advised not to assume the same answers would apply to their own case, which may have a different set of facts. Licensees who wish to enquire about their own situation may write to the Board and request an opinion. The excerpts contained in this section have not been approved or endorsed by the Board and should be used for general guidance only. Reliance on these excerpts is not a defense or bar to any investigation by the Board concerning a violation of the Act or Rules of the Board.

Use of Titles

..IN EXEMPT AGENCIES

Q. What title may I use as an employee of an exempt facility? (F803)

A. As an employee of MHMRA, which is an exempt facility, you are exempt from the Act and Board rules and you may use whatever title that agency assigns you to use. However, this is not to say that because of this exemption you could then use this title to provide services to the public outside of your MHMRA employment

...FOR SPECIALTY SERVICES

Q. I offer forensic services. May I use that specialty title? (F803)

A. You don't meet the requirements of Board rule 465.6(d) that would allow you to use the specialty title of forensic psychologist because the cut-off for the degree was 1977 and relevant coursework is required. The Board would suggest that with your background, you should pursue specialization status from an organization which bestows this kind of title. According to the Board rule you could then use that title, as long as you include the name of the organization as well.

...BY RETIREES

Q. What title do I use if I retire or go "inactive" with my license? (P601)

A. In accordance with Texas law a licensee who is either on inactive status or retirement status may not legally provide psychological services with that license. A person who is on inactive status should refer to himself as a licensed psychologist who is on inactive status. A person who is retired may wish to refer to himself as a formerly licensed psychologist who is now retired. Persons who are on inactive status or who are retired should not have business cards that identify them as licensed Psychologists. Cards for some other type of business or stationery should not reflect the person as a licensed psychologist but simply as a Ph.D. or Ph.D. in Psychology. Here, again, the goal is to protect the public from any misrepresentation of the person's credentials to provide psychological services.

EXEMPT AGENCIES

...AND PERMITTED PRACTICES

Q. At our university practicum center may we test people from outside the university? (C801)

A. The Psychologists' Licensing Act does not apply to "...the activity or service of a person, or the use of an official title by the person, who is employed as a psychologist or psychological associate by a governmental agency or regionally accredited institution of higher education if the person performs duties the person is employed by the agency or institution to perform within the confines of the agency or institution." Therefore, this section of the Psychologists' Licensing Act provides an exemption for persons who are psychologists or who are providing psychological services in an exempt facility. The determination of what activities you are employed to perform rests with the exempt facility and its policies. Your questions should be addressed by the university.

...AND LICENSURE REQUIREMENTS FOR UNIVERSITY PRACTICUM SUPERVISORS

Q. Do I need to be licensed to supervise a university practicum course in which students evaluate patients? (H504)

A. Because your supervision of the students in the evaluation of a patient is part of a course that you are teaching at a regionally accredited institution of higher education, the exemption in the Psychologists' Licensing Act would apply to you. While Board rules require that students seeking to fulfill internship requirements be supervised by a licensee of this Board, there is no specific rule that requires practicum courses to be supervised by a licensee. However, please be aware that the Board would always encourage institutions of higher education to have any psychological services that are provided to the public through a counseling center or other means to be supervised by a licensee of this Board. Also, if you provide such services and are not licensed, informed consent to the patients should make this status clear......and exemption from complaints.

Q. May a complaint against me be filed with TSBEP if I work in an exempt agency? (L402)

A. Attorney General Opinion JC-321 advances the proposition that so long as an employee of an exempt facility is performing services within their "scope of employment," the Board does not have the authority to pursue a complaint filed against the employee for such services. However, there may be activities done by the employee that could fall outside of their scope of employment. Therefore, the Board will continue to investigate complaints received and make such determinations on a case-by-case basis.

TEST DATA

..AND RELEASE OF SCALED SCORES

Q. What constitutes "raw data" and is it appropriate to release scaled scores from standardized tests? (W102)

A. On June 3, 1999, the Board adopted Rule 465.1 Definitions. In this rule, test data is defined as follows: (14) "Test data" refers to testing materials, test booklets, test forms, test protocols and answer sheets used in psychological testing to generate test results and test reports. Throughout the Board rules, the phrase "raw data" is not used, but rather "test data." With respect to scaled scores, Board rule 465.22 (c)(4) states: "Test data are not part of a patient's or client's record. Test data are not subject to subpoena. Test data shall be made available only to another qualified mental health professional and only upon receipt of written release from the patient or client or pursuant to a court order."

...AND RELEASE OF PROJECTIVE RESPONSES

Q. Is a sentence completion form a test? I believe parents are entitled to a copy of the sentence completion form containing their child's answers. (S505)

A. Board rule 465.5(b), Practice of Psychology, includes examples of the activities that, when performed by a licensee, are subject to Board rules: (1) conducting or administering testing that requires the use of psychological education, training, knowledge, or skills; (3) projective techniques, including, but not limited to, Rorschach, Thematic Apperception Test, Roberts Apperception Test, Sentence Completion tests and Holtzman Ink Blot. The Board, then, clearly considers Sentence Completion Series a test. There are copyrighted parts of the Sentence Completion Test forms that are "test data." They should not be released to parents. However, the parent is entitled to the test results and to the report that the licensee produces as result of the test.

" EXTENDERS" OF PSYCHOLOGICAL SERVICES

....AND TESTING PERMITTED

Q. Which types of tests may be administered by unlicensed assistants? (R204)

A. Board rules 465.3, 465.4, and 465.5 are the rules to which your inquiry most relates. In accordance with these rules unlicensed persons under the supervision of a licensed psychologist may administer, proctor and score non-projective tests provided that the duties do not require psychological education or involve the provision of psychological services. The Board has never identified tests that may and may not be administered by non-licensed persons. No list could be all-inclusive and the Board cannot maintain such a list in rule form. However, the Board can clarify for you what it considers to be the kinds of non-projective tests that require a psychological education. Tests that do not require a psychological education would include those that do not require any kind of independent, professional judgment. This is to say, that if part of the test requires monitoring/recording the client's reactions and body language in a subjective manner during the test, i.e., and therefore not mechanical or electronic recording, the test should not be administered by a non-licensed person. In other cases, the non-licensee could be trained by the psychologist in the administration of the testing and grading of the test. Those tests that require a certain kind of setting to be maintained for the administration of the test would probably best be administered by a licensed professional. However, it is conceivable that the licensee could have a specific testing area that always maintains the appropriate setting, for example free from extraneous noise, well lighted, etc. An unlicensed administrator could then only have to monitor this setting and identify any irregularities in the environment that occur during testing.

...FROM OUT-OF-STATE

Q. May an individual completing requirements for licensure in another state provide psychological services under the supervision of a licensed psychologist in Texas? (N1103)

A. In accordance with Texas law, an unlicensed person in this state can only provide the services as set forth in Board rule 465.4, Employment of Individuals Not Licensed by This Board. However, if you will be working in an exempt setting you are not bound by the rules. The only other way that you could provide the services that you indicate would be to enroll in an internship program or a practicum course at a regionally accredited institution of higher education that would require you to provide these services and would monitor the provision of such services.

...WHO ARE EDUCATIONAL DIAGNOSTICIANS

Q. May I hire an Educational Diagnostician to give intelligence and academic achievement tests which will be included in my broader psychological report? (Y602)

A. Educational Diagnosticians are credentialed to provide services in the public schools of Texas. It is not clear from your inquiry if you are providing services to a public school through a contract. If so, it would be permissible to use tests conducted by the Educational Diagnosticians of that school in fulfilling your contract to provide psychological services in the public schools. However, if you are asking if an Educational Diagnostician can conduct the tests you indicate for use in your private practice, you would need to comply with Board rule 465.4. The Educational Diagnostician would be considered the same as an unlicensed individual in this rule since that credential is only appropriate for the school setting. Therefore, according to this rule, the person could only perform services that do not require psychological education or involve the provision of psychological services.

...WHO ARE LPCS OR LMFTS

Q. May I hire an LPC or an LMFT to provide counseling in my private psychology practice? (S602)

A. In accordance with Board rule 465.4(a) psychologists may employ or utilize individuals who are licensees of another profession to provide only activities or services permitted by the applicable licenses. This rule also requires that the services and activities may not be described or represented to the patient or client as psychological services and the licensee must be clearly identified to the patient or client as a licensee of the applicable profession who is providing services pursuant to that individual's own license. Therefore, psychologists are permitted to use the services of other licensees, provided that this rule is followed.

PROVIDING SERVICES OUTSIDE LICENSURE

...SUCH AS COACHING

Q. I would like to begin an independent "coaching" practice, not using either of my LSSP or LPA licenses. I would be interviewing normal functioning clients and providing structure, support, and feedback to them in order to facilitate the attainment of their goals. (S505)

A. You indicate that in your provision of coaching services, you would not mention your licenses. This would be required in order not to misrepresent yourself to the public. Additionally, it would be a conflict of interest to provide coaching services to students in your school district that you also serve as an LSSP or to those patients that you might also see under the auspices of your LPA license. The Board suggests that you carefully read the section of the Psychologists' Licensing Act that defines the practice of psychology in your efforts to ascertain the legality of your providing what you define as coaching to the general public without the use of your licenses. Please understand that the Board cannot give you approval or clearance in your endeavors. Regardless of the services that you provide to the public, if a complaint were to be filed against you while you are still licensed with this Board, the Board would investigate the complaint to determine if you were in violation of the Act and rules.

...SUCH AS TRAINING MINISTERS

Q. I have been asked to train selected members of my church to become Stephen Ministers (Christian care ministers), offering caring involvement to shut-ins or other church members going through personal crises. The ministers would refer individuals with more severe mental health problems to an appropriate professional. Would the Board consider my activities to be providing services as a psychologist? (M802)

A. The Board's primary concern is protection of the public. Part of this protection regards misrepresentation to the public. If you embark upon Stephen Ministries, it would be important for you not to misrepresent your participation as part of your provision of psychological services under your license as a psychologist. There is also the issue of dual relationship. Ideally, persons to whom you provide services as a Stephen Minister should not be patients to whom you provide psychological services since this could constitute an unethical dual relationship. Further, those ministers that you supervise would be supervised through your credential as a ministries trainer, not as supervisees under your license as a psychologist. It is unclear if Stephen Ministries would fall under the exemption to the Psychologists' Licensing Act, Section 501.004(a)(4) for clergy or under (5) concerning voluntary activity for a charitable nonprofit organization. Both of these exemptions are dependent on the person not referring to himself as a psychologist or the services as psychological.

...SUCH AS OPERATING A MH CONTRACTING BUSINESS

Q. *May an LSSP operate a business that provides a range of assessment services to Texas public schools? Specifically: (1) May our business contract with the schools to provide assessment services by LSSPs in our employment? (2) May our business hire other professionals such as Speech Pathologists or Educational Diagnosticians to provide services for private schools, making it clear that these are not psychological services? (3) May a person who is both an LSSP and an Educational Diagnostician offer IQ and achievement assessment in a non-public school if that person identifies himself only as an Educational Diagnostician? (H205)*

A. Unfortunately, the Board cannot definitively respond to most of your questions. Laws and rules regarding the establishment of businesses should be accessed through the Secretary of State's Office. As you know, this Board does not regulate hospitals or businesses that provide psychological services, but rather only persons who are licensed to provide psychological services. Any violations of the Board rules by licensees of this Board would be subject to disciplinary action by the Board. If it is your business to hire other professionals, again you would need to present the services that your business provides in such a way that this Board's rules and other boards' rules are adhered to by your employees who are licensees of those boards.

Please remember that psychological services can only be provided by licensees of this Board or persons fulfilling the requirements of internships or practicums in order to be licensed by this Board. Anyone else that provides psychological services is in violation of the Act and will be investigated by the Board. As you are aware, an LSSP is a license that can only be used in the public schools. Psychological services in the public schools can only be provided by LSSP's, LSSP interns, and doctoral level psychologist interns. Specifically, Board rule 465.38 states that the assessment of emotional or behavioral disturbance, for educational purposes, using psychological techniques and procedures is considered the practice of psychology.

This letter is for guidance purposes only. It cannot be used as immunity if a complaint is brought against you.

OFFICE PRACTICES

...AND DETERMINING WHO IS THE CLIENT

Q. When I do forensic evaluations, who is the "client" from whom I should seek informed consent? (R601) (C402)

A. TSBEP defines patient or client as "a person who consults with or is interviewed by a licensee for a diagnosis, evaluation, or treatment of any mental emotional condition or disorder... regardless of whether the patient or some other individual or entity paid for the consultation or interview" (Rule 465.1(7)). A psychologist may have a contractual arrangement with an attorney, court, or state agency, but the "client" remains the person to whom the psychologist is providing services. Of course, the forensic evaluator has additional duties outside of the patient-therapist relationship that are spelled out in Rule 465.18. These duties, which may impinge on confidentiality, record keeping, or other ethical rules, need to be provided to the client through informed consent. Those persons whom you evaluate are considered your clients pursuant to the Board's definition of "client." The court or probation department may employ you and may be the end-user of the information, but the client is the person to whom psychological services are given. That being said, you may be in a situation where informed consent is effectively precluded by court order, i.e. the psychological services are provided to the client with or without his or her consent based on the legal or clinical context presented. Therefore, you should follow the dictates of Board Rule 465.11(h) and describe the nature of your services and the obvious limits on confidentiality in the situation.

...AND RECORDS

Q. I would like to propose that TSBEP amend their rule about record retention so that practitioners could give records directly to the patient or get the patient's permission to destroy the records. (C204)

A. Current Board rule 465.22(d) requires that records be maintained for 10 years after the last contact with the patient unless the patient is a minor in which case the records should be kept until 10 years after the age of majority. As currently written, this rule is mandatory. By simply giving the records to the patients there are several difficulties that might arise. You could become the receiver of a lawsuit for psychological services that you provided and yet you would no longer have the documentation to counter the lawsuit. The same situation would ensue if a complaint was filed against you with the Psychology Board and you had no records of the patient. If the Complainant had some proof that you did indeed provide services but you had no records, then the Board could take action against your license. There is also the problem of test data, i.e. exam protocols and exam materials, which are not part of a patient's records but which cannot be released to the patient by Board rule 465.22 (c).

Therefore, it would be another direct violation of Board rules to release this type of information to the patient. Under no situation should test data be released to a patient as this could compromise the validity of the tests themselves. The purpose of retaining patient records, as stated in Board rule 465.22 is to provide continuity of care to the patient, should they seek psychological services in the near future. While the Board sympathizes with the bulk of records that may accumulate in a lengthy practice, it would point out that licensees are free to keep records in electronic format or on microfilm, so that the storage required is significantly reduced.

...OUT OF ONE'S HOME

Q. Is it possible to have a psychology practice out of one's private home? (K504)

A. There's no rule that prohibits a home office; however, caution should be taken because there is the possibility that clients might fail to distinguish professional services from the private, personal life of the provider leading to the appearance of an unethical dual relationship.

...IN ACCOMMODATING DISABLED CLIENTS

Q. In accepting a potential client with disabilities, to what extent is a psychologist obligated, by law or otherwise, to provide accommodations such as an interpreter or special equipment? And who pays for these accommodations? (H505)

A. Many of the issues about which you inquire concern the Americans with Disabilities Act (ADA), a federal law. This Board is not the best source of information regarding disability issues of this sort. Also, you may want to consult an attorney who specializes in ADA issues. However, the Board would offer you the following information: Board rule 465.9(a) and (b) require that licensees provide only services for which they have the education, skills, and training to perform competently. Additionally, competency includes the ability to provide services concerning an individual that takes into account characteristics of that individual, including age, gender, ethnicity, national origin, disability, language, and socio-economic status. Therefore, a licensee must take the disability of a client into account to determine if the licensee can provide competent services. A psychologist must not provide services to anyone if he or she believes that his training or experience is insufficient to provide competent psychological services. Referral to another practitioner who is better qualified to provide services is the best course of action. Generally, the preference of the client should be adhered to and an interpreter be utilized if requested. Ultimately, if the client does not want an interpreter, and if the psychologist does not believe that adequate and competent services can be provided without an interpreter, then the psychologist should refuse to provide services. The billing issue for an interpreter is one that the psychologist must discuss with the client and include in informed consent.

Some agreement must be reached as to who will reimburse the interpreter and at what acceptable rate. For specific assistance, the Board would refer you to this website: *www.dars.state.tx.us* (Department of Assistive and Rehabilitative Services and the Office of Deaf and Hard of Hearing Services). Here you will find information about how to secure an interpreter and the rates that the different certification levels require.

...IN SELLING A PRACTICE

Q. As attorneys, we are requesting a formal opinion regarding to whom a psychologist can sell his practice? The psychologist employs different mental health professionals who practice under their respective boards' rules. (S503)

A. In general, a psychologist may sell a practice to any potential buyer. The disposition of practice rule says "a licensee has the right to sell his practice to another licensed psychologist;" however, there is not a negative implication that psychologists are the only class of potential buyers to whom a practice could be sold. Please note that the disposition of practice rule must be read in connection with the Board rule concerning termination (465.21). In another words, the transfer of the patients themselves must be to another qualified mental health professional that could, theoretically, treat the patient safely and competently.

With that in mind, here are the concerns that accompany the different scenarios in your letter: (1) A psychologist licensed in another state could buy the practice, but could not advertise himself, nor could he provide any services in Texas. If he were provisionally licensed in Texas, he could not engage in independent practice, but would have to operate under the supervision of a licensed Texas psychologist. (2) An LPA could theoretically own a practice; however, LPA's cannot independently practice. (3) MD's, LMSW-ACP's, LPC's or a combination of such licensed mental health professionals may own practices and may independently practice their own professions. Patients (in compliance with Rule 465.21) could be transferred to these individuals, assuming that the types of patients were within the scope of practice of the various professions. (4) Sale to a professional corporation is fine, especially if the person to whom the patients are referred is the psychologist within the professional corporation. If not, then see the answer to (3).

The Board does not license professional corporations, so it would depend on the individual to whom the patients are initially referred. In short, the disposition of practice rule cannot be read in isolation. The psychologist selling the practice will necessarily be terminating patients, so the real considerations come in Rule 465.21 (reasonable steps to facilitate transfer of responsibility to a qualified service provider, appropriate pre-termination counseling and referrals, etc.)

SUPERVISION

...OF THE FORMAL YEAR OF EXPERIENCE FOR LICENSURE AS A
PSYCHOLOGIST

Q. I have questions about doctoral level supervised experience. (1)
May a clinical psychologist supervise a counseling psychology intern? (2) May
the requirement for two full-time equivalent interns be met by individuals at
different training levels? (3) Must the internship site be APA approved? (F802)

A. (1) The Board accepts documentation of experience by a supervisor
trained in clinical psychology with appropriate training and experience supervising
an applicant in counseling psychology and vice versa. (2) The requirement that
there be a minimum of two full-time equivalent interns at the internship level
of training during the training period was enacted in accordance with national
standards for psychology internships and to fulfill the requirement that at least
one year of supervised experience be a formal internship or the equivalent
thereof as opposed to the other year of experience in which the supervision
requirements are more loosely defined. Although Board rules do not require that
both interns be at the same level of training (i.e., one intern could be doctoral
level while the second intern is master's level), all interns must be graduate level
psychology interns in order to meet the requirements of Board rules. (3) The
Board does not require either the academic institution or the internship to be
approved by the American Psychological Association.

...OF THE FORMAL YEAR OF PSYCHOLOGY EXPERIENCE IN A "VIRTUAL"
INSTITUTE

Q. We would like to create a formal psychology internship experience
for a practicing LMFT at our MH institute. While our institute has physical
facilities, to some degree, it is a "virtual" institute, consisting of any location
where our institute faculty practice. (1) May we augment this individual's MFT
practice with supervision and training experiences in psychology to meet the
Board requirements? (2) May we count the time she spends seeing patients at
her private office? (B601)

A. While the Board cannot pre-evaluate requirements in the absence
of a formal application pending before the Board, we will attempt to address
your questions in the order in which they appear in your letter. (1) The Board
is concerned with your concept of "augmenting" the practice of a marriage and
family counselor with an internship in psychology. If your plan is to supervise her
LMFT private practice and consider her activities and services "psychological,"
please be aware that this is not legal. Services delivered or billed under her MFT
license are MFT services and may not be called "psychological."

Therefore, such an arrangement would not meet Board rules. If your plan
was to supplement her LMFT practice with separate psychological activities and

services, please be aware that any clients she sees must belong to the supervising psychologist. It would be confusing to the intern's current clients if you planned to have them suddenly become the patients of a supervising psychologist. While marriage and family therapy is considered a part of psychological services, please note that Board rule 463.11 requires that the internship must constitute an organized training program that is designed to provide the intern with a planned, programmed, sequence of training experiences. Also, the primary focus and purpose of the program must be to assure breadth and quality of training. (2) There may be no more than two placement sites for the intern, thus a multi-site "virtual institute" does not appear to meet this requirement. In the situation you describe, you would need two or more full-time psychologists on staff who serve as primary supervisors at the private practice.

By on staff, these psychologists must be employed full-time by the private practice. Also, one staff licensed psychologist must be actively licensed in the jurisdiction where the internship takes place during the internship period. This staff licensed psychologist is responsible for the integrity and quality of the training program and must be present at the training site for at least 20 hours per week. At a private practice internship it is assumed that the primary supervisors will be the licensed psychologists whose private practice is being used as the training site.

The plan you have suggested does not appear to meet requirements of Board rule 463.11(2). The Board would advise you to be cautious in going forward with this internship and perhaps to talk with formal internship programs at universities to understand the types of internships that readily meet the Board's requirements. If you have not already done so, you may wish to obtain an application packet for provisional licensure as a psychologist and an application packet for licensure as a psychologist from the Board. Each is available for a fee of $15 and a written request to the Board office. These forms allow you and the applicant to know exactly the questions that are asked of supervisors and applicants for these types of licensure.

...WHEN PAID FOR BY THE SUPERVISEE

Q. May I pay for a psychologist to provide additional supervision since my pre-doctoral internship site has only one licensed psychologist? (R503)

A. Although there is no rule prohibiting your paying a psychologist to provide supervision for you it is not advised due to the high potential for an unethical dual relationship. The Board does not favor such an arrangement primarily because of the threat to the supervisor's objectivity. Board rule §463.11 requires the internship agency to have a minimum of two full-time licensed psychologists on the staff as primary supervisors.

...*AND DOCUMENTATION OF THE FORMAL YEAR OF EXPERIENCE*

Q. Does the Board require university transcript documentation of supervised clinical internships? (A1102).

A. Board rules allow the formal year of supervised experience to be completed pre-doctorally or post-doctorally. Also, Board rules do not specifically require that the formal year be through a university although that is usually a requirement for a doctoral degree. Therefore, there is no requirement that the doctoral transcript include documentation of the formal internship. While the Director of Internship Training in the rules usually refers to a university professor, the rules do not specifically require this. Therefore, a formal internship completed outside of a university would have a Director of Internship Training who would have to attest that the various specifics of the formal internship meet Board rules.

...*AND REQUIREMENTS FOR THE INFORMAL YEAR OF EXPERIENCE*

Q. I have questions about the post-doctoral internship. (1) When can I begin counting hours toward the post-doctorate? (2) What professional activities are required? Are research activities acceptable? (3) Must the site have a formal post-doctoral training program? (L602) (B803)

A. (1) The official transcript must state the date the psychology degree was awarded or conferred. Therefore, the Board goes by the date that is provided on the transcript, regardless of whether the date indicates conferral or award. Most transcripts have only one date. If a transcript has two dates, one for conferral and one for award, the Board will accept the earlier date for the purposes of meeting this rule requirement. This in turn means that you cannot start your post-doctoral year until after the date on your transcript.

(2) Any provision of psychological services, regardless of the specialty area, could be used to satisfy the requirements for the post-doctoral year of supervised experience, provided that it adheres to other applicable Board rules. The post-doctoral year does not require that services be provided directly to patients. The Board considers research a type of psychological service that could be provided during this year. Research activity and teaching are not precluded as supervised experiences. However, if, as you say, private practice is your goal, it would be better to use your post-doctoral year to further enhance your training in the area in which you intend to be most competent. The two years of supervised experience is a graduated step from formal coursework to complete independent practice and, therefore, should be obtained in an area and setting that will be of most benefit to the intern. This in turn protects the public.

(3) You have completed your formal year of supervised experience. Your post-doctoral year requires that the supervising psychologist has agreed to adhere to the Board's supervisory requirements.

...OF A PSYCHOLOGY POST-DOCTORATE IN HER LPC PRACTICE

Q. I'm an LPC working for a United Way Agency that has hired a firm to supervise my post-doctoral psychology internship. Is this acceptable? (G702)

A. Please be advised that we cannot pre-evaluate qualifications for licensure in the absence of a formal application pending before the Board. However, the following may provide useful information. In the situation for supervision presented in your letter there are several areas of concern. It appears as if you are practicing independently using your license as a professional counselor and that you wish to use your LPC practice to meet the requirements for licensure as a psychologist.

In considering this situation you should realize that as the supervisee, your counseling patients would become the patients of your supervising psychologist in that they would be receiving psychological services under the psychologist's supervision and that the licensed psychologist supervisor(s) would be ultimately responsible for their care. The Board would also bring to your attention that your supervision must also be under the direct supervision of an authorized licensed supervisor at all times. You indicate that you practice in a United Way Agency and that they have hired an outside firm to supervise you for licensure. This would appear to be a remote and, therefore, difficult scenario for adequate supervision.

Also, the Board requires that all clients or patients who receive services from unlicensed persons (anyone not licensed by this Board) must be informed of the supervisory status of the individual and how the patient or client may contact the supervising licensee directly.

...IN MORE THAN ONE PLACEMENT SITES

Q. May individuals completing post-doctoral clinical internships in one agency also be hired by school districts part-time to provide clinical assessments under the supervision of an LSSP? (M704)

A. While the Board does not pre-evaluate supervised experience, it can provide you with some information. The post-doctoral year can be in no more than two placements. It is conceivable that a public school could be one of these placements. Direct supervision must be provided by a licensed psychologist. However, any part of the post-doc year that is provided in the public schools must be supervised by an individual who is both an LSSP and a licensed psychologist. Board rule 465.3(b) requires the individual who is fulfilling post-doctoral experience to be under the direct supervision of an authorized supervising licensee at all times.

...AND REQUIREMENTS FOR SUPERVISION BEING ON-SITE

Q. How many post-doctoral supervision hours are required to be on-site? (S1103) (B803)

A. An unlicensed individual must be under the direct supervision of an authorized supervisor at all times. While Board rules do not further define "direct supervision," an off-site licensed psychologist for an unlicensed person is not sufficient supervision. Again, the intent is that the supervisor is always available to the supervisee. The Board strongly recommends that any exceptions be rare and as brief as possible and that that the supervising psychologist always be available for contact by the supervisee during the provision of psychological services. Such on-site exceptions might be a week's vacation by the supervising psychologist, during which time a back-up local licensed psychologist should be immediately available to the supervisee.

We strongly recommend that your supervisor should be at the facility where you are providing services while you are providing services. Your supervisor should not work out of a different office. Such a situation would lend itself to misinterpretation by the public that you were practicing independently. There are no specific rules regarding post doctoral supervision hours. Board rules do not set a specific number of hours, but rather indicate by rule that supervision should occur "at all times."

Documentation of supervised hours is the responsibility of the supervisee and the supervisor. The supervisor will have to attest to the number of hours of supervision that occurred weekly. Also, the supervisor is asked how many one-on-one supervision hours occurred weekly, although there is not a specific number of one-on-one hours required.

...AND ADVERTISING FOR SERVICES

Q. I am currently under post-doctoral supervision by a licensed psychologist and would like to advertise so that more clients will seek our services. (C1103)

A. In regards to your advertisement, as an applicant for licensure, you must adhere to Board rules. Board rule 465.6 prohibits advertising that is false or misleading. Your proposed advertisement is misleading in that it appears that you can independently provide psychological services to the public. The potential patients are the supervisor's ultimate responsibility, not yours. To meet the requirements for licensure as a psychologist, the individual must represent oneself to the public as an intern or resident or other title which clearly indicates that the individual is being supervised. There is no such title indicated in your advertisement.

...for *LPA* licensure in an *LPC* practice

Q. I have been asked to supervise an LPC so that this individual can obtain 450 hours for licensure as a psychological associate. She would like to obtain the 450 hours in her LPC practice and pay me directly for the supervision. I am employed elsewhere, not in her practice. (V802)

A. In the situation for supervision which you present there are several areas of concern. It appears that the person requesting supervision from you has an established independent practice as an LPC. She now wishes to use this practice to meet the 450 hours of supervision by a psychologist required for her application for licensure as a psychological associate. In considering this situation you should realize that as the supervisor, her counseling patients would become your patients receiving psychological services and therefore your ultimate responsibility since you are the supervisor.

Also, the Board requires that unlicensed persons providing psychological services must be under the direct supervision of an authorized licensed supervisor at all times. While direct supervision is not further defined by rule, it should be inferred that this means close supervision. There is no Board rule which specifically requires the supervisor to be on-site. However, as you indicate that you practice elsewhere, this does appear to be a remote and therefore difficult scenario for adequate supervision. There is no Board rule prohibiting payment for supervision although it is not generally advised because of the potential for unethical dual relationship.

...of *LPAs*

Q. I have been an LPA, working in a hospital setting for many years. My current supervisor will only allow me to work when he is on-site. This seems overly restrictive and cuts into my hourly pay. (R204)

A. According to Board rule 465.2, it is the responsibility of the supervising licensee to determine what level of supervision is appropriate for the supervisee. Since the licensed psychologist supervisor is ultimately responsible for the services provided, he or she should determine what level of supervision each psychological associate requires.

Beyond this rule, the Board does not advise regarding specific supervisory situations. Of course, you are aware that you may negotiate to obtain supervision from another licensed psychologist who, for various reasons, might ascertain that you would be able to practice with less supervision.

PRACTICE IN THE SCHOOLS

...AND *LSSP* LICENSURE WITHOUT THE PSYCHOLOGY DEGREE

Q. I have a master's in school counseling. If I complete the remaining courses needed for the master's in psychology, my university will give me a letter stating that I have completed these courses. Is this sufficient for the Board's LSSP degree requirements? (S503)

A. You must have a graduate degree in psychology and if your transcript does not state this then you would not meet this qualification for licensure. However, there are alternative qualifications that you may wish to pursue which are provided in Board rule 463.9. If you obtain certification as a National Certified School Psychologist, the Psychology Board considers this certification as having met the educational qualifications for licensure. Therefore, you may want to pursue this certification before applying for LSSP licensure with this Board

...AND *LSSP* INTERNSHIP SUPERVISION PART-TIME

Q. Is it appropriate for districts to "contract" for supervision for LSSP interns when that supervisor is not full-time? (G1104)

A. Board rule 463.9 (c) requires that "direct, systematic supervision must involve a minimum of one face-to-face contact hour per week or two consecutive face-to-face contact hours once every two weeks with the intern". Board rule 465.38(4) requires that "Direct, systematic, face-to face supervision" must be provided to LSSP interns. Additionally, Board rule 465.3(b) states that unlicensed individuals providing psychological services pursuant to 501.260(b)(3) must be under the direct supervision of an authorized supervising licensee at all times.

...AND *LSSP* INTERNSHIP SUPERVISION FROM OFF-SITE

Q. Must supervision be on-site? (A504)

A. With respect to supervision, Board rule 465.2(b) states that supervisors provide an adequate level of supervision to all individuals under their supervision according to accepted professional standards given the experience, skill and training of the supervisee and the type of psychological services. This rule allows the supervisor to adapt the supervision standards to the skills of the specific individual that is supervised. Also, the Board would point out the important difference for the supervision of LSSP interns, per Board rule 463.9(c) that states "Direct, systematic supervision must involve a minimum of one face-to-face contact hour per week or two consecutive face-to-face contact hours once every two weeks with the intern."

This type of supervision is not further defined, but clearly, the intent is that supervision is an important aspect of the provision of psychological services in the public schools by any of these individuals and a significant part of the supervision provided must be on-site, immediate, and routine. Therefore, while it is not specifically against Board rules for any of the categories of providers of school psychological services to provide services without an on-site supervisor, this is not the optimum situation and would have to be justified by the supervisor in view of the qualifications and skills of the individual being supervised.

...AND OWNERSHIP OF TEST PROTOCOLS

Q. Who owns the original test protocols used in an evaluation, the school district or the psychologist contracted to test the child? And who owns the responses to projective tests? (M505)

A. You may want to contact an attorney with expertise in school law. Licensees comply with all applicable state and federal laws affecting the practice of psychology. Prominent education laws are listed in Board rule 465.38(7). In the event of a conflict between state or federal statutes and Board rules, state or federal statutes control. However, if there are no applicable state and federal laws, the Board rules would apply. Specifically, Board rule 465.22, Psychological Records, Test Data, and Test Protocols, deals with maintenance, access, and retention of records by licensees.

Test protocols are not part of the client's records, but should be maintained by a licensee or other responsible entity. Also, in the absence of applicable state and federal rules, records and test data shall be maintained for a minimum of ten years after the last contact with the client. If the client is a minor, the record period is extended until ten years after the age of majority. In accordance with Board rules, it is not who "owns" the records, but who should "maintain" the records and protocols in compliance with applicable state and federal laws and Board rules. Who will maintain the records and the protocols should be clearly stated in the contract for psychological services.

...AND EMPLOYMENT OF NON-*LSSP*s

Q. May a school district employ licensed psychologists who do not hold the LSSP to practice within the limits of their training and competency as long as these services do not encompass the full scope of school psychology services? And may these psychologists employ LPAs to provide services under their supervision? (M303)

A. A school district could contract with a licensed psychologist who is not an LSSP to provide specific types of psychology, but not school psychology. This kind of contract would have to be on a short term or part time basis and cannot involve the broad range of school psychological services. In this scenario, the licensed psychologist could utilize a licensed psychological associate to provide the specific type of psychological services for which the school has contracted (but not school psychology services).

...AND CONTRACTING OF LPAs

Q. As an LPA, may I work on contract for a school district doing diagnostic work? (P505)

A. State law requires that psychological services in the public schools be provided by LSSPs. Board rule 465.38(3) clarifies that in certain instances schools may contract with licensed psychologists and licensed psychological associates to provide specific types of psychological services, other than school psychology. Therefore, as an LPA you may not contract with a school district to do diagnostic work. Under Board rules, LPAs may not practice independently. Therefore, any patient that an LPA provides services to is ultimately the responsibility of the supervising licensed psychologist.

...WITHOUT PASSING THE NATIONAL EXAM

Q. If individuals do not pass the national school psychology exam, is there any way they can work for a public school? (J401) (R1102) What if they have already interned for two years and still haven't passed the national exam? (R403)

A. Unfortunately, the Board cannot waive the requirements of the Psychologists' Licensing Act or Board rules. Persons who provide school psychological services in the public school must be enrolled in a formal university internship or practicum course, hold LSSP trainee status with the Board, or be LSSPs, or they may not provide school psychological services in the public schools. Persons may continue to be considered interns only so long as they are enrolled in a formal program. The required internship may last for as long as two years or as short as one year. The formal program requirement is necessary to protect the public to ensure that someone from the training facility is directly supervising the applicant.

Therefore, the Board suggests that students who find themselves in a hiatus period be allowed to enroll or re-enroll in an internship program or practicum that would enable them to be supervised by trainers from the institution of higher education while they continue to provide psychological services in the schools. There are various ways that such courses could be structured and, of course, those would be up to the individual schools. There may even be the possibility of structuring an internship program with supervision to extend say for up three months past the final grade for the course if the student has made an acceptable grade. However, an individual who has completed two years of LSSP internship and still not passed the national exam should not be allowed to continue work as an LSSP intern.

The Board maintains that the protection of the public is at stake, and therefore does not choose to implement a less rigorous set of requirements. An individual who has passed the national exam and been approved by the Board becomes an LSSP Trainee. The trainee status allows the applicant to provide psychological services in the public schools for up to one year, during which time they must take and pass the Jurisprudence Exam. When that exam is passed, the license is issued.

...AND ACTIVITIES PERMITTED

Q. What services are LSSPs competent to perform? (P602) Can they provide psychological counseling? (H205) Can they do neuropsychological assessment? (A504)

A. Competency of a practitioner is determined by the practitioner himself or herself, by a supervisor of that practitioner if applicable, and by the Board if a complaint is filed against a licensee. In addition, a client may have an opinion as to the competency of the practitioner. In a school setting, all of these determinations are important and should be considered. Also, what might be a competent practitioner for one client is not for another, depending on the skills and competencies of the practitioner and the needs and conditions of the client. Therefore, decisions as to the provision of psychological services and the competency of the practitioner in each scenario must be justified and the justification documented.

LSSPs may provide psychological counseling or neuropsychological assessment to students in public schools provided that the licensee is competent to provide such services. An LSSP, who is competent to provide counseling because of training and/or experience, can provide counseling in the public schools. Such counseling is not required to be supervised unless the LSSP is practicing within the first year of licensure. However, the Board would recommend that on-going psychological counseling not directly and specifically related to the child's functioning in school would most appropriately be provided by a licensee of this Board whose private practice is primarily to provide counseling and therapy. Neuropsychological assessment is typically regarded as a specialty within the field of psychology.

Therefore, the most competent neuropsychological services would be provided by a licensee who primarily provides neuropsychology and who has had extensive training in this specialty. However, there is no specific Board rule against any licensee of this Board providing neuropsychological testing provided that the licensee has adequate training to provide such services.

... AND INFORMED CONSENT

Q. What is required for "informed consent" in a school district assessment? (M1101) Must I have parent consent to share test results with the child client? (S504)

A. You may be interested in an article titled "LSSPs Adhere to State and Federal Education Laws" in the agency's newsletter dated Summer 2001 (Vol. 14, No.1), which is available on our website, www.tsbep.state.tx.us. We believe this information will assist you in understanding the complexities of this issue. Adequate informed consent is one which clearly alerts the client to the specific types of assessments and evaluations that are to be done and to the limits of confidentiality for the records that will be created. Such parent consent would include any plans to share test results with the child client. However, you with the guidance of your legal counsel for the school system should decide what constitutes informed consent in accordance with state and federal education standards.

Q. *My school district would like to test a child. The mother is opposed, but the father has given informed consent. What should our legal and ethical response be? (C505)*

A. The Board would recommend that you seek advice from our district lawyers regarding the requirements of state and federal laws concerning the situation that you set forth. Their legal advice would be the guide as to how you can proceed. Board rule 465.37 states that licensees comply with all applicable state and federal laws affecting the practice of psychology. In the event of a conflict between state and federal statutes and Board rules, state or federal statutes control. Board rule 465.11 requires informed consent for psychological services. If according to state and federal laws you have obtained the required informed consent from the father, then you have met the requirements of this rule.

...UNDER A DIAGNOSTICIAN TITLE

Q. *As an LSSP, I've been hired as an Educational Diagnostician but I'm asked to provide school psychological services, including supervision. Does it jeopardize my license as an LSSP to perform school psychological services while having the job title of diagnostician? (S1104)*

A. The Board is not concerned with the classification of your employment with the school district. However, to provide school psychological services in the public schools of Texas, a person must be an LSSP. Also, to supervise an LSSP you must hold the LSSP license. Therefore, it is misleading to the public if you do not refer to yourself as and use the title of LSSP. There is no problem with you being hired as an Educational Diagnostician, but if you provide psychological services for the school, you should use your title of LSSP.

DOING BUSINESS WITH TSBEP

...BY FAX

Q. *May I fax my renewal form to the Board? (N505)*

A. The Board does not receive renewal forms by fax because the renewal form must accompany the required fee. The last sentence on the green renewal reminder card now sent to all licensees states: "Renewals may not be submitted by FAX because the renewal fee must accompany the forms."

...AFTER A CHANGE OF ADDRESS

Q. *I moved and my renewal notice was not forwarded to my new address. Would you waive the late fee? (G205)*

A. Addresses of record can only be changed by licensees. The Board is required to charge late fees in accordance with the Psychologists' Licensing Act.

...REGARDING CONTINUING EDUCATION

Q. *Does membership on a hospital ethics committee count for the ethics CE requirement? (G205)*

A. Board rule 461.11 (c) lists activities permitted for CE.

Q. *Will the Board accept as CE professional meeting activities for which no certificate is provided? (R704)*

A. Board rule 461.11 requires that CE be documented by the signature of an official of the providing organization.

TSBEP Disciplinary Actions

January, 2000, to May, 2005

Infraction	Number of Licensees disciplined
Violations of Continuing Education (CE)	42
Unsubstantiated Forensic Statements	13
Inadequate Informed Consent	11
Inadequate Record-Keeping	10
Inappropriate Sexual Relationships	10
(4 with current clients; 4 former clients; 2 students)	
Improper Denial of Client Records	5
Unethical Dual/Multiple Relationships (non-sexual)	5
Breach of Confidential Information	4
Criminal Conviction/Failure to Report	4
Failure to Report Child Abuse	3
Failure to Respond to TSBEP	3
Unlicensed Practice by Licensee	2
Inadequate Treatment Plan	2
Negligent Supervision	2
Failure to Report Sanctions Received from non-TSBEP Sources	2
Other *(failure to complete TSBEP-assigned disciplinary sanctions; incompetence in emerging area of treatment; inappropriate restraint of child client; inadequate preparation of client for termination; improper delegation of projective testing to LPC; impaired professional)*	6

Disciplinary actions are compiled by the Texas State Board of Examiners of Psychologists (TSBEP) and are available to the public under the Public Information Act. Specific information about the violations is published in the Board's newsletters. In the Spring, 1999, Newsletter, the Board published a categorization of pending complaints that enabled practitioners to see trends in the kinds of complaints received by the Board.

At that time, 44% of complaints involved continuing education violations, 38% involved general practice complaints, 12% involved complaints about custody cases, 3% alleged sexual violations, and 3% involved other areas. The above table and the titles of violations were developed by the authors with the goal of illustrating the kinds of professional problems for which licensees have been sanctioned by TSBEP over the past five years.

It should be noted that some licensees were disciplined for more than one type of infraction and the numbers in the table reflect those multiple violations. The table is not approved or endorsed by the Board and should be used for general guidance only. Additional information about the complaint process is found on the Board's website (*http://www.tsbep.state.tx.us*).

INDEX

ORDERING INFORMATION

Additional copies of *Texas Law and the Practice of Psychology* are available from the publisher. Orders may be placed by phone, by mail, by FAX, or directly on the web. Purchase orders from institutions are welcome.

❏ *To order by mail:* Complete this order form and mail it (along with check or credit card information) to Bayou Publishing, 2524 Nottingham, Houston, TX 77005-1412.

❏ *To order by phone:* Call (800) 340-2034.

❏ *To order by FAX:* Fill out this order form (including credit card information) and fax to (713) 526-4342.

❏ *To place a secure online order:* Visit http://www.bayoupublishing. com.

Name: _____

Address: _____

_____

City: _____ ST: ___ Zip: _____

Ph: _____

FAX: _____

❏ VISA   ❏ MasterCard   ❏ American Express

Charge Card #: _____

Expiration Date: _____

Signature: _____

Please send me _____ copies at $35.00 each _____

Sales Tax (Texas residents) _____

plus $4.50 postage and handling *(per order)* _____$4.50

Total $ _____

Bayou Publishing
2524 Nottingham, Suite 150
Houston, TX 77005-1412
Ph: (713) 526-4558/ FAX: (713) 526-4342
Orders: (800) 340-2034
http://www.bayoupublishing.com

TEXAS PSYCHOLOGICAL ASSOCIATION

For additional resources provided by the Texas
Psychological Association, visit the TPA website at:

http://www.texaspsyc.org.

Texas Psychological Association
1005 Congress Avenue, Suite 410
Austin, TX 78701
(512) 280-4099
(888) 872-3435

admin@texaspsyc.org